THE
HOLISTIC
YOU

THE HOLISTIC YOU

INTEGRATING YOUR FAMILY, FINANCES, FAITH, FRIENDSHIPS, *and* FITNESS

RABBI DANIEL LAPIN
and
SUSAN LAPIN

WILEY

Published by John Wiley & Sons, Inc., Hoboken, New Jersey.
Published simultaneously in Canada.

For general information on our other products and services or for technical support, please contact our Customer Care Department within the United States at (800) 762-2974, outside the United States at (317) 572-3993 or fax (317) 572-4002.

Wiley also publishes its books in a variety of electronic formats. Some content that appears in print may not be available in electronic formats. For more information about Wiley products, visit our web site at www.wiley.com.

Library of Congress Cataloging-in-Publication Data is Available:

ISBN 9781394163489 (Cloth)
ISBN 9781394163519 (ePDF)
ISBN 9781394163502 (ePUB)

Cover Design and Image: Wiley

SKY10052790_080723

We humbly dedicate this book to our extraordinary children:

Rebecca and Max Masinter
Rena and Yoni Baron
Rachelle and Zev Stern
Ari and Menucha Lapin
Ruthie and Asher Abraham
Miriam and Anshel Kaplan
Tamara and David Sasson

With limitless admiration for what you have all become
and
with boundless appreciation for all you have done

Contents

Preface

O ur seven delightful but rambunctious children intrigued us with their interactions. Their play varied immensely depending on who was in the game that day. The same child behaved in one way in conjunction with three of her sisters, in an entirely different way when playing with two other sisters, and when her brother was involved, things went in an entirely different direction. The interactions were as interesting as the individuals. We began seeing the happiness of our family as the product of how well our system of individual components interacted. As important to us as the individual development of each child was, we learned that the way they interacted with one another was equally important. We realized that our family is a system.

We laughed at this observation during our date night conversations and began comparing it to other systems like the operation of, say, an airline. We never chose which airline to fly based solely on what jets made up their fleet. Neither did we make our travel choices only on schedule convenience, ticket price, or frequent-flyer club affiliation. We somehow would integrate many of these factors, along with others such as safety records, and arrive at a choice because an airline is a system, and the interaction of all the components is as important as any component by itself.

We aren't sure which one of us first raised the idea of our very lives being systems. That realization, the heart of this book, surged into being spontaneously like a burst of laughter between close friends. Of course, our marriage was also a system. Which meant that like any system, the quality of our marriage was also not just the sum of its parts, but it was the product of our interactions. It was not either one of us that latched on to that idea about a life system—it was us, our marriage. Similarly, it was not the engine or the steering wheel that got us to our destination on our recent road trip, it was our car.

For us, with our deep connection to two thousand years of ancient Jewish wisdom and to the individuals, families, and communities that this accumulated body of data has sculpted throughout time and space, it was easy to identify the five key components of a life system. We then catalogued hundreds of people we had helped to guide through times of tribulation and challenge only to discover that for more than 90% of the individuals we reviewed, their troubles were a direct function of failure to integrate the five key components of their lives.

It turned out that just as we strove to put each of our children on to his or her appropriate life path, they had astonishingly put us on to the productive path of understanding how life's key components, Family, Finance, Faith, Fitness, and Friendships all interact. At the same time, while our children granted us a stake in the future, we opened their eyes to the past. Not surprisingly our research quickly revealed that most of the perplexing puzzles of the 5Fs could be best resolved by looking backward in time rather than forward.

Many things, like raising children for instance, are best accomplished by consulting the past. Others, like designing anti-lock braking systems for motorcycles, are best achieved by peering into the future. The past, for instance, has little to contribute in the quest for faster quantum computing. The future, however, is unlikely to shed any light on how best to civilize the human male's sexual obsessions. Technological development emphasizes how rapidly the world is changing, while at the same time it camouflages how little things have really changed. Human greatness born of handed-down wisdom and experience still counts for something, although we confuse it with technical proficiency. The latter could, in principle, be programmed into a machine while the former is unique to human beings.

The 5F system at the heart of *The Holistic You* is a pathway to human greatness. Traveling that pathway is one of life's greatest adventures. We welcome you to join us as we move forward into the future while maintaining a spotlight on the past. We pray that the life of every reader of this book will be dramatically enhanced by implementing the principles herein.

Rabbi Daniel & Susan Lapin
Maryland, 2023

Acknowledgments

One reason it can be hard to teach a toddler to say "thank you" is because acknowledging gratitude is like declaring a dependency. In the Lord's language, Hebrew, the word for expressing gratitude is the same as the word for confessing. "Thank you" means that I confess I needed you and I needed and value what you have done for me. For little people, it can be hard to acknowledge a need for others.

We, on the other hand, joyfully acknowledge our dependency upon so many others and our delight at the privilege of collaborating with them on this book. Our family deserves much gratitude for so often having had to yield to the book's priority. Many is the family occasion that we missed or for which we arrived late on account of our dedication to the book. They understand our unquenchable desire to make ancient Jewish wisdom accessible to as many people as possible and uncomplainingly make allowances for it.

Kevin Harreld at Wiley is as much a parent of this book as are we. Without his vision, encouragement, and guidance it simply would never have come to life. We appreciate him greatly. Kevin's amazing colleagues at Wiley shepherded us toward the finish line. You would not be holding this book in your hands without the steady stream of directives and patient professionalism of Susan Cerra and her team.

Our editor, Sheryl Nelson, has known us for years and still agreed to undertake the task of polishing our torrents of verbal enthusiasm into this now very readable book. A great editor doesn't just change; a great editor improves, and this Sheryl certainly did.

Emma Fialkoff, an accomplished author in her own right, heads our production team and has shared many late night hours with us as we struggled with one or another aspect of the book's architecture. We recognize that we are not the easiest of writers to work with and she deserves much credit not only for what she did but for how she did it.

There would have been no chance of our having been able to concentrate for such extensive periods on this book exclusively unless we felt confident that our office would continue to run smoothly and effectively. That it did so is due to three remarkable women who are not only accomplished professionals but who have also become cherished friends. Crystol Garrison could easily be managing any large multinational corporation. That she has instead chosen to be the crucial lynchpin of our organization for so many years fills us with wonder and appreciation. We doubt that we could manage without her because in addition to all she accomplishes, she also brings out the best in us. Jessica Solberg Black is the personification of competence. Those words are often used to describe a soulless bureaucrat, but Jessica could hardly be more different. She is not only startlingly creative but successfully stimulates similar creativity among her team members. Ellen Joyce Garcia is the calm and experienced engineer deep down in the engine room of our ship. She keeps the machinery throbbing with purpose and power as our enterprise plows through the oceans and is a pleasure to work with.

Dina Bengio is our truly remarkable personal assistant who uncomplainingly makes problems vanish and frustrations evaporate. We are still trying to discover areas in which she possesses less than extraordinary experience and ability.

We close this altogether inadequate attempt at expressing our gratitude with a great big thank you to God Almighty without whom we doubt that we would have found one another and without whom nothing our marriage has achieved would have come to pass.

Rabbi Daniel & Susan Lapin
Maryland, 2023

About the Authors

For nearly two decades, Rabbi Daniel Lapin and his wife, Susan, led the Southern California congregation they planted and where they met and married. After counseling crowds of young people through career crises, dating dilemmas, and marriage mysteries by applying ancient Jewish wisdom to solve contemporary problems, word of their work began spreading beyond their own community into both Jewish and Christian circles. Their seven best-selling books, daily television show, weekly podcast, and the resources they create make their inviting, Bible-based approach to life's challenges accessible to people of every background. They are well-known speakers for Jewish, Christian, and business groups in the United Kingdom, Switzerland, South Africa, Ghana, Nigeria, Korea, China, and throughout North America.

While Susan grew up in New York, Rabbi Daniel was born and spent his early childhood in South Africa. His parents, the distinguished Rabbi and Mrs. A. H. Lapin, dispatched him to England and Israel even before he turned 13 to immerse him in Scripture. Though not a particularly studious young man to start with, he did eventually find himself intensely intrigued by the Bible, economics, physics, and mathematics, which he subsequently taught at Yeshiva College. As he puts it, "These disciplines explain how the world *really* works."

Rabbi Daniel and Susan Lapin have been blessed with seven children whom they greatly admire and who are now building their own young families. The Lapin children were homeschooled on Mercer Island, Washington, and the family enjoyed annual holidays boating off the coast of British Columbia. Several of the Lapin children joined their parents on an exciting Pacific Ocean crossing in their own sailboat, and some are now homeschooling Lapin grandchildren. The Lapins recently relocated to Maryland where they live in one of the most vibrant Jewish communities in the United States.

Chapter 1

Meet the 5Fs

Imagine going to see the dermatologist, hoping to deal with the rash on your face. It is itchy and unsightly; you are desperate to get rid of it. After an examination, you are delighted when the doctor tells you that she has just the cream that will clear everything up. As she enters the prescription into the computer, you casually ask if the medication has any side effects.

"Oh, yes," she says. "It can cause an irregular heartbeat and damage your kidney function. But your skin will be beautiful!"

You can't get out of that office fast enough.

On your way home, you stop at the garage to ask the mechanic why your car is accelerating slowly. He offers to rev up your motor. However, you may want to find a new mechanic if he doesn't confirm that your car's other parts will integrate with your newly tuned motor.

A motorcar is a complex system consisting of an engine, wheels, brakes, suspension, and many other components. These are exquisitely matched to work smoothly in conjunction with one another. A car with a wonderful engine but poor brakes and an underperforming suspension drives less well than a car with a weaker engine but with all its components designed to work together as a system.

Get a second opinion before signing the repair ticket.

The genius of any system is so much more than the quality of its components—it's really a question of how well all the components play together. Here is one more example.

Let's imagine you are an ambitious entrepreneur with a plan to start manufacturing and marketing widgets. You tell your executive recruiter to find you the very best production engineer available. You interview him and are quickly convinced that he could easily set up a widget manufacturing facility. Next, assuming the role of chief executive officer, you recruit the best marketing manager available knowing full well that he or she will become a wizard at selling widgets. Now you find yourself a qualified chief financial officer and finally you hire a chief operating officer. You sit back to watch the profits rolling in. With such top-rated personnel in place, how could it fail?

Easy! During your first day, your financial officer bursts into your office shaking with indignation that the production guy spent 15% over budget for some new machinery. (The production engineer tells you that a plus or minus 15% margin of error in projections is perfectly normal.) Your sales manager informs you that there is no way she can market the flawed widgets that are being turned out by the factory. (The production engineer insists that all widgets coming off the line are exactly to design specifications.) All these competent specialists start developing deep antipathies toward one another. After all, each is perceived as preventing the others from excelling at their jobs. It now begins to dawn on you why chief executive officers are well paid. Pulling together all the disparate personalities and welding them into a unified team fully committed to a common goal is not easy. Though quality components are a great place to start, building a system is far harder than obtaining good components.

We sometimes see this when sports teams, businesses, or movie productions bring in a "star," often for a cost of millions of dollars. For many years, the Seattle Mariners were a rather lackluster team in spite of having enjoyed the services of baseball greats like Randy Johnson, Ken Griffey, Jr., and Alex Rodriguez. When they lost those three stars, the Mariners enjoyed a season such as they had never before experienced. They did this without a single star, just a team of good, solid players working together.

So too in our own lives. Happiness can elude us when we have a "star" player—for instance, a well-developed professional life—if the rest of the team (family, friendship, faith, and fitness) have limited or no place in that picture. Having a relationship with God is hugely helpful, but even He insists that we need family, finance, fitness, and friends as well.

Overdeveloping one aspect of our lives, or putting another on hold because we think we can only focus on one at a time, is like trying to drive with an engine but no brakes. Our lives are fundamentally impaired when we take this approach. Instead, it pays to think about how we can invest in our life system as a whole—giving regular attention to all of its key components.

We have been fortunate, over the years, to meet and talk to many of the hundreds of thousands of people who have attended our speeches, read our books, and taken part in our mastermind groups and classes, both in person and online. Whether they live in North or South America, in Africa, Europe, or Asia, we find that many of their concerns are similar. Once basic physical needs are secure, people seek to find a life worth living. That is easier said than done.

Too often, students tell us of wonderful years they spent pursuing and achieving one goal only to wake up one day to the realization that they are older and have missed out on other vital parts of life. Other individuals, who aim at having it all, are baffled at how to balance the many different calls on their time and energy. Many people realize that the direction they received during their education and training and from the general culture was incomplete at best and largely faulty.

Ancient Jewish Wisdom

People of different ages and backgrounds ask us about dealing with sibling rivalry and inheritance squabbles. They ask us about resolving tension between work and marriage. They ask us about diminishing financial stress during inflationary periods. They pose questions about friendships, about marriage and children, about sex, about work and money, and about almost anything else really relevant to life that you can imagine. Do they turn to us because they think we are more intelligent or better educated than they are? No. They turn to us because they believe that we have had exposure to a valuable branch of knowledge that can change their lives.

What is that branch of knowledge? We call it ancient Jewish wisdom. And we specialize in this ancient Jewish wisdom that relates to the things that people care about on a very practical level. Ancient Jewish wisdom encompasses a vast body of data based upon the written Five Books of Moses and an accompanying multi-millennial transmission of elucidation.

One reason there are five books is related to why there were Five Commandments upon each of the Two Tablets of the Law. While we have developed the habit in society of calling the stones that Moses brought down from Mt. Sinai the Ten Commandments, that actually doesn't correlate with how they are referred to in the Bible. There, they are called the "Ten Commandments" (more accurately, the Ten Statements) only a few times. However they are called the Two Tablets more than 30 times. Two and five are more important numbers when relating to the revelation on Sinai than 10 is. The stone tablets actually supply only five principles, but those principles are explored on each of the two tablets, with two examples being given of each principle. Number one and number six show two facets of one principle, number two and number seven do the same for the second principle, and so on.

As an example, the second commandment on the first tablet not to have false gods corresponds to the commandment on the second tablet not to commit adultery. Both relate to the importance of not betraying sacred relationships. The only difference is that one relates to our relationship with God, the other to our relationship with a spouse.

Why five? The lens of ancient Jewish wisdom associates specific qualities with different numbers. Five is the number that converts the abstract to the realm of the real and tangible. It is a number associated with revelation, when something internal is brought forth and manifested in the world. Translating the immense catalog of theoretical principles that we find in the Bible into livable and practical guidelines requires distilling them into five dimensions.

The same transition from abstract to reality is signaled by the five fingers we have on each hand. Responding to the utterly abstract creative thoughts of our souls, the brain issues electronic signals that travel down our arms and culminate at the five fingers which move to actualize everything. Whether it is writing words with a pen or moving a mountain of mud with a mighty bulldozer, which responds to the operator's delicate hand movements, our hands concretize what we think of doing. Whether in poetry or in the Bible, the phrase "work of your hands" is familiar and resonates with us.

Not only does each number have a conceptual association in ancient Jewish wisdom, but Hebrew letters each have a numerical value. Even page numbers in an Israeli cookbook or novel might show letters for pagination rather than numbers. For example, instead of seeing 149 at the bottom of a page, the reader will see three Hebrew letters—a kuf, a mem, and a tet—with the respective values of 100, 40 and 9. Those fluent in Hebrew make the same type of immediate leap from the letter to its associated number value as do motorists when they immediately translate a red light to the command "stop."

The fifth letter of the Hebrew alphabet, the letter "heh" has a numerical value of 5 and is also the letter that, when added to a noun, converts the noun to a feminine one. One feature of femininity is translating the abstract into reality. There are few better examples of this concept than a woman's body receiving the potential life force transmitted by her husband and then transforming it over the course of 9 months into 7 pounds of real baby.

Similarly, as we sculpt our lives, we need to know how to act in order to align our lives with the abstract values we wish to live by. The actual behaviors we need to modify fall under the five main headings of Family, Finance, Faith, Fitness, and Friendship. These are the key life areas that when crosslinked with one another constitute the essence of a fulfilling and satisfying life.

These five categories form the core of this book.

Introducing the 5Fs

Following is a list with a brief explanation of each F. Admittedly, these explanations are meant to serve only to introduce the pillars, certainly not to explain them exhaustively. That is what we will do over the course of this book.

Family: These are the relationships we have with parents, siblings, spouses, children, and other blood relatives or relatives through marriage. From another perspective, we speak of family as the relationships that result from sexual connection. When we share a joyful multigenerational family gathering, as awkward as it might be to contemplate, we sometimes forget that the only reason that we are there together with uncles and aunts, and cousins is because many years ago Grandpa and Grandma's eyes met, they formed a bond, and found ecstasy in one another's arms.

Finance: This covers relationships with our possessions and with our money in all its forms. It includes human connections that revolve around money. Employers, employees, customers and clients, work associates, professional associations, and vendors all contribute to this heading.

Friendship: This includes friends or people we connect with through shared interests like hobbies or sports, church, or our children's education. Political and social groups with which we associate and charity organizations in which we actively participate also fall under this category. Likewise, the experience of "community" that many people feel through association with a religion is part of the friendship pillar. Most relationships with people who are linked to us through neither family nor money fall into this category.

Faith: Faith refers to our relationship with things that cannot be measured in a laboratory. Faith may be a commitment to integrity, say, or the love and esteem of others that we feel. Whatever beliefs play a role in our lives or whatever set of values that governs our decision-making fall under the Faith heading as does, obviously, a relationship with God.

Fitness: This pillar refers to everything having to do with our bodies—our anatomy, physiology, and biology. It helps combat the common tendency of many of us to be overly cerebral. Fitness covers our health and how we maintain it. How we eat, breathe, excrete, drink, make love, and eventually die are covered in detail in ancient Jewish wisdom.

When psychologist Abraham Maslow tried to capture the totality of all the needs and drives of the human being, he came up with his hierarchy of five needs: physiological, safety, belonging, esteem, and self-actualization. We also interface with the world through our five basic senses: touch, smell, taste, hearing, and seeing.

It is equally natural that the number of separate pieces that make up the totality of our lives should be five. In his 1890 work, *Principles of Psychology*, William James, often called the Father of American Psychology, wrote these words:

...a man's Self is the sum total of all that he can call his, not only his body and his psychic powers, but his clothes and his house, his wife and children, his ancestors and friends, his reputation and works, his lands and horses, and yacht and bank-account. All these things give him the same emotions. If they wax and prosper, he feels triumphant; if they dwindle and die away, he feels cast down, —not necessarily in the same degree for each thing, but in much the same way for all.

In James' words, we see all five of our categories; family, finance, and friendships are clearly listed, while fitness and faith are included in his phrase, "body and his psychic powers."

Years before Abraham Maslow or William James, the Bible alluded to these five categories. After escaping from his less-than-holy father-in-law Laban's home and having conducted a scary meeting with his brother, Esau, Genesis 33:18 tells us that Jacob comes to the city of Shechem.

Here is the NIV translation of the verse:

After Jacob came from Paddan Aram, he arrived <u>safely</u> at the city of Shechem in Canaan and camped within sight of the city.

The Amplified Bible, Classic edition says:

When Jacob came from Padan-aram, he arrived <u>safely and in peace</u> at the town of Shechem, in the land of Canaan, and pitched his tents before the [enclosed] town.

This is the translation of the American Standard Version:

And Jacob came in peace to the city of Shechem, which is in the land of Canaan, when he came from Paddan-aram; and encamped before the city.

Each of the translations we see above are valiantly trying to distill ancient Jewish wisdom on the word "shalem" into one English word. Does it mean *safely*? Does it mean *in peace*?

Yes and yes, but it means more than that as well.

This is how we would present the first four words of the Hebrew verse. (Translating the rest of the verse would take another few paragraphs!)

"And Jacob came SHaLeM to the city of Shechem."

When Jacob comes "shalem" to the city of Shechem, ancient Jewish wisdom actually tells us that he came *complete*. It further details that he was complete in his faith (despite living in Laban's idolatrous home), complete in his body/fitness (despite limping after having wrestled with an angel only a few verses earlier), and complete in his finances (despite attempts by his father-in-law to cheat him and the gifts he lavished on his brother, Esau). His family, which at this point was his social circle and community, is with him as well. All five of our 5F areas are presented in that one sentence: family, faith, fitness, finances, and friendships.

The Lord's Language

To understand this better, we need to take a few minutes to explore more of the amazing properties of the Lord's language—Hebrew. You are probably familiar with the word we cite above, *shalem*, as it is used in its variation, *shalom*. You see, vowels are of secondary importance in Hebrew. In that language and in a Bible Torah scroll, SHaLeM is spelled exactly the same way as the word SHaLoM, the word SHLoM, and by adding a suffix, the word SHLeiMuT.

In English, we don't spend time trying to understand why we use one word, "bark," to talk about the sound a dog makes and also about the outside of a tree. In Hebrew, however, when one word has multiple meanings, that fact is significant.

Consider the English words PiN, PaN, PiNe, PeN, oPeN, and PuN. Obviously a writing implement, pen, has no relationship to a cooking utensil, pan, and a pin has nothing to do with a pun. But in the Lord's language, Hebrew, those six words would all be spelled PN, and what is more, every variation arrived at by inserting different vowels would all be closely connected with one another in terms of the concepts they connote.

What does the previous verse from Genesis tell us that we can apply to our lives today? Let's zero in on the fact that this word, SHaLeM/SHaLoM, means *payment* as well as *completion* and *peace*.

If a customer simply takes a pair of shoes from a store, there is no *completion* and *no peace* between the customer and the seller. When she takes the shoes, an imbalance is created—she has received something from the store owner without giving something back in return. To achieve peace, she must first pay for those shoes. This levels the imbalance. She has made the store owner whole again by giving money in exchange for the shoes. Only then can peace reign.

Were she to walk out of the store without paying, there would be little peace. Instead there would be a charge of shoplifting and considerable turbulence for all involved. Peace is far preferable but can only be attained when we correct the imbalances that are naturally created when we give and receive from one another. Payment is one of the ways to correct this imbalance.

Not only does peace depend upon payment for things taken, but it has to be fair and market value payment. This is the genius behind the Fifth Amendment to the American Constitution. In it, we find the words, "nor shall private property be taken for public use without just compensation." The wise Founders clearly understood how peace depends upon just compensation. In fact, in colonial America, many of the leading pastors and statesmen not only knew Hebrew but had correspondence and friendships with leading rabbis of the day. Given the familiarity with Hebrew that many of them enjoyed, it is likely that they also understood that peace and payment are the same word.

The meaning of shalom when used as a greeting simply flows from all these meanings. When we greet a new arrival or bid farewell to him by uttering the word shalom we are expressing the hope that we shall both enjoy the full tranquility that can only come from totality and mutually discharged obligations.

Think of your life as a system with five chief components: (1) the health and proper operation of your body; your physical Fitness; (2) your social relationships and community affiliations; your Friendships; (3) your close and intimate relationships; your Family; (4) your work, income, assets, and possessions; your Finances; finally, (5) your state of spiritual awareness; the condition of your Faith. The truth is that for every one of us, if we have a great and loving family life and a circle of good friends, good health with few money worries, and we also feel spiritually integrated, well, we have very little in life to complain about. We have found a way to maintain balance among the components of our lives. We are at peace and complete.

Unlike Drs. Maslow or James, we are not psychologists. It is only fair to let you know from where we draw our approach. We are the fortunate recipients of a more than three-thousand-year-old heritage that dates back to Mt. Sinai, called the Torah. In it, God revealed rules for best living in His world, a comprehensive theory of the totality of existence. As we noted, it comprises five volumes: Genesis, Exodus, Leviticus, Numbers, and Deuteronomy. Moses actually received two component parts of the Torah from God: the written book known as the Five Books of Moses and an oral transmission that explains what the surface narrative truly means. Following Moses' time, the books of the Prophets (such as Malachi) and the Writings (such as Psalms) were added, forming what is known as the Hebrew Bible. This too has a written component and an accompanying oral transmission.

This vast body of Torah data reached my (RDL) father, Rabbi A.H. Lapin of blessed memory and my mother, Maisie Lapin of blessed memory, and in due course, over many years, they passed much of it on to me. In the years following our marriage, Susan was blessed to learn from them as well, adding on to her own family's transmission. My parents made great sacrifices so that I could study with many outstanding teachers, some of whom were my relatives at the great rabbinical seminaries in the United Kingdom and Israel. These included my great-uncle, Rabbi Eliyahu Lopian of blessed memory, acknowledged as one of the outstanding Torah transmitters of his generation.

You might say that those of us who continue this chain are subjects in a continuing longitudinal study that has been in progress for more than two thousand years and has been closely observed as it has covered over one hundred generations. The Jewish people's triumphs and disasters, virtues and vices have been meticulously followed in many countries and in many eras.

The Secret of Jewish Success

It is incontestable that Jews consistently play an outsized role on the stage of world history. When the state of Israel was founded in 1948, there were about the same number of Sri Lankans as Jews in the world. Today there are considerably more people in Sri Lanka, formerly known as Ceylon, than there are Jews. Yet, whether in news, media, business, entertainment, or geopolitics, one hears far more about Jews and Israel than about Sri Lankans and their beautiful island.

From notorious anti-Semites to venerable sages, and from scholarly academics of every national and religious background to neighbors down the street, pretty much everyone agrees that there is something unique about the Jewish people.

In his book *Beyond Good and Evil,* the German philosopher, Friedrich Nietzsche (1844–1900), wrote "…I have not met a German yet who is well disposed toward Jews…. The Jews, however, are beyond any doubt the strongest, toughest, and purest race now living in Europe."

Mark Twain likewise once wrote: "If the statistics are right, the Jews constitute but one quarter of one percent of the human race. It suggests a nebulous puff of stardust lost in the blaze of the Milky Way. Properly, the Jew ought hardly to be heard of, but he is heard of, has always been heard of. He is as prominent on the planet as any other people, and his importance is extravagantly out of proportion to the smallness of his bulk…."

Mark Twain was wrong. Jews do not constitute even one-tenth of 1% of the human race. But he was quite right to observe that Jews have survived and thrived in different epochs, different countries, and under difficult circumstances. Whether it is starting out in poverty and building wealth or maintaining strong families and communities, the Jewish people persevere. Unlike other cultures that span thousands of years, there is tremendous continuity. Only academically trained people can pick up Chaucer and easily understand his words written in Middle English. Being a modern speaker of English isn't that helpful. When my (RDL) father tried to use his high school Greek while disembarking from a plane in Athens, the customs official looked at him as if he was, well, speaking Greek—and not a variety that the official recognized. However, stop any modern Israeli Jewish child on the street and show him a verse from the Torah or the words of the prophet Jeremiah, and he will be able to read it fluently and translate it.

If our great-great-great (add as many greats as you'd like) grandparents were to walk into our house, they would not recognize many of the foods we eat and ingredients we use. Soy sauce? Artichokes? Spaghetti? These had no part in their diet. However, the only thing they would care about would be whether the food was in accordance with the dietary laws as given in the Torah and agreed upon through the ages. Being assured of that fact, they would happily sit down and join us for a meal. We would all start the meal with the exact same words of blessing and end it with exactly the same words. We trust they would feel at home.

This supernatural continuity and success comes not from genetics but from the strength of basic permanent principles that often remain part of the culture for a few generations even when, sadly, the Bible that is the source of these principles has been abandoned. The one and only thing that has played a consistent part in Jewish life for more than two thousand years is the Torah, which in Hebrew means *the teaching*. Jewish supernatural success comes from the strength of timeless truths that remain etched into the culture.

What about Jews who apparently have no connection with the Torah, you might ask? In fact, in most generations that includes the majority of those identifying as Jews. Many outwardly successful Jews are not religious and pay no homage to the teaching that we are suggesting is the true source of their success.

The answer is that the fumes in a gas tank last a long time. If we cut a beautiful flower off its plant and bring it indoors, we seem to have done a clever thing. No longer do we need to step outside to enjoy the bright colors and intoxicating fragrance—it's right there on the table. However, the next day we notice the flower is less colorful and its perfume a little fainter. Later the flower fades and shrivels. Its sisters out in the garden are still magnificent. This is the sad fate of the severed flower.

The first few generations of Jews who walk away from Jewish observances and practices while still feeling a warm connection to their origins often contribute magnificently to the world and, as a group, enjoy personal and economic success. They have strong values and morals, cherish family, and work hard even if they do not recognize that their views are Bible-based. They are like our severed flower just after it has been brought inside.

Eventually though, their descendants no longer identify with the Torah, and they culturally assimilate into the larger world, moving further away from their heritage. Historically, this has often happened under coercion, as when about 50% of the Jews in Spain converted to Catholicism after 1391 under the threatening sword of the government. Nowadays, this is usually a voluntary assimilation. Individuals may retain a connection to the importance of education, charity, or community—ideas that give them a step up in the world for a bit longer—but slowly, they lose the benefits of their heritage. Sadly, they often become the biggest advocates of an anti-God world view, promoting secularism in both politics and culture.

Yet, since the days of Moses on Mt. Sinai, there has always been a portion of the Jewish people who remain planted in the soil of the Bible. In the twenty-first century, as in every earlier century, a core group of Jews, perhaps 15% of the overall total number, still confine their diet to the kosher rules of the Torah, the Five Books of Moses. In this, what they eat and what they refrain from eating is the same as what Jews in the time of Jesus did. Likewise, each spring (in the Northern hemisphere) these Jews celebrate Passover just as Moses Maimonides celebrated it in Spain more than eight hundred years ago and just as Rabbi Akiva and his friends did about two thousand years ago.

When Jews of this type in twenty-first century Montreal, Canada, marry or divorce, they do so in exactly the same way that Jews in tenth century Mainz, Germany, did. The same is true with prayers and how they teach children to read and understand the Hebrew of the Bible. All of these rules, rituals, and restraints, along with many more, spring forth from the Torah and its accompanying oral tradition. While perhaps not every single Jew in this category thrives, in each generation this group seeds the core group that continues the picture of exceptional Jewish continuity and success.

Much of what built Western civilization is based on this heritage. Both John Selden and John Locke, English scholars of the seventeenth century upon whose work the Founders of the United States of America depended for their ideas, and upon whose writings indeed much of Western jurisprudence is based, were knowledgeable students of this ancient Jewish and Hebrew wisdom.

Since we married, our life's work has been to teach timeless truths and core values from this tradition, making them accessible to anyone interested. We have found that people can immediately apply many of these principles to benefit their life regardless of their background or faith. This wisdom can be thought of as a general theory of the totality of all existence—a set of theorems or permanent principles that apply everywhere and in all times.

How Holistic Systems Work

As we introduced earlier in this chapter, one crucial life principle that often gets overlooked is the idea that the core areas of our lives do not each stand alone.

We (sometimes painfully) learn of the importance of the 5F system by accident. Newly minted dentists find out that having the best equipment and the finest degree means little unless they also know how to manage the business side of their offices and can put patients at ease. Couples who are deeply in love face the reality that being in debt strains relationships.

On the flipside, we may accidentally discover that success in one area of life often helps other areas. Since people like to do business with those they know, like, and trust, having many friends helps increase one's bank account. A healthy bank account, in turn, gives one breathing room to engage in civic activities that then increases one's circle of friends.

Not only does healthily developed Finance assist in the creation and maintenance of a healthy Family, but the counterintuitive reverse is equally true. Married men dramatically outperform their single brethren on the financial front.

Orison Swett Marden's name rings very few bells today. However, he was a household name in late nineteenth century America, and his influence still lingers. In a brilliant, best-selling book on motivation, he wrote these words:

> Over the door of every profession, every occupation, every calling, the world has a standing advertisement: "Wanted—A Man." …Wanted, a man who is symmetrical, and not one-sided in his development, who has not sent all the energies of his being into one narrow specialty and allowed all the other branches of his life to wither and die….

There is an inherent love in the human mind for wholeness. In a healthy body, the lungs and heart are both working well, and the minute electrical impulses that trigger the pumping of the heart's ventricles hum along reliably at about 70 impulses a minute. The kidneys are doing exactly what they should be doing, and all other organs are also operating normally. Nobody would suggest that as long as the heart is behaving properly, we need not pay attention to the lungs or brain. We all recognize that our bodies are complex systems. Not only must all components effectively interact, but the appropriate and balanced development of one aspect of health actively enhances the operation of another. Improved diet may reduce weight and also boost energy. Small improvements in posture may enhance digestion. Exercise may increase cognitive performance. In all, when we look to grow in one area of health, it is more appropriate to think of our efforts as improving all of our health through one particular avenue.

The challenge is that many of us are not in the habit of viewing life in a holistic way. Sometimes, we make the mistake of thinking only sequentially. A person inexperienced at how the world really works might mistakenly assume that it is best to first focus on making money and only then, having achieved a measure of financial security, focus on marriage and family, perhaps leaving friendships and faith for later in life. Alternatively, a young person might think that college and life during her 20s are a time to focus on friendship and fun. Life will get serious soon enough. Relationships and making money can wait. The journey we're on together in this book will take us into compelling explorations of how our 5Fs interact and how we can achieve successful living when we develop all five holistically.

For the sake of clarity, we will mention that each of the 5Fs has many components that are appropriate at different times. Our family means our parents and siblings, grandparents, aunts, uncles and cousins, before we move on to a spouse and children. While the Torah transmitter, Maimonides, advises men to prepare their field—meaning having a way to earn a living—before getting married, one needs to pay attention to refining one's character as one attacks that financial pillar. Knowing that one will soon be looking for a wife and anticipating having children keeps a person focused on the broader picture rather than just examining one's bank account.

Certainly at times we have to hunker down and focus our attention disproportionately on one area. However, knowing that we are working within an inclusive system changes how we approach even those phases of our lives. When we keep the bigger picture in mind as we tackle what is appropriate at the time, it keeps us on a straighter path.

There is no such thing as "having it all worked out." Life needs constant attention. Bicycling around Stanley Park in British Columbia is one of our family's favorite activities. We experience gorgeous vistas, observe boats entering and exiting Vancouver Harbour, spot seals, and are serenaded by birds. We also come across what seem to be gravity-defying rock formations by the shore. Talented artists spend hours patiently balancing rocks, forming mesmerizing structures. Some of the rocks they use are large, and some are small; some are smooth, and others are cragged, but all the pieces intersect, and the formation stands.

These rock-creations may last for hours or days, but eventually, they fall as the result of crashing waves, roaring winds, or the malicious action of a human being. After all, gravity is a reality.

There can be minutes and hours, sometimes even days or weeks or months when our lives resemble those rock structures. We love and are loved, we are at peace with ourselves, others, and the world. Our bank accounts are solid, and we are challenged just enough by activities and work to feel stimulated, but not so much that we are overloaded. We picture God smiling at us (we may call it karma or fate), and our bodies function smoothly without calling attention to themselves. Yet, those moments do not last.

Our goal in this book is to provide guidance both for maximizing those stable times in our lives and for coping with the internal and external winds that inevitably assail us.

Please note that we are not merely observing that a full life must of necessity contain a number of different elements. We're going much further. In fact we are introducing the reality that growth in each element facilitates progress in the others. Omitting one because it is considered less important results in harm to all the other four as well. One important permanent principle is the compelling reality that the many departments of our lives are all essentially unified. If you're not feeling well, it is really difficult to put your best foot forward at work. If you are estranged from your family, romantic relationships are more difficult to form. If you are severely short of money, some of your friends will avoid you almost as if they can smell your desperation. If you ignore your body or your spiritual needs, everything will be more difficult. The most important tool available to us is simultaneously advancing the different areas of life. Integrating these five important parts of life will take you to new levels of achievement.

In order to avoid a sense of prioritization that is almost inevitable when presenting items in list format, we prefer placing the 5Fs, Faith, Finance, Family, Fitness, and Friendship, equidistant to one another on the circumference of a circle. This way, there is no recommended order. Furthermore, we view each F point on the circumference as joined by straight lines to each of the two Fs opposite it. In other words, each of the 5Fs links with each of the other four categories.

True Yesterday, True Today, True Tomorrow

It is a natural tendency to view our own times as unique. In every epoch people think that things are truly different. After World War I, people believed that wars would never again be fought. They even named it the War to End All Wars. After World War II, people promised that genocides would never again be allowed while the world looked the other way. After the terror attacks of September 11, 2001, people said that the world would never be the same. After the stock market collapse and the international recession in early 2009, people said that everything had changed. During the COVID-19 epidemic of 2020, we heard once again that the world will forever be different. All these statements were correct while at the same time they were all wrong.

Of course, things do change. Change is a constant. However, the more that things change, the more we need to depend upon those things that never change. With two of its words for the passage of time, the Lord's language, Hebrew, reflects precisely this contrast between gaining freedom to change while being anchored to the unchangeable. The two words are *shana* and *chodesh*, year and month, respectively. The Hebrew year, in contrast to our civil calendar or the lunar one followed by Islam, is based both on the solar cycle *and* on the lunar cycle. Perhaps not surprisingly, the word for year, shana, also is the verb to repeat. This is exactly what a cycle does; it repeats again and again. In other words, the year suggests unchanging cycles, each year following on the one earlier in exactly the same way.

In contrast, chodesh, the Hebrew word for month, also means new, fresh, and different. The moon grows and shrinks, waxes and wanes, looking different each and every day. In this way, ancient Jewish wisdom teaches the necessity of viewing time as both an opportunity to maintain continuity by remaining anchored to the constants of life while simultaneously grasping each opportunity for change and renewal.

Timeless truths never change. War and genocide are not becoming obsolete. People will always travel and trade. Diseases come and go. Human beings are social creatures who thrive when surrounded by loving family and friends. It is mainly the superficialities that change. Occasionally they change dramatically. For instance, modern technology has changed exponentially since the start of the twentieth century. That sometimes camouflages how little the permanent principles have changed. My grandfather traveled away from home for business about the same number of days a month as I do. He and I both felt the tension between wanting to earn a living and wanting to be home with family. That important reality is unchanging. All that changed is that he traveled by noisy buses and slow trains while I travel at airline speed in air-conditioned comfort. He ranged up to a few hundred miles from home, while I regularly travel thousands of miles. He spent nights on the road in boarding houses and nondescript inns, while I stay in comparatively luxurious hotels. But the bottom line is, like me, he was traveling in order to bring money home. The details are very different, but the needs and motivations are the same. Though a hundred years and two oceans separate us in time and space, our lives are remarkably similar. What is important is learning what is a timeless truth and what is merely superficial change. That is exactly what Bible-based, ancient Jewish wisdom does so well.

Have you ever struggled to do something only to discover later that a bit of knowledge would have made your efforts so much easier? We have, ranging from the inconsequential to the notable. Certain trivial things that stymied me (SL) for years, such as how to fold fitted sheets, became easy once I watched, paused, and rewound an online video. To be sure, my inability to fold fitted sheets barely impacted my life. I get a short-term kick out of seeing an orderly closet, but the appearance of my linen closet makes little difference in important or even minor aspects of my day-to-day existence. Life was going along just fine without that.

Other information matters a lot more. If you plan to boat in the Pacific Northwest as we regularly do, it helps to know that there are tremendous tidal variations. Certain passages should be traversed only at slack tide. Now, a boater may insist on the freedom to go where he wants to go, when he wants to go. But he may find himself going backward, going aground, or even capsizing. Replace that boater with a captain of any sex, race, nationality, income, or educational level, and the rules of the sea will still hold true.

Likewise, if you are interviewing for a job, you can increase your chances of being offered a position by taking a few preliminary steps. Whether it is researching the company, following the proper format for a resume, or dressing appropriately for an interview, most of us have no problem acknowledging that there are proven ways to up the odds of being hired. We can all agree that showing up looking disheveled, without having read the job description, and knowing nothing about the company is not likely to lead to a job offer.

Why is it so easy to understand that when it comes to boating or interviewing there are certain inviolable principles and rules, or at least strongly suggested guidelines, and yet it's so difficult for us to accept this when it comes to interactions between men and women, money, work, community and spirituality? (Spiritual is not the same as religious—more on this later.) Why do we have such a hard time believing, in other words, that there are rules to how to best live our lives? And just as we are all free to anchor without checking the tide table, or to show up hungover to a job interview, some life choices are less likely to achieve either a safe or satisfactory result for us.

Partially, because when you are boating or interviewing, you know pretty quickly if you've made a mistake. If you capsize or don't get the job for which you applied, you know that the attempt was unsuccessful. When it comes to our lives, we often don't recognize missteps until years down the road.

This lack of clarity, in part, is due to the fact that we may not be sure what we're targeting. How do you know if your life is successful if you're not clear on what a successful life looks like? One of our goals for this book is to encourage you to not only ask yourself that question, but to seek out those from different age groups, experiences, and viewpoints who can widen your horizons as you formulate your answer.

What's more, while six books on getting a job may each feature different approaches, they aren't going to drastically differ on basic ideas. None of them are going to suggest, for example, going to a job interview at an old-school, prestigious law firm dressed in your sweats. Yet, we can find wildly varying ideas as to how we should behave and what we should do when it comes to friendship, career, marriage, children, and life in general.

To some extent, these varying ideas are a product of the changing opinions and beliefs of a generation. And almost every generation thinks that while people certainly believed in ridiculous ideas in the past, their own generation is so advanced that the things it touts must be true. We can read about the tulip craze of the 1600s and the popularity of phrenology in the nineteenth and early twentieth centuries, and we are smugly sure that we would not fall for similar economic bubbles or false science. We shake our heads at advertisements from the 1930s and 1940s telling us that 9 out of 10 doctors recommend a certain brand of cigarette, but insist that anything that 9 out of 10 doctors today say must be accurate. We may (justifiably) bristle at pompous, old-fashioned statements explaining that women don't have the intellect to be lawyers, but do we recognize the hubris in insisting that the current generation, for the first and only time in history, doesn't have its own fallacies and fabrications?

Perhaps we should spend some time asking which of our follies our own descendants will cite when feeling superior to us. When it comes to living our lives, the stakes are too high to fall in line unthinkingly with current beliefs.

This book presents ideas that many today might attack as outdated, objectionable, deplorable, and bigoted. But calling something names doesn't refute an argument. It certainly doesn't expand one's thinking or allow one to adjust one's ideas even slightly.

Much of what we are about to tell you will be contradicted by almost every university in the world. That doesn't worry us. If we were talking about nuclear physics or quantum mechanics, it would be legitimate to ask whether we had the backing of other scientists. And recently developed knowledge in the field would suggest that a textbook from, let's say, 1920 should not be accepted as the final word. But when it comes to human nature, to relationships between parents and children, the nature of male-female relationships, or the nature of earning money, technological advances blind us to those unchanging truths that continue to influence us, whether we are conscious of them or not. Research, while useful, can leave us in a constant state of flux and panic as we try to constantly adjust our approach to keep up with the latest "discoveries." In fact, when it comes to getting the most out of life, ancient wisdom is often more useful than articles touting the latest finding in psychology.

Given the contradictory nature of the information available— whether from science, religious tradition, or popular culture—how are we supposed to make a choice about how to live? Can we afford to plumb each source to the depths until we hit the bedrock of truth, if such a thing is even possible? Certainly an examined and thoughtful life is a good idea. But what about the life that is happening in the meantime?

Herein lies the dilemma. We need to make major life choices before all the data are in. This is true in most areas of our life. Every year, thousands of students saddle themselves with debt and commit hours of their lives to educational studies without a guarantee that they will want to devote themselves to that field or that it will be a good fit for them. Entrepreneurs start new businesses without knowing if their ventures will succeed. Couples marry and have children without a crystal ball into the future telling them that they will be glad they made that choice. Anyone who waits for certainty before starting out on a road will find him or herself always standing behind the starting line. If you never attempt things because you're holding out for certainty, you will be holding out for a long time.

For those of us with robust egos and good educations, many of the concepts in this book arouse instinctive pushback. These ideas force us to question how much we can rely on our feelings and intuitions as well as the messages beamed at us by the surrounding culture. If you can cope with the possibility that even some of the ideas in this book might be true, read on. After all, your happiness just might be at stake.

Chapter 2

Connect for Success

Here is the opening sentence of a well-known book:

Aaaaa b ccc ddd eeeee gg hhh Iiiiiii kk lll nnnn oo p rrrrr sss tttttt ww y

Would you like to read the rest of the book? Probably not. Written as they are, the letters are meaningless. They will capture our imagination only once they are cunningly joined together to make words.

Arranging the previous letters intentionally as George Orwell did in the opening to his book *1984*, introduces us to a world where people must pretend that the senseless makes sense: "It was a bright cold day in April and the clocks were striking thirteen." Now, perhaps, you might be intrigued and ready to read on.

Letters by themselves are just random squiggles on a page. Once they are combined into words, their power is overwhelming. Whether we are speaking of *Uncle Tom's Cabin*, the book that Massachusetts senator Charles Sumner credited with electing Abraham Lincoln to the presidency, or whether we are reading a lover's note, it is the almost unlimited combination of letters into words and words into sentences and sentences into paragraphs that affect us.

Isolated musical notes set no hearts pumping. Strung together they move us to tears, set our toes tapping, and elevate or lower our spirits. An array of spices and cooking ingredients clutter our counters. Mixed together they provide food to warm our stomachs and delight our tongues.

Even the elements in the periodic table only become useful once they are combined. Almost everything we need and enjoy, including air and water, is made from combinations of elements rather than individual ones. Hydrogen and oxygen combine to make the water we drink while the air we breathe is composed of nitrogen and oxygen, plus traces of argon and carbon dioxide and more. It is difficult to think of anything we use that isn't made up of more than one element. Amazingly, elements that are poisonous in themselves, such as sodium and chlorine, join together to make a wondrous creation that is necessary for life and that adds spice to our food—salt.

We live in a world of connection. This is as true for human beings as it is for letters, musical notes, and elements. The premise of our 5Fs is that to live our fullest lives we need connection—with other people, with ourselves, with spiritual reality, and with the physical world around and within us.

What happens when connections disintegrate? Most of us have experienced the blue screen of death on our computers. We are immediately unlinked from the work we were doing, from the people with whom we interact online, from having instant access to our bank accounts, and much more. We are frustrated and annoyed, and we face a niggling doubt about how we would manage if there was a major system outage for a prolonged period of time.

Similarly, most of us have faced an electrical system blackout, perhaps as the result of a storm. In an astonishingly short space of time, we may find ourselves in physical danger from cold. As we huddle in our coats and blankets gauging how often we can safely open our warming freezers and wondering how we can heat food if we don't have a gas stove, our wants and needs become centered on life's most basic elements.

Just as we see what happens when civilization's connections are severed, so too we understand the peril when our body's neural connections disappear. Scientists estimate that the brain sends and receives information regularly using somewhere in the neighborhood of 100 trillion connections from tens of billions of neurons. One neuron may have as many as 7,000 connections with another neuron. When, sadly, someone suffers from a stroke or a disease like Alzheimer's that severs many of those connections, the results are dire indeed.

What is true for society and for our bodies is true for our overall well-being as well. The more connections we make and the more linked these connections are to each other, the better life we will enjoy. When tragedy strikes us personally, we will be better prepared to compensate. Losing a job and being left without an income is devastating. Having friends and family who will lend a helping hand can be a lifesaver. A serious health challenge can be debilitating. Folks who feel God walking with them through the crisis talk of the strength that gives them. Having expendable money makes coping with many crises easier, turning problems into mere expenses. We could go on showing how each of the other 4Fs makes a crisis involving any one particular area more easily bearable.

What Makes Us Happy?

While many of us think of nomads as long-ago wanderers that we learned about in history class, technology has sprouted a new group— digital nomads. At any time, thousands of people are traveling around the world with little more than a backpack and a laptop computer. They choose a location, enjoy the surroundings, and live in short-term rentals. Then they move on. As long as they can connect to a reliable Wi-Fi signal, they can work anywhere. These people work as YouTubers, marketers, virtual assistants, Amazon resellers, website designers, software developers, and at dozens of other occupations.

The accounts given by digital nomads of their on-the-move lifestyles speak glowingly of the sense of liberation they feel. There is nothing tying them down or restricting their schedules. Many sold their furniture and gave away or discarded clothing, books, and belongings, freeing themselves from possessions. And we, their readers, viewers, or friends, are led to believe that digital nomads live lives to be envied.

Yet, it turns out that while many enjoy the nomadic lifestyle for periods ranging from a few months to a few years, it is hard to find people who have been living as digital nomads for much longer than that. Why does such an apparently attractive lifestyle appear to work only temporarily? Being able to live in any exotic city at your whim or in a beautiful remote beachfront village and to be able to move on to the next appealing destination whenever you feel like it seems an ideal life. So why does it appear to be almost nonexistent as a permanent lifestyle? Why do virtually all of those living this appealing life eventually settle down?

In the same way that objects dropped tend to fall downward, human beings have a desire to be moored. Just as gravity is a perfectly natural force, so too it is natural for digital nomads to eventually resume a more conventional lifestyle with possessions and social commitments. It is perfectly normal to feel a need for long-term, physical connection with people, places, and possessions: not split-second virtual digital connection, not constantly changing experiences, but solid connection with the world around us. Though it's true that some people have a greater degree of wanderlust than others, almost all human beings recognize the benefit of having the attachments and securities of settled life. Paradoxically, though our impulse may be to settle down, advancements in technology and changing social norms encourage and enable us to be more mobile than ever.

Even those of us who aren't seduced to become digital nomads by the idea of constantly seeking new places and experiences are much more mobile than previous generations. Before World War I, most of those living in the United Kingdom had never traveled more than 50 miles from their homes. In the past, those in the military who frequently moved their families every few years were the exception. Most people married and settled down assuming they would stay in the same city for life. All sorts of inventions, from the telegraph to the internet and from bicycles to airplanes, had the unexpected consequence of making a certain amount of mobility not only easier, but desirable and even necessary.

Over the past few decades it has become far more normative to grow up in one city, go to college in another region of the country, and start one's career in a third location. Many of us view it as normal that moving to a new state or country may be part of our life plan. Not unrelated at all, getting married and having children, which used to be taken for granted as a step into adulthood, is increasingly less common. Where most people used to be members of a faith community, that choice too is a path less taken. Earning a living and establishing lasting business relationships seems to be harder to do than it was a few decades ago. Who stays at one company for 50 years anymore?

But what is the result of all this moving around? Perhaps people gain a higher degree of worldliness. But at what cost? Scores of articles and books report a startling increase in loneliness, sadness, and anxiety in many lives. Could these phenomena be related?

In 1938, Harvard commenced a longitudinal study of adult development. It carefully got to know the life details of 724 young volunteers since they were teenagers, and then, year by year it continued studying them and their lives. (President John F. Kennedy was one of the original cohort.) Some of the original participants are now in their 90s, and the study, currently led by Dr. Robert Waldinger, the fourth director since 1938, is also following their children and grandchildren.

The study's purpose was to discover which factors contribute to successful lives. The central importance of relationships to overall happiness clearly emerges from the study. Said Waldinger, "When we gathered together everything we knew about them at age 50, it wasn't their middle-age cholesterol levels that predicted how they were going to grow old, it was how satisfied they were in their relationships. The people who were the most satisfied in their relationships at age 50 were the healthiest at age 80."

In other words, the subjects' physical health was tied to the quality of their relationships. It should come as no surprise that wealth also correlates with relationships. Financial success, claim the scholars, depends chiefly on warmth of relationships. In other words, it turns out that flourishing in life in general depends upon close ties with family, friends, and community. Life success has less to do with fame, wealth, social class, IQ, genes, or anything else.

This famous longitudinal study is widely deemed reliable and highly indicative of reality. That isn't surprising considering that it has been in process consistently for the best part of a hundred years and has so far covered three generations.

Connecting Through Time and Space

At this point we would like to add another dimension to the 5F picture—time. While the oral transmission was first taught by God to Moses on Mt. Sinai, over the years it became clear that certain pieces might eventually get lost. In the third century, Rabbi Yehuda (Judah) HaNasi (the Prince) began the process of writing down key words and phrases that would serve to spark memory. Unlike the five books of Moses, he divided his writing into six volumes, known collectively as the Mishna. These actually divide into three groups of two. The first pair deals with how we relate to the world around us and are called *Seeds* (Zeraim) and *Time* (Moed).

What is that about? Seeds are the way that life spreads over space. When seeds waft on the wind or are carried about, new areas sprout fruits, vegetables, and flowers. The solitary oak tree can become a forest. Seeds also spread life over time, as new embryos are fertilized and future generations are born. Over only a few generations, two individuals can have more than one hundred descendants. These two sections of the Oral Torah deal with connections that spread over space and time. As early twentieth century physics determined, space and time constitute the totality of the physical world.

Connecting in a healthy way means not only connecting to different parts of our lives today, but also to the past and to the future. In other words, a truly connected person acknowledges the people and traditions that came before him and "seeded his life," as it were. He connects to parents, ancestors, history—a heritage—rather than seeing himself as an isolated entity. Likewise, the connected person looks toward the future and takes responsibility for it—both by "seeding it" with the children that will form future generations, and preparing for it, whether by building generational wealth or instituting programs and initiatives that will outlive him.

This is a huge challenge for our individualistic culture. For one, education and media today teach us to look at previous generations as a step below us rather than as people to admire. We are encouraged to dismiss anyone who does not share our views, no matter how long ago. There is no consideration given to the idea that not only might we be entirely wrong but that people are complex beings rather than bank statements. On a bank statement, if one started with $100 and spent $25, their account will show +$75. If they spend $125, their account will show −$25. The final sum is what matters. Human beings do not work like that. The actions of a person who did some wrong things and some great ones do not cancel each other out. Together, they make up the whole of the person, who can be appreciated for the good she did while sorrowing at the bad. The entire idea of "canceling" an entire person for a misguided view or mistake reeks of arrogance and immaturity. One result is that many young people look upon their parents and previous generations as ignorant and unenlightened compared to themselves.

Furthermore, modern culture glorifies instant gratification. Building a future, which takes real investment and work, is very hard when you see the be-all and end-all of life as constantly being happy. If we're hungry, we go online and have food delivered to us within an hour. We get impatient if a text isn't responded to within a few minutes. The idea, long held in society and strongly encouraged by religion that we have a responsibility to those who came before us as well as to those who will come after us, is weakened in a world that encourages us to see the individual in the present—me, myself, and I and how I feel today—as of primary importance.

We see our culture's disregard for connections across time play out in many arenas. Statues of great historical figures are pulled down because they did not share the sensibilities of an 18-year-old today. Eradicating the history of nations is in vogue. On a personal level, in a shocking trend, women and men under the age of 30 are choosing to be sterilized, severing their strongest avenue for connection to the future. The numbers of childless young women seeking information about tubal ligations and the numbers of childless young men seeking vasectomies is higher than ever before.

As one 19-year-old said, "I want time alone, time with my partner, and time to travel and spend money on luxury. And I don't think there's anything wrong with that. It's my life and I'm not hurting anyone."

We disagree. If connection is the key to flourishing life, then each person who opts out of connecting, whether with other people or with their past and future, is contributing to a lesser world. What is more, as countries in both Europe and Asia have discovered, their nation's very survival is at stake when the numbers of births dips below the replacement rate. The pillars of society crumble when too many people choose to be indifferent citizens. One example of this indifference is not having children or not raising them to value their country. As much as we may boast, "It is my life," everyone's life is affected when the surrounding society collapses.

Go ahead and list the 10 most important relationships in your life. Some will be family and others will be business and work relationships. There will probably be a few friends on the list too. Family relationships are fairly well defined. The obligations and expectations of those relationships are, for the most part, known quantities. Business relationships are also clear, governed as most are by contracts. But what about friends? What are the obligations of friendship? What are the reasonable expectations of friendship? While the Five Books of Moses are packed with rules and rituals that shape both family and business relationships, it is notably light on any mention of friendships. We know what employees owe their employers and vice versa, and we know what parents owe children and what children owe their parents, but if we ask people what they owe their friends, the answer could be, "It depends on the friend."

Everyone knows the answer to the question, "For how long will your parent be your parent?" If asked for how long a marriage is intended to last, the correct answer is, "This is forever." But if one is asked for how long one's friend will be one's friend, the prudent answer is, "I don't know." The true answer might be, "For as long as we both want to be friends."

The fine Irish poet William Butler Yeats penned a well-known line:

There are no strangers here; Only friends you haven't yet met.

The words hint at a perplexing truth, namely that the line between friends and strangers can be a bit blurry. Which presents us with a puzzling problem: how do we build lasting frameworks for friendships? Ancient Jewish wisdom provides a pathway by noting the parallels between the first two commandments given in the Torah and the last two of its 613 commandments.

#1: Have children

Be fertile and increase. . . (Genesis 1:28)

#2: Circumcision

You shall circumcise the flesh of your foreskin. This shall be the sign of the covenant between Me and you. (Genesis 17:11)

#612: Annual gathering, a sort of State of the Union Address

Gather all the people—men, women, children, and the strangers in your communities (Deuteronomy 31:12)

#613: Everyone must have his own copy of the Torah

Therefore, write down this prose (Deuteronomy 31:19)

The first two commandments link the individual to both the past and the future. God wants me to reproduce, carrying on to the future. Furthermore, I'm directed to circumcise my sons. This is an immensely powerful, emotional ceremony that locks me and my descendants to the past.

The last two commandments link the nation to the past and to the future. We're told to hold an annual gathering at which we all—men, women, and children—listen to the Torah and relive our history. The Torah's final instruction directs each member of the nation to write our own copy of the Torah, the document that links us to each other and to our national destiny going forward into the future.

Thus, we see that the Torah, the constitution of the Jewish people, is bookended by a pair of rules that give the individual his or her life context, and another pair of rules that give the nation its life context. As an individual, I am not an alienated orphan dropped into a cold lonely life. I am linked to the future by my children, and I am linked to a past by the timeless covenant of Abraham. The nation, in turn, is also linked to its destiny in the future and its origins in the past.

Many Americans and Europeans fear greatly for the future of their countries because new citizens, whether by birth or immigration, are no longer taught to value the country's origins. Current citizens no longer share any sense of a purposeful national future.

When past and future are shared with others, friendships often result. Each stranger can truly be a friend, "you haven't yet met." When people's ideas excite them today but have no bedrock in the past nor sustainable hope in the future, strangers can walk together temporarily, but true friendship is unlikely. For friendships to thrive, our lives need to be firmly rooted in the past and foreseeable in the future.

Ironically, though many today sever their ties to the past and future in the name of "better connection" to a partner, or a fuller life in the present, the lack of connection with the past and the future often goes hand-in-hand with a lack of connection to the present as well. In 2019, an American study from YouGov of 1,254 US adults ages 18+ found that while 9% of baby boomers say they have no friends and the same percentage say they have no acquaintances, 22% of millennials cite no friends while 25% say they have no acquaintances. While the study question excluded family members and "partners," those numbers are troubling.

Family isn't faring well either. The United Kingdom organization, *Aging Well Without Children*, estimates that by the year 2030 about 2 million adults over the age of 65 in the UK will never have had children. Other first-world countries face similar problems. However, despite the organization's hopes that the British government will fill in the gaps, governments cannot solve loneliness and mandate loving care. The government of Scotland has just budgeted £10M to "tackle social isolation and loneliness." Individual families do that in ways that no bureaucracy can mimic. There is also a direct correlation between being alone and an increase in needing medical care.

Professor David Spiegel, chair of psychiatry and behavioral sciences at Stanford said: "Numerous studies have shown that social isolation is associated with increases in all-cause mortality risk to the same degree as smoking or high cholesterol levels. Individuals tend to die after rather than before their birthdays and major holidays, suggesting some ability to postpone death for a short period to reach a meaningful goal. Conversely, depression and the associated social withdrawal/alienation is an independent predictor of shorter survival with cancer and heart disease.... We are social creatures, and we manage stressors better when we are not alone with them."

In 2023, US Surgeon General Vivek Murthy proposed six solutions to what he defined as a loneliness epidemic. One of them included creating more accessible public transportation. We are skeptical that this, or any other of his recommendations, reaches in any way to the core of the problem because his solutions do not mention the words, church, synagogue, religion, or marriage. This book presents an entirely different perspective.

The bottom line: many in the modern world are in a crisis of disconnection, and the results are not pretty. The good news is that each of us has the choice not to follow these trends.

Fundamentals of Connection

Whether you believe, as we do, that the Bible is the word of God, or whether you think of it as ancient literature, the fact remains that the Bible has shaped world history. No book has been more influential in molding Western civilization than the Bible. Much of what we take for granted in our daily lives stems from this book. It is only because these ideas are so ingrained in our culture that we don't think about their origins. As traditional religion shrinks, we see that ideas we used to think of as automatic and normative, such as the assumption that men and women will marry and have children, a respect for private property, and a belief in the greatness of the human spirit, are falling away.

As Christianity spread over the globe, first as Catholicism and then also as Protestantism, ancient Jewish wisdom was often part of the message. This was sometimes overtly recognized, as English poet John Milton acknowledged, or in the Ainsworth Bible that accompanied the Pilgrims to America. Other times, it went unrecognized but was still influential. Cultures shaped by the Bible emphasized different things than did countries in which the Bible was alien. One of these ideas was connection.

This idea is embedded in the Hebrew of the Bible. Most of us understand that much is lost when we read great pieces in translation. To truly get the full impact of Dostoevsky's novels, one needs to read them in Russian. Shakespeare's words best speak to our hearts in English, while a love poem in French may fall flat in another language. The language of the Bible is Hebrew. While the Bible has been translated into more languages than any other book, and as of September 2022 what is commonly known as the Old Testament can be read in 724 languages, none of these capture the entire picture that the Hebrew alone conveys.

One failing is that most translations follow the advice of third-grade English teachers rather than opting for accuracy. Barring a compelling reason, writing advice says not to begin sentences with the word "and." God had such a compelling reason—connection. In the original Hebrew, more than 50% of the sentences in the Five Books of Moses start with the Hebrew letter "vav," which serves as a prefix that means "and." After the opening verse, "In the beginning God created the heavens and the earth," each of the succeeding 33 verses describing Creation begin in the Hebrew with the letter "vav." All of Creation is connected, one step leading to the next. This emphasis on events, actions, and generations being connected to that which comes before them and after them is a crucial point in God's word. The world is not random.

When we look at the Bible through this lens, we see the unfolding events in a new light. We are being taught, step by step, how to build connections with others and with the world itself.

The Bible lays this message out early on with the statement, "It is not good for man to be alone" (Genesis 2:18). God is sharing a profound piece of information with us. On a surface level, He is talking about Adam's matrimonial future, declaring that Adam cannot live a "good" life unless he joins in a loving union with a wife. On a deeper level, we are being told something that applies to all aspects of our lives all the time: our existential need for other people. Throughout our lives, we need to seek to build connections with others. We need to push back against isolation and loneliness. This is foundational to successful living.

A question regularly explored in the academies of ancient Jewish wisdom is this: surely, God could have started the world with two people. Look closely at Genesis 2:18–2:19, and you will see a perplexing problem. Once God makes the declaration, "It is not good for man to be alone," we would expect the next verse to introduce us to Eve. Instead, we take a zoological detour for Adam to meet and name the birds of the sky and the beasts of the field. Only once Adam experiences loneliness and cannot alleviate it with any other creature on the planet, does Eve make her appearance. Once again, we can see the Bible either as rather poor literature or alternatively we can read it as God's guidebook for living.

Doing the latter explains why none of the 5Fs we mention have to do with pets. Being around animals has many advantages. While working animals such as cows or horses provide obvious benefits, owning a pet also has many plusses. Pets are a source of affection and provide an opportunity for humans to be givers. Taking care of pets' needs can be good for our physical and emotional health. However, Genesis 2:19 reveals a truth that many in our day find antiquated: a relationship with an animal cannot replace a relationship with a person.

Like us, you probably have heard people talk about their "children" only to discover they are referring to their cats and dogs. Contemplate for a minute how over the past years dogs went from being utilitarian workers to being "man's best friend" to being a "fur baby." You may have heard of a new yoga studio or spa opening only to find out that it was meant for those with four legs, not two. Perhaps you even have seen an ad for neuticles, fake testicles for one's neutered dog or cat. Do you think that the expected increase in pet ownership among 18- to 34-year-olds might be related to the decrease in marriage and children? This is one of the areas where you need to decide if a Creator provided "best practices" direction or if following the crowd is a better idea. A vote for the former suggests that a relationship with an affectionate, loving, and responsive animal can augment a balanced, healthy life, but it is not a necessity for having one. On the other hand, affectionate and loving human relationships are necessary.

Sex and Money

As we move on through the text, we uncover the climax of the account of the creation of man, which includes God's incentives to people for connecting. Almost irresistible rewards await the person who succeeds at connecting with others: the joys that stem from achieving success in the areas of Family and Finance.

We mentioned how the first pair of volumes of the Mishna, the code of the Oral Transmission, focuses on connection through space and through time. We are now ready to discuss the next pair that deals with two types of human relationships: sexual, which is to say Family, and Financial.

". . .and they shall become one flesh," (Gen 2:24) promises the ultimate in sensual pleasure for connecting deeply with another one of God's children in accordance with His instructions. True, sex can be abused, forced, or engaged in casually and improperly. But that is a case of humans abusing a Godly gift. The best and most satisfying way to engage in a sexual relationship is with a covenantal, long-term partner with whom one shares a life of mutual giving and receiving. In such a life, sex becomes the growing expression of true union, in which physical pleasure mirrors emotional connection. More shallow forms of sex may provide temporary physical stimulation, but they seldom satisfy fully. Sex grounded in marriage also expands our world through family.

Because of their own actions, Adam and Eve are no longer going to remain in the Garden of Eden. Ancient Jewish wisdom teaches us that Adam gave an anguished cry: "I was connected to you, God, in a way that animals are not. You highlighted my humanity by granting me free will, the ability to make decisions by choice rather than instinct. You gave me a directive about not eating from one tree. I failed. I am now little better than an animal—instinctively eating when I am hungry."

In response to that acknowledgment and cry of repentance, God forgave Adam and gave him and his descendants a chance to do better and use their human abilities. Genesis 3:19: "With the sweat of your brow you will eat bread" is not part of the punishment but the granting of a second chance.

In Biblical nomenclature, bread stands for money. Even today, many cultures use the words "bread" or "dough" as colloquial terms for money. How do you excel at economic interaction? First of all, planting wheat, harvesting it, grinding it into flour, and baking it into bread are too much for one person to do. We require the cooperation and collaboration of a number of people. We do that by using the uniquely human ability of speech to communicate with others, cooperating together rather than using our bodies to threaten violence. Furthermore, one must commence the process well before one is hungry, so exhibiting forethought and the ability to delay gratification are necessary. True, economic interaction can be abused, forced, or engaged in casually and improperly. But, once again, that is a case of humans abusing a Godly gift.

Adam's children can descend to the level of animals and live lives of strife where might makes right. Or they can live lives of abundance by making "bread," the metaphor for money, the fruit of economic collaboration by working with others over the long term.

Looking at Genesis once again, we see the very first human interaction is one man to one woman—husband and wife. This core quickly expands to children and other direct descendants. You could say that Genesis is the story of learning how to be a family. We see conflict between husbands and wives, interactions between parents and children, and struggles between siblings. Cain and Abel, Isaac and Ishmael, Jacob and Esau . . . getting along with one's brother seems to be a challenge that humankind must learn how to manage.

Each narrative having to do with the just mentioned characters has a message for us. Let's take a deeper look at Cain and Abel and understand what they are teaching us.

Those of us with busy families, who live in crowded cities, or who shop in cramped stores have probably all dreamed, on occasion, of being surrounded by fewer people. Just imagine easily getting a parking spot or not needing to stand in line to ring up an item. Imagine not being put on call waiting when you try to reach your bank by phone! It sounds heavenly. At least until we think about it some more.

When the English novelist Charles Dickens visited a prison outside of Philadelphia in 1842, he witnessed prisoners being held in solitary confinement. He wrote that most people are incapable of recognizing the full extent of the torture and agony of being incarcerated alone. He insisted that the mental torture of solitary confinement was far worse than any torture that could be inflicted upon the body.

What does this have to do with Cain and Abel? Were Adam and Eve and Cain and Abel real people? How about Jacob and Joshua, Moses and Miriam? Yes. However, the Bible is not a history book or a collection of biographical sketches. The only incidents in people's lives that are mentioned are those that contain needed information for people in all places and at all times.

To begin understanding the story of Cain and Abel, let us start by examining the name of one of our key characters. As we've said, each Hebrew word in the Bible unpacks into life lessons. Likewise, every Hebrew name in the Bible has a meaning that conveys something about the essence of the person or place being named. Cain, or more accurately in the Hebrew, Kayin, means "acquisition." This signifies that Cain's entire essence was acquisitiveness. He wanted to acquire more and more. Anything that another human being possessed was something that he saw as being taken away from him.

After Cain's parents, Adam and Eve, are banished from the Garden of Eden, death is a reality. Though the text doesn't tell us explicitly about the reason for Cain's fight with Abel, ancient Jewish wisdom fills in the blanks and provides a logical explanation for the fight. Now that death is a reality and Adam is aging, Cain and Abel are left as the future inheritors of the whole world. Mulling this over, Cain decides that acquiring the whole world is better than only acquiring half. He doesn't consider his brother, Abel, to be a beloved partner. He is a competitor who must be eliminated. The result of that thinking is the world's first murder.

Cain's understandable but mistaken presumption is that the road to wealth and happiness lies in owning everything. Sadly, we can think of people today who have exactly the same attitude. They too look at their brothers—other people—with envy and resentment.

God's response to Cain's action is based on the idea that the punishment always fits the crime. Sometimes, as in this case, the punishment helps us understand what the motivation for the crime was. Cain's penalty has two parts: "When you work the ground, it will no longer continue to yield its strength to you. A vagrant and a wanderer is what you will be" (Genesis 4:12).

How does this punishment fit the crime? There are two ways that land serves us—agriculture and development. You can plant crops, or you can build a structure that you will use or that will be used by others who will pay you rent. The world Cain was so bent on acquiring is now useless to him. Nothing he plants will grow. What's more, he will be constantly on the move, making durable relationships with others impossible. We see that the essence of Cain's sin was not recognizing his need for other people. As the owner of the entire world, he will be the poorest, saddest man around. Abel was not his adversary; he was his ally.

We wait to see if Cain learns from his conversation with God that he should interact and cooperate with other people, not kill them. Genesis 4:13–16 provides the answer. Recognizing his sin and repenting, Cain asks for and receives a reprieve. He is allowed to stay in one place, and he settles in the land of Nod. What does he do next? He brings new life into the world.

Bright Screens, Dim Minds

We are going to digress for a moment here because we hear some of you asking questions, "Who was Cain's wife? What other people are there to interact with him?" To explain why the answers to these questions are actually irrelevant, we need to point out a mistake we often make when trying to visualize events and people in the Bible.

As hard as it can be to accept, let's all try to agree that since Adam and Eve ate of the fruit from the tree of knowledge of good and evil (for that is its full name), good and evil have been commingled in pretty much everything. A life-saving medication comes with warnings about the many unwanted potential side effects. In a far-off land, an earthquake kills thousands, but it also stimulates rigorously enforced new safety building codes, which saves many lives in the future. It is hard to think of bad things that bring absolutely no good in their wake, and it is even harder to think of nominally good things that contain no seeds of evil. Even welcomed and amazing technologies have negative side effects that we may only become aware of down the road.

Before movies boasted synchronized sound, which didn't arrive until *The Jazz Singer* in 1927, about 90 million cinema tickets were sold in the United States each week. Remember that the entire population of the United States was then just a touch over 100 million! Then came television. When World War II ended in 1945, there were almost no television sets in America. By 1951, only six years later, nearly 20% of American homes had a television. By 1960, more than 90% of American households had televisions. No invention had ever penetrated so deeply into American culture quite as quickly as television. By comparison, it took telephones about twice as long to penetrate 90% of American homes. Computers and mobile phones, penetrated slightly more quickly than television had done.

It is undoubtedly wonderful to be able to reach for a small hand-held device in one's pocket and watch, in real time, events transpiring half a world away. While that is an amazing technological achievement, it can also do harm. What harm have television and other small screen devices perpetrated? One less discussed consequence is the cognitive push to see everything in concrete, full-color images. We became less able to understand and manipulate abstract ideas, some of which cannot be visualized by our limited human brains.

Many of us grew up with toy arks, populated by plastic Noahs and a variety of animals. We may have done art projects depicting Joseph's coat of many colors. The problem comes when we don't deepen our knowledge of the Bible as adults. We still picture that ark or coat when we read the associated Bible verses. With that childish view, we try to see Bible "stories" in the same way that we would watch a movie. We get caught in the details rather than appreciating the picture.

An example from mathematics illustrates this point. The square root of a number is that smaller number which, when multiplied by itself, yields the original number. The square root of 9 is 3 and the square root of 25 is 5. But actually 9 has two square roots, +3 and −3 because a negative number multiplied by a negative number gives a positive answer. So both +5 multiplied by itself and −5 multiplied by itself yield +25. All that is easy to understand.

However, there is a very useful concept that is used a lot in mathematics—the square root of −1. Well, what is it? Since +1 multiplied by itself gives +1 and −1 multiplied by itself also gives +1, how do I visualize on the number line something that when multiplied by itself gives me −1? It is impossible. Nonetheless, it still exists as an abstract concept. What is more, it is a very useful abstraction when dealing with higher mathematics. The ubiquity of screens in our lives makes it harder for us to deal with non-seeable abstract things such as this.

Perhaps the most harmful factor in trying to grasp the complexity of the Hebrew Bible is the perfectly normal tendency to want to imagine how each description would look on a screen. Trying to figure out who Cain's wife was is an example of this. For understanding the critical message for successful living today, that doesn't matter. With that in mind, let's return to Cain.

Not only does Cain bring new life into the world, he names the baby *Chanoch*, meaning *education* and *dedication*. He has learned his lesson. He has been educated about the gift of people and understands that the best way to prosper is not to eliminate others, but to cooperate with them—to connect. He dedicates his life to bringing people together, building the world's first city, a place where people gather.

This is not to say that time alone sometimes is not beneficial. The key word is "sometimes." The treasured evening silence of a quiet apartment differs from the lonely, isolated misery of a lonely apartment in no materialistic way. Imagine an intelligent, sentient fly on the wall. He will see two scenes that seem remarkably similar. He might see an individual sitting on the couch, a cold drink at his side. Yet, one scene depicts a person relishing a few silent moments in between one day that was filled with human interaction and fulfilling experiences and the next day that will be filled with human interaction and fulfilling experiences. The fly moves to another room where he sees someone who looks just like the first person. Yet this individual has no one in his life who knows or cares what he did yesterday or what he will do tomorrow. He is not on the couch for a few fleeting, cherished moments of quiet, but almost never leaves that couch. Although our fly doesn't understand, the two views are worlds apart.

I Need You; You Need Me

The book of Genesis continues to lay out family relationships for us, and as families grow, they become clans and tribes and nations. First we have siblings, a generation later we have cousins, then second cousins, and so on. Within a very few generations, instead of recognizing everyone as family, we find the need to get along with those we no longer consider to be close relatives. Two of our 5F categories, Friendship and Finance, describe ways that we reach out to those who are beyond Family. The 5F structure recognizes that the category of Friendship must include not only our close friends, but also our wider communities and greater society. To thrive, to have sewers and power plants, armies and industry, we need systems for getting along with those we may never be related to and in many cases, may never meet.

One powerful way to connect with others is through money—what we label as Finance. Ancient Jewish wisdom written down more than 2,000 years ago tells of the sage Ben Zoma who, standing on the stairs at the Temple Mount, looked down and saw bustling crowds. He didn't worry about not finding a parking spot for his donkey or whether the apples at the fruit store would be sold out. Instead, he recited a blessing that sounds strange to our ears.

Blessed is the One Who knows all secrets (God) and blessed is the One (God) Who created all these people to serve me.

That sounds rather egocentric, doesn't it? Not at all.

Ben Zoma goes on to explain that a man alone needs to plant, sow, and reap. He needs to grind flour, sift, knead, and bake. He needs to raise sheep and shear, card, spin, and sew clothing. You get the point. He is grateful to God for making so many people, each of whom has his or her own talents, needs, and desires. This leads them each to specialize in a field such as raising dairy cows or harvesting rice or manufacturing clothing, which they then offer to Ben Zoma in exchange for something that he does that they need or a medium of exchange such as money that can be used to purchase what they need. In this sense, we are all created to serve others, and others are all created to serve us.

There is a Jewish prayer, sort of a mini-grace that we recite after we have enjoyed a snack. This is the translation:

Blessed art You who created many people and their deficiencies. On all You created by which to keep all alive, blessed is the Eternal Life.

This prayer elaborates on Ben Zoma's thoughts. You know that person who got the last spot in the elevator so that you need to wait for the next one? Maybe she is the accountant who will save you hours and money by preparing your tax return for you. The maid whose existence you barely notice when you stay at a hotel? She allows you to come in after a long work day and collapse on a tidy bed in a clean room. The personnel director who did not hire you but who might remember the thank-you note you wrote her for her time? She may think of you when an associate of hers mentions an opening in his company. The Friendship-Finance connection of the holistic you recognizes how much better your life is because you and I benefit from our family, our friends, and from the relationships we form through finance. Adding more people to those networks powers a better life. Perhaps a subsistence farmer or a survivalist can exist from day to day, but neither lives a life of expansiveness. Not surprisingly, the fitness—health—of the isolated person suffers as well, something we will discuss in more detail in a later chapter.

Samuel Colt started his eponymous gun company in 1830. We ask you to use your imagination to picture this scene. Colt has a work table in Connecticut, and shall we say, six men are sitting around the table, all making revolvers. Each man takes a piece of steel, drills it out, makes a barrel, and uses another piece of steel to craft a trigger. After each man makes a trigger guard followed by a receiver, he then engineers the cylinder, and finally, he assembles all the components he's built. He proudly signs his name on the handle of the revolver and puts it in the box to be taken out and sold. When payday comes, Samuel Colt jots down how many revolvers each worker made and proceeds to pay them accordingly.

One day, Samuel Colt presented a shocking new idea to this group.

"We're going to do things a little bit differently now," he said. "You there at that place on the table, you're only going to make barrels." He instructed another man, "You are going to work only on the wood handle." To the third man he said, "You are going to make trigger guards, only trigger guards all day." The next man was told to build firing hammers, and the man seated next to him was slated to build revolving cylinders. Finally, the last man was instructed to assemble the revolvers by taking one of each part needed and putting them together. The group didn't like this idea at first. They changed their minds when payday came around.

Can you imagine how exciting it was for the group to discover that they had produced 10 times more guns than they had ever made in any other week! Their pay went up commensurately. At the end of the eighteenth century, economist Adam Smith described this idea, that of division of labor in his groundbreaking book, *The Wealth of Nations*.

The advantages of this type of specialization make sense. As Smith wrote, "When the whole force of the mind is directed to one particular object, as in consequence of the division of labour it must be, the mind is more likely to discover the easiest methods of attaining that object than when its attention is dissipated among a great variety of things."

Yet, greater productivity because of specialization and division of labor is not the only benefit. Greater human connection is another one.

Devotees of the Bible recognized the wisdom of specialization all along. Think about Jacob at the end of his life, the end of the book of Genesis (Genesis 49:1–28). What does he do? He gathers his sons together as he's about to die and says, "Boys, come here, I want to bless you." Now if we were writing that book we might have dealt with it in one verse: "Boys, I'm 147 years old, good luck to you all, serve the Lord, take care of each other. I'm out of here. Goodbye." You could say all of that in one long verse.

That is not how the Bible reads. Look at the end of Genesis, and you will find 30 verses of a very long goodbye. Jacob starts off, "Reuben, this is my blessing for you. Simon, this is my blessing for you…." Every single son gets a different blessing. Why? Jacob is expressing the idea of unity through separateness. The only way to make sure that the children of Israel would stay together is if Jacob made them all specialists. He gave a different blessing to each son to make absolutely certain that they would need one another.

Amazingly, Moses does exactly the same thing at the end of Deuteronomy (Chapter 33). We find another 30 verses. Each tribe gets its own distinctive specialized blessing to create its role in the future of the people of Israel. This makes absolutely certain that everybody would need everybody else. It's a very beautiful concept.

In the earlier example of Samuel Colt, think about the way everybody was making guns up until then. What is the reaction of five men around the table when Tom doesn't show up for work one day? They might think,

> Who cares? Tom's not here, fine! We're all just going to carry on making our guns. Since each one of us gets paid by the piece, all that will happen is that Tom won't get paid today.

The level of care and concern between those men around the table is how much? Zero.

What happens when the group switches to division of labor and specialization? When Tom doesn't show up for work, what happens? Everybody rushes over to his house to find out what's the problem—can they help him? Give him an aspirin? Bring him back—because if he isn't there, none of them can get paid. He's vital! He is needed to make one of the components that goes into the revolver. And as Adam Smith noted, as each employee focuses on one task, he discovers short-cuts and ways to do his job better and faster. This leads to the blessing of financial abundance. From our perspective, it is one of the rules God built into the world that rewards us for caring for one another.

If I made everything that I needed by myself, do you really think I'd care about the company that crafts the shoes I favor? As it is, I pray for them, I watch their stock, I want them to thrive! The same is true for the car manufacturer whose autos I prefer, and the same is true for all sorts of companies, stores, and practitioners that I patronize. The suppliers of these things are in my prayers every day because I'm not independent. I need them all to flourish, and I want to pay them fairly. I want them to do well because I want them to be there to supply me tomorrow as well. These aren't my family, they aren't my friends, but through the miracle of finance, I care about them.

Friends and Stuff

Throughout history certain groups have tried to limit their exposure to outsiders. We can look at royal families ranging from ancient Egypt to more recent times and see that they often married within their own ranks. Pharaohs married their own sisters and even their own daughters. If we examine the blood ties of Europe's royal families we see that Tsarina Alexandra of Russia (1872–1918) was a first cousin of George the Fifth of England (1865–1936) and that the royal families of Spain, Monaco, the United Kingdom, the Netherlands, Sweden (among others) all link back to King George II who ruled Great Britain and Ireland from 1727 until 1760. This inbreeding led to an unusual number of hereditary illnesses.

Perhaps this helps explain why family is not enough. Just like certain genetic characteristics are shared among family, families tend to share interests and proclivities. Though having strong family characteristics may be wonderful, we will always need to expand ourselves by connecting to others outside our immediate circle. Don't get us wrong. Family is vital, but we grow by being pushed out of our comfort zone. Friends, with their different backgrounds and perspectives, help us do that. As long as we share a core group of values so that there is trust among us, we enhance each other's lives.

Looking at South Korea today, it is hard to believe that back in 1960, her gross domestic product per capita was about the same as Ghana's. That is to say that the average Ghanaian was as economically productive as the average South Korean. By 2020, South Korea's gross domestic product per capita had grown to be more than 14 times that of Ghana. What changed during those 60 years for one country more than the other? It was during those decades that South Koreans embraced Christianity en masse. This made a difference because sharing a belief with someone else is a far more dependable basis of friendship than sharing a fondness for tennis or baseball statistics. One way of exploring the difference between the economic performance of different countries is by measuring what we think of as the circle of trust. A society in which people tend to trust only family members and tribal affiliations is always going to lag behind the economic productivity of societies with far broader circles of trust. After all, money is created when two people effect a transaction, and most of us tend to prefer doing business with those we know, like, and trust. Yes, friendship is really important and does impact finance both on a national scale and on an individual level.

We see a fascinating clue to the importance of friends in the haunting book of Job. While the book deserves much attention, our focus here is not on whether it is an allegory or how to understand the interaction between God and Satan. Let's accept it on its surface value and note that God granted Satan the power to hurt Job in any and every way other than killing him.

And the Lord said to Satan, behold, he is in your hand, but spare his life. (Job 2:6)

Tragedy follows. Satan strips Job of everything. Job loses his family, his fortune, and his health. Soon, his three friends come to console him.

Now when Job's three friends heard of all this evil that had come upon him, they came ... to mourn with him and to comfort him. (Job 2:11)

Wait! Why did Satan not also rob Job of his friends? After all, he took everything else. He took his home and his business. He took his children and his health. If his goal was to leave Job with nothing, surely he should also have taken his friends? This would strip Job of even the consolation of friends mourning with him.

Our friend Rabbi Yaakov Horowitz shared a profound insight from ancient Jewish wisdom with us: being deprived of friends is a sentence of death. Thus, according to God's directions to Satan that Job's life must be spared, Satan lacked the power to deprive Job of his friends. This would have been equivalent to killing him. There is a 2,000-year-old aphorism well-known to learned Jews: "Either friendship or death."

This sounds heartwarming, but does it make sense? After all, stipulating healthy relationships, most of us would choose family over friends if we had to make that terrible choice. That is true. But we don't always have the choice as refugees from war-torn countries or victims of heinous crimes know. Sometimes, our families are taken from us. Parents, siblings, spouses, and children can die or be far from us. Yet, unless you are in solitary confinement, you can always make friends. No matter your age or situation, no matter how difficult approaching strangers can be, making friends is within your power.

Having explored some of the importance of Family, Finance, and Friendship, we'll take a look at another aspect of Finance—stuff. While most of us accept the idea that being connected to family and friends and paying attention to our physical health is important, many people are uncomfortable about connecting with money and the material possessions money allows us to have.

We assume that most, if not all the people reading this book feel no irresistible urges to carve an idol from wood or stone and bow down to worship it. It seems as if the second of the Ten

Commandments, "Do not make other gods for yourself," is one of the easier ones to keep for those raised in a Jewish or Christian heritage.

Let's not breathe a sigh of relief too quickly. Ancient Jewish wisdom makes clear that anything that controls us can be considered an idol. Are you incapable of keeping control of your temper when someone cuts you off in traffic? Anger is your idol, the thing that directs your behavior. Does your desire for approval lead you to gossip viciously about a friend (or anyone else) as your entree into the "in" crowd? Being accepted is your idol. Are you unable to stop eating, smoking, drinking, or buying things? Modern medicine may call these addictions, but that is another way of saying that those things have become our idols. They are directing us instead of us directing them. It is not a coincidence that among the 12 steps of Alcoholics Anonymous and the other similar groups is an acceptance of a higher authority. Only God or another higher authority can displace the one that is currently being obeyed.

The urge to accumulate money and possessions can certainly be an idol. But it is not automatically so, just as marble in itself is not an idol nor is alcohol. And while one can live a perfectly fine life without marble, money is in a different category; it is a vital blessing.

Yours, Mine, but Not Ours

The Hebrew Bible makes an unequivocal case for private ownership. Clearly, as we saw with Cain, valuing things above people is a mistake. What is less often understood is that *not* valuing things, or elevating communal ownership over private ownership, is also a mistake. Where do we see this?

We can point to many places including Micah 4:4 where the prophet, picturing a glorious future, directly after talking about swords being beaten into plowshares and there being no more war, mentions:

And each man shall sit under his vine and under his fig tree . . .

This picture of perfection doesn't mention people sitting under communal vines and fig trees, but each person under his own privately owned tree. Similarly, we can argue that the entire Biblical system of charity is based on individuals giving from what they themselves have, not a system where everyone produces and gives into a common pot from which everyone then receives what (the group thinks) he needs.

We see one of the strongest affirmations of ownership by comparing two similar Biblical commandments. Leviticus 19:16 states that we may not ignore a person in desperate need: "Do not stand by the blood of your fellow." The first four verses of Deuteronomy 22 parallel this idea by telling us that when we see a lost animal or object we may not ignore it; we have the obligation to pick it up. We cannot pretend that we don't see it and just pass by.

When discussing the rules of returning lost property, ancient Jewish wisdom makes clear that only one part of this obligation relates to caring for another person. It is true that just as we would appreciate the return of an item we lost, so should we return things to our neighbor. However, it goes deeper. There are items that we normally have no expectation of being able to return. For example, if we come across a $5 bill on the street, and we did not see someone drop it and no one else is around, we are told that we are obligated to pick it up (leave aside complications such as fear of germs or it being laced with cocaine). Were we to post a notice, "Money found at the corner of Pine and Oak," no one would be able to identify it convincingly as their missing money in contrast, let's say to a piece of jewelry that could be described. If it was much more money, say $1,623, we could publicize that we found an amount of money and only the person who lost it could tell us the total and even the denominations that make up that total. But $5? Most people will never even know it is missing, and if they do discover the loss, they will not expect to get it back. Nonetheless, our focus is on the person who sees it. This Bible verse encourages us to pick it up rather than ignoring it and leaving it ownerless. The ideal world is one in which most property is owned by private people. You may have been raised with an offshoot of this idea, that of picking up litter and disposing of it properly. Even though you didn't make the mess, our mothers recognized that allowing an area to become a version of a public dump diminishes safety and living conditions for all of us.

The distinguished Peruvian economist, Hernando de Soto, identified one of the paramount distinctions between more and less successful economies to be how dependably each country recorded ownership of property. In many less-developed parts of the world, as little as 3% of a country's land is owned by individuals, the remainder by various state interests. What is more, another characteristic of developed societies is an accurate survey or mapping of the land in order to be able to describe the exact land covered by a title deed. Even in the twenty-first century, in many countries, trying to discover who owns a particular plot of land can be almost impossible.

Among many truths about property, ancient Jewish wisdom recognizes three that are applicable to our discussion here:

1. Nobody looks after other people's property as well as he cares for his own.
2. Property that belongs to "everybody" actually belongs to nobody.
3. Ownership of property confers stature upon the owner.

In order to persuade oneself of the veracity of the first two of these three truths, one need only compare the condition of most post offices, run by a government that evidently does not care much about customer satisfaction, with the condition of most FedEx offices managed by a corporate board of directors and owned by shareholders who really do care whether the company is pleasing its customers. Or perhaps we might somewhat guiltily compare how we treat the rental car we're using for 2 days with how we look after our own cars back home.

Now it is true that some are persuaded by the idea that we are moving into a non-owning economy. For instance, the notoriously narcissistic World Economic Forum, which meets annually in the Swiss ski resort village of Davos, issued a list of eight predictions for the world in 2030. One prediction made by Danish parliamentarian Ida Auken was that nobody would own anything. Populations would rent, lease, or borrow everything they needed, she added. With the growing popularity of ride-sharing services such as Uber, and the trend for companies to acquire software subscriptions rather than owning their software, it is easy to suppose that the World Economic Forum is on to something. However, in their hubristic belief that human nature can and will be changed by their enlightened leadership, they overlook the perfectly natural human desire for ownership.

Many of us try to spurn this human urge in the name of religious asceticism or anti-capitalism, or in pursuit of what is perceived as a form of spiritual purity. And we do need to make sure that we are not elevating material possessions out of proportion. However, that is different from not appreciating how, used correctly, they can elevate our lives. Wanting to set a table nicely, to dress attractively, and to own special books rather than borrowing them are good impulses, not bad ones.

Sometimes, our rejection of "things" is nothing more than a desire to simplify life. An entire industry of tidy-up and organizing specialists help clients get rid of things they don't really use. Nonetheless, while decluttering may be necessary for many of us in today's consumeristic age in which we are inundated with more products that we can use, it's important to remember that possessions are not inherently bad. Even decluttering guru Marie Kondo discovered that a messy home filled with children and all that comes with them is preferable to a pristine home without them. There is a surge of subconscious warmth and satisfaction from saying "our house," "my company," or "my horse" and so on. That coincides with wanting to protect and take care of that which gives us pride.

Patterns of Connection

Along with other spiritual ailments, disconnection often results in alienation. While the need for human connection and for connection to our possessions is far more intuitive, the truth is that we also need connection to the larger world. Science is one pathway to understanding the physical world around us, and here, too, connection plays a role. In fact, science is based on the quest to find patterns, the connection between various things. Noticing how objects fall toward the earth led to the understanding of a force that pulls them there—gravity. Noticing what happens to a bulb attached to a coil of wire when a magnet moves near that coil led to understanding electricity. A pattern of connection suggests unity between the connected phenomena and a widespread pattern of unity suggests an overall unity. For instance, for no easily discernible reason, the way electrostatic forces behave is identical to how gravitational forces behave, although they are entirely different forces. The two formulae have the same appearance.

Similar unifying relationships are found in chemistry with reactions becoming astonishingly predictable once the periodic table was identified by John Newlands in 1863. For the next hundred years, more and more of the natural world began to be explained in terms of reliable mathematical relationships. Whether it was optics, mechanics, motion, electricity, or any other measurable aspect of the world, things fell into place extending all the way to the cutting edges of thermodynamics, relativity, and atomic physics. The idea that everything in the physical world should be reliably ordered was so amazing and so unexpected that, later in his life, Albert Einstein worked on identifying the one explanation for everything; he called it the unified field theory. A few decades later, Stephen Hawking was irresistibly drawn toward the same conclusion—that there must surely be one central unifier, as it were—he called it the theory of everything. Neither man actually found it because what they both unknowingly sought was God.

Astronomer Johannes Kepler (1571–1630), who, years before Einstein and Hawking, discovered secrets of the planets' orbits, expressed the views of many of his fellow scientists when he said:

The chief aim of all investigations of the external world should be to discover the rational order and harmony which has been imposed on it by God and which He revealed to us in the language of mathematics.

Kepler was followed by Robert Boyle, who found the patterns linking pressure and volume of gasses, Faraday and Maxwell who did the same in electricity, and Compton and Walton in light and atomic physics, respectively. The latter, a Nobel Prize winner, aroused no protest when he declared that "science was mainly a way of finding out more about God," Renowned scientist Francis Collins led the international team that mapped the human genome. Of that work, Collins said: "We had now seen the language that God used to speak us into being." All these scientists and many more, including the great Isaac Newton in the seventeenth century, were Bible-believing Christians.

It made sense for so many of the scientists who laid out the foundations of modern science to have been God-centric people because if one God created everything, then exploration of His creation would surely lead to unveiling an understanding of the Creator Himself. From their earliest youth, they all knew the opening verse of the Bible: In the beginning, God created heaven and earth. Just as when we want to know more about an artist we study his works and when we want to know more about an author we read what he wrote, religious people who want to know more about God study the rules and patterns that He built into his work—the world.

That coherent patterns govern physical phenomena in our world is in itself surprising, though of course, we today are so accustomed to it that we take it for granted. But earlier on in the period of scientific discovery, we can see that cultures and people of Christian background discovered far more about the nature of the physical world than everyone else put together. They enjoyed a head start, as it were. They knew that they were searching for something that certainly existed—unity. It turned out that they were correct. It was all true, provable, and the unshakeable foundation of everything that was to follow.

Let's apply some of this thinking to our understanding of the 5F principle. When we seek a wholeness in our lives, we need as much as possible in our lives to connect and to be unified, while each part still retains its singular integrity. What do we mean?

Let's pick two categories: Finance and Friendship. It is easy for us all to see that thinking of a fun evening out with friends while in the middle of analyzing a spreadsheet at work makes us less efficient at our job. Similarly, obsessing on tomorrow's office meeting while out for an enjoyable evening with a friend will hamper both our enjoyment and our friendship. One solution to this type of conflict is to declare a priority. At this point in my life (perhaps my early 20s), I want to have a good time with friends. I will work at this and that, earning only enough to cover a few months of living, and spend those months enjoying exotic experiences and hanging out with different people.

Alternatively, I might say that while I know that friendship is important, my priority now is advancing in my career so, while regretful, I need to miss major events in friends' lives and fall out of touch while I hyperfocus on work.

Neither of these are ideal choices. The first leaves us scrambling to assemble skills that are valued in the marketplace years behind others, while the second option offers us a healthy bank account and dwindling numbers of people who truly care about us.

We can analyze every other 5F crosslink in the same way. However, very few of us are professional jugglers. Keeping five balls up in the air is not something we instinctively know how to do. But, when it comes to our 5Fs, we need to learn how to do that for our most successful lives.

Chapter 3

Seeing the Invisible

As anyone (like us) who has befriended or married someone from a different region, let alone a different country, knows, words mean different things in different places. A few years after immigrating to the United States, my (RDL) mother asked a friend to pick up six strawberry jellies for her. Her friend happily undertook the errand, returning with six jars of jelly, ready to be spread on bread. My mother was flabbergasted. After a confusing back and forth, it became clear that to my mother, jelly meant a box containing powder that one stirred with boiling water to make a sweet, jiggly substance. To her American friend, jelly was a synonym for a clear jam.

We don't want to make a similar mistake. For this book to serve a useful purpose, we need to share a common language. In Chapter 1, we mentioned that spirituality is not a synonym for religion. We would like to elaborate on that so that when we say that we humans live in a world made up of both a physical and a spiritual reality, we all agree on what we mean. For the purposes of this book, we classify Spirituality and Faith under the heading of Faith. (Four Fs and one S didn't pack the same punch!) Once we understand that the category of Faith intersects with the other 4Fs, Faith and Spirituality hover over almost everything we discuss.

One of today's most prevalent proclamations is, "Hear ye, hear ye. Science is truth, and truth is science."

There are quite a few problems with this rosy view of science, but for our purposes, one stands out. People who cite science as the end all and be all, presuppose that science can answer all questions. In that case, we don't have to pay any attention at all to other areas of human pursuit, including philosophy and religion. We can and indeed must rule them out as irrelevant because only science reveals the truth.

Yet, science, when you think about it, like any lens, is limited in what it can explain. Specifically, science is limited to things that can be observed and measured.

How many important traits like loyalty, perseverance, optimism, happiness, courage, compassion, willpower, self-discipline, integrity, attraction, altruism, and others can be either observed or measured by scientific standards? Yet, these qualities are hugely important in our day-to-day lives.

When you hire someone, or you go into a partnership with somebody, or marry somebody, physical characteristics like height, weight, skin color, the amount of hair on their head, and their shape may or may not be relevant, but they're not nearly as important as the non-physical characteristics that we listed. The things that are most important are not truly measurable. We say these things are spiritual.

In other words, spiritual doesn't mean Godly or holy, or anything like that. It simply means non-measurable by scientific means. If you could devise some sort of machine or app or even a psychological test that could reliably measure somebody's integrity, optimism, or resilience now and in the future, or for that matter whether two people who fall in love will remain faithful to each other, or whether a military recruit will demonstrate steadfast loyalty under fire, the world would beat a path to your door, and you could name your price. But though there have been many efforts over the past several decades to create "operational definitions" of these qualities, or to find indirect ways to "quantify" qualities like happiness or perseverance, the qualities themselves will never truly be measurable. By definition, spiritual characteristics are intangible.

When a pregnant woman visits an obstetrician, the doctor can tell her (or will soon be able to tell her) physical characteristics of the baby. Do the baby's organs look normal? What is the baby's blood type? How much is the baby likely to weigh at full term? Will the baby catch cold quickly? Yet if the mother asks whether her baby will be a loyal friend or a devoted daughter, she will be met with silence. Those qualities are spiritual.

Science is an admirable instrument. The application of science, namely technology, is also amazing and astounding. But these are tools. You can't measure whether your freezer is working by using an oven thermometer. There's nothing wrong with an oven thermometer. It's just the wrong instrument for your freezer. And the important part of using tools is recognizing that you have to use the right one.

I (RDL) have an old Craftsman crescent wrench in my toolbox. It's a fantastic tool. And it's really, really useful. But my Craftsman crescent wrench is not at all useful for fixing a broken window or repairing an electrical connection to my lamp. It's the wrong tool. It doesn't mean it's a bad tool. But no tool can do everything. Science is no different from any other tool.

Science cannot define truth because truth must encompass everything. To operate a business effectively, you need both a physical and a spiritual perspective. To run a marriage or raise children effectively, you need both a physical and a spiritual perspective. To keep your body healthy, you need both a physical and spiritual perspective. Even to have lasting friendships requires both a physical and a spiritual perspective. This is why the F of Faith that includes an understanding of the spiritual world is an integral part of the holistic you.

The Blindness of Science

In our times, we are accustomed to the idea of specialists. A modern economy depends upon each participant doing one thing very well and very efficiently. A plumber wisely hires an auto mechanic to repair his car. A lawyer doesn't try to do her taxes on her own. But that isn't the whole story.

A recent medical school graduate has an array of knowledge at her fingertips that would astound the general practitioner of less than a century ago. For that, we are grateful to science.

Yet, the newly minted doctor today is often missing an understanding of the spiritual elements. The rural doc who paid a house call and saw a widower's empty fridge, messy home, and dying plants might have prescribed getting a dog or joining the local Rotary club rather than an expensive array of medicines. This doctor might not have been a religious man. He may even have identified himself as an atheist. But, whether he knew it or not, he was attuned to the spiritual aspects of health. In the area of mental health, science is at an even greater disadvantage as a tool because whether we are facing serious problems like schizophrenia, major depression, obsessive-compulsive disorder, or addiction, we remember that there is no brain scan or blood test to date able to diagnose a mental illness.

Likewise, high blood pressure and low vitamin E levels may partially be physical symptoms of a spiritual problem—loneliness. Having more ways to quantify the precise blood pressure and levels of vitamin E is nice, but it may not be as valuable as the warmth and all-encompassing eye of the physician who perceives the nonphysical elements at play. Science and technology that allow us to run ever more tests can mask what actually lies at the root of the problem.

Many doctors and scientists who ignore spiritual realities in their personal lives nonetheless are aware of uncomfortable phenomena that are difficult to understand using only laboratory tests and instruments. We will discuss some of these, such as placebos, a bit later in this book.

The real divide today is not between religion and science. As we mentioned earlier, that idea should raise skepticism from anyone who knows the names Isaac Newton, Johannes Keppler, Robert Boyle, or modern scientists like Dr. James Tour, professor of nanotechnology at Rice University, and biologist and physician/geneticist Dr. Francis Collins, former director of the US National Institutes of Health (NIH). The real divide today is between atheism and science. Occasionally, scientists acknowledge that science is the philosophical lodestone of the faith of secularism. The following quote is long, but it is worth reading carefully. Richard Lewontin (March 29, 1929–July 4, 2021), an evolutionary biologist and self-described atheist, said:

Our willingness to accept scientific claims that are against common sense is the key to an understanding of the real struggle between science and the supernatural. We take the side of science in spite of the patent absurdity of some of its constructs, in spite of its failure to fulfill many of its extravagant promises of health and life, in spite of the tolerance of the scientific community for unsubstantiated just-so stories, because we have a prior commitment, a commitment to materialism. It is not that the methods and institutions of science somehow compel us to accept a material explanation of the phenomenal world, but, on the contrary, that we are forced by our a priori adherence to material causes to create an apparatus of investigation and a set of concepts that produce material explanations, no matter how counter-intuitive, no matter how mystifying to the uninitiated. Moreover, that materialism is absolute, for we cannot allow a Divine Foot in the door.

Dr. Lewonton is admitting that materialism (secularism) has become its own religion. Many of its parameters are set by an absolute and faithful belief that there is no God. Scientists who want to be accepted by their peers and obtain funding must follow that belief. While we laypeople may have thought that, by definition, science is open to new information and advances, to testing and reassessment, and to understanding that today's "truth" may not be tomorrow's, that is not the reality for many credentialed scientists today. In effect, they are abusing the word "science." If we cannot ask questions or explore new paths because we are committed to saying the science on a certain issue is "settled," then we are making a statement of faith, not one of true science.

That too many of today's "scientists" ascribe to a fervent faith system is increasingly evident in many areas, but for decades that idea has pervaded any discussions of evolution. Professors and students who questioned the *theory* of evolution on college campuses were treated as heretics. They were forbidden to mention any scientific flaws it might have or to ask challenging questions about it. Evolution was not about science; it was about demanding that everyone bow down and proclaim, "There never was a God, there is not a God, and there never will be a God." (This conflict is not the topic of this book, but if you suspect that we are exaggerating, material on the subject is easy to find.)

Does It Really Matter?

What is relevant for this book is that how we choose to explain human presence on planet Earth really impacts our lives. Whether we explain our arrival in terms of a lengthy process of unaided materialistic evolution or whether we choose to believe in a Creator has real consequences for how we live. Very few people consciously think about these consequences, but our subconscious is deeply influenced by these ideas and the decisions we make.

Our attitudes affect how we approach every area of life. Once, when we were sailing in the Caribbean, we tied our dinghy up at a rickety and shaky dock. As we walked ashore, the wood under our feet wobbled precariously. While ending up in 2 feet of warm Caribbean water wasn't a terrible thought and was even appealing, our attitude changed entirely when we saw sharks circling the dock. We gingerly and nervously took each step until our feet firmly touched land.

Similarly, whether or not we think that business is fundamentally immoral and is nothing but a question of "survival of the fittest" colors all our business interactions. We will act very differently if we see business as a way to use our talents to serve God's other children. Obviously, our relationships to others and whether we view other people as potential friends or potential stepping-stones to our egocentric goals is affected as well.

When it comes to raising children, evolutionary theory has major consequences. If we are descended from apes, then our children and all the members of the generations that follow us are one step higher on the evolutionary ladder. They are more improved and greater than we are! If, on the other hand, God lovingly created man and placed him on earth, and if He revealed His presence at Mt. Sinai, then each successive generation is one step further from that revelation. The older generation is the custodian of wisdom that it can convey to youth.

To clarify the practical implications of this dilemma, let me (RDL) tell you what happened to a great rabbi, one of my finest teachers. On a trip to Israel, he found himself seated next to a man who headed an Israeli socialist and anti-religious labor movement. Soon after the plane took off, a young man, seated several rows behind, came forward and said, "Rabbi, let me take your shoes; I have your slippers here.

You know how your feet swell on the airplane." A few minutes later, he returned and said, "Here are the sandwiches your wife sent. I know you do not like airline food."

This went on in similar fashion for some time, and finally the head of Israel's socialist labor movement turned to my teacher and said, "I don't get this. I am so impressed with your son. I have four sons. They're grown now. But in all my life I don't recall them ever offering to do anything at all for me. Why is your son doing all of this?" And the rabbi said, "He isn't my son; he's my student. Had my son been here you would really have seen service. But you must not blame yourself. Your sons are faithful to your teachings, and my sons are faithful to my teachings. It is simple, you see. You made the decision to teach your sons that you are descended from apes. That means that you are one generation closer to the ape than they. And that means that it is only proper and appropriate that you acknowledge their status and that you serve them. But, you see, I chose to teach my sons that we came from God Himself. And that puts me one generation closer to the ultimate truth, which means it is only appropriate that they treat me accordingly."

Finally, we must acknowledge another huge implication of choosing whether there is a God or not. A Harvard professor and leading evolutionist, Stephen Jay Gould said in his closing comments for an evolutionary documentary for David Suzuki, "Now that we know we were not made in anybody's image, we are free to do whatever we wish." Who among us has never felt that desire to know that we can choose whatever behavior we want with no concern that it might be wrong?

Through its word for truth, EMeT, the Hebrew language reveals an additional reason why science cannot be the equivalent of truth. EMeT is made up of the first letter of the Hebrew alphabet, the final letter of the Hebrew alphabet, and the middle letter of the Hebrew alphabet. Haven't we all had the experience of hearing one version of a story, or perhaps only a piece of a story, and coming to the wrong conclusion? Maybe we heard parts of the story in an incorrect order. Parents quickly learn not to make a judgment based on a statement such as, "He pushed me." It makes a difference if the pushing took place after, "I punched him in the nose," or maybe after, "I was about to run into the street after my ball." By focusing on only part of a picture, we lose the larger vision.

By definition, science must always be open to examining new and conflicting ideas. Doctors with closed minds are a fact of history. Whether we look at the medical establishment's rejection of Dr. Semmelweiss's exhortation in 1850 that doctors should wash their hands between treating patients, or we read about the doctors who ignored Sister Kenny's groundbreaking treatment of polio patients in the first half of the twentieth century, scientists and doctors are human beings with egos and financial interests. Advances in science have always come at the expense of having to reject earlier ideas. While educators love to mention the Catholic Church's rejection of Galileo and his ideas, they are not as quick to elaborate that, frequently, new ideas are rejected by the scientific community for bad reasons that have nothing to do with traditional clerical authority.

As science mixes with politics, trying to reach the truth becomes more difficult. Particularly when dealing with areas of sexuality, the compulsion to prove what one wants to prove is overwhelming. Similarly, during the COVID-19 years, almost everyone in the world was affected by policies that sprang from various beliefs. There is no getting away from the presence of beliefs in how we approach our physical lives.

The crucial question is whether we believe we should be guided by our morals and values derived from accumulated wisdom and from traditional cultural institutions like religion or only by our own reason and thoughts. It colors issues as varied as how we approach abortion and assisted suicide, body piercings, and what we eat. Are our bodies on loan from God, or are they ours to do with as we see fit? An adherent to the faith of secular fundamentalism will, by definition, see things differently than a more traditional individual.

Why Do We Blush?

Looking at our lives only through a physical lens means that many of the things that we human beings do are irrational. An evolutionary biologist can explain why a mother bear will protect her cub even at risk to her own life. That same reason might explain why a human mother will act in the same way. However, even while we and animals share activities such as eating and excreting, we do them in different ways. While human babies eat and excrete at will, as we grow up we confine those activities to appropriate times and places and surround them with ceremony. No dog comes across a lovely bone and, although tempted, refrains from eating it so that he can share it with his best friend. No deer places monogrammed towels and soap in the shape of shells in the location where he defecates. We don't know how evolutionary biologists would explain those human behaviors, but we can share the view of ancient Jewish wisdom.

In a refrain you will see repeated throughout this book, we cannot prove that the Bible is God's word, and no one can prove that it isn't. It is a statement that cannot be answered scientifically. However, each of us must choose (deciding not to choose is by default the same as choosing) according to which option we will live our lives. From the perspective of ancient Jewish wisdom, one of the main goals of the first two chapters of Genesis, as well as a priority in the rest of the Bible, is distinguishing between animals and people.

In his book, *The Expression of the Emotions in Man and Animals*, Charles Darwin (of natural selection fame) wrote: "Blushing is the most peculiar and most human of all expressions." Indeed it turns out that of all the creatures on the earth, only humans reveal embarrassment upon the largest organ of the human body—the skin.

What is our God-centric explanation for blushing being a uniquely human phenomenon? It is that shame and embarrassment are uniquely human characteristics. This may sound strange, particularly to those who love their dogs. Western culture anthropomorphizes animals and trains us to think of them as human equivalents starting from our youngest ages. We read stories about moose, elephants, lions, dogs, birds, and even aardvarks to our toddlers and these animals think, talk, and act just like human beings. Broadway shows and movies like *The Lion King*, accompany us as we grow older. One of our own favorite authors is Alexander McCall Smith. Smith's *44 Scotland Street* series features a dog named Cyril. The author expresses Cyril's thoughts and emotions to us, and as we often do with our own dogs, his reactions mesh with human ones. Yet we have no series written by dogs doing the equivalent about humans.

We may overlay our humanity on dogs and other creatures, but ancient Jewish wisdom suggests that while animals certainly have instincts and they feel emotions such as fear and happiness, other characteristics, including embarrassment, are reserved for humans.

Genesis 2:25 introduces the concept by telling us that Adam and Eve were naked but experienced no embarrassment because of that fact. By Genesis 3:10, embarrassment enters the picture, and in response, they clothe themselves. What happened? There was no temperature change or other physical reason for needing clothes. What did occur is that innocence had been lost, just as Paradise had. And with the loss of innocence, a need for clothing was introduced.

Why? Have you ever noticed that a healthy body is a body that you don't notice? When everything feels fine and nothing is in pain, we don't really pay attention to our bodies. But slice open a finger or develop a migraine, and you will definitely start to notice that finger or your head. Prior to Adam and Eve's sin, there was no separation between the body and the soul. The body acted as a clear container, reflecting the soul within it, and was completely unnoticeable. With sin entering the scene, the body became clouded—like a glass surface that is suddenly noticeable due to the dust adhering to it. And when Adam and Eve noticed their bodies for the first time, they felt the immediate instinct to cover them. Physicality that reflects no spirituality is slightly awkward for us. This spiritual awkwardness is the source of our embarrassment. What we are embarrassed by, we feel the need to hide.

It is fascinating that one of the Hebrew words for clothing is LeVuSH. In Hebrew, the B and V sounds are expressed by the same letter. Furthermore, in Hebrew you will recall, if two words are spelled the same even though their meaning seem to be totally unrelated, they are in fact telling you different dimensions of one unified idea. The idea that concepts that share words are related and meant to be understood together is a basic truth of the language.

Because of this, the fact that LeVuSH, meaning clothing, is the same word as L'BoSH, meaning "for embarrassment" is crucial. (Remember that Hebrew has no vowels in the written language.) Clothing is one way that we manipulate our physical bodies in order to affect our spiritual selves. We cover ourselves to alleviate the basic embarrassment we feel in our nakedness. What's more, the type of clothing that we wear can make us feel more strongly that our exterior matches our divine interior. Anyone who has felt smaller sitting in a skimpy hospital gown recognizes that our clothes affect our perception of ourselves. The way we are dressed can make us feel powerful and dignified, or it can make us feel weak and small.

Adam and Eve's embarrassment and subsequently clothing themselves reflected that, after disobeying God's command, their bodies and souls were no longer completely in harmony with each other. That was an uncomfortable feeling. We live with that legacy until today.

Our bodies and our souls are not two disconnected entities. Like the double helix of DNA's molecular structure, they are intertwined, interlocked, and interconnected. On a basic level, our souls need our bodies in order to function in the world. On a deeper level, our emotions, behaviors, and thoughts have a physical effect on us.

Our skin is actually one of the easier ways to recognize this interconnectedness. Many people know that their skin responds to their being under mental or emotional stress. For instance, psoriasis, eczema, and hives are among the skin conditions known to be aggravated by nonphysical causes such as mental or emotional stress. In other words, our skin is as sensitive to our spiritual welfare as it is to our physical. A physiological reaction may be caused when we are affected by a spiritual problem. The health of our skin is as likely to be helped by harnessing our thoughts and emotions as it is by popping pills or lathering lotions.

Ancient Jewish wisdom teaches that God chose to have our bodies show an outward sign of our embarrassment to help us feel genuine discomfort at sin. A blush is a very literal way of making our body stand out—as it did in Eden after Adam and Eve sinned for the first time. Blushing reminds us to tune into our embarrassment and not overlook our mistakes. The man who proudly proclaims, "nothing embarrasses me," is essentially an outlaw. By contrast, embarrassment helps us to distinguish between good and evil and between desirable actions and reprehensible behavior. This is crucial to a happy life and to a successful society.

The Spiritual Aspect of Everyday Life

Much more of our lives is driven by spiritual considerations than we might recognize. Understanding this changes how we behave in some areas of our lives. We might ask whether an employee asking for a raise really wants extra money or is he chiefly being driven by wanting to feel more valued? Would giving him a larger office and an expanded job function satisfy him as much as an increase in pay? Is the young child behaving abominably because of hunger or exhaustion (physical) or because of feeling embarrassed (spiritual) at an earlier criticism we leveled at him in front of a neighbor who had dropped in for a quick visit?

Two men or two women may have identical professional and work histories. They are the same age with the same qualifications and work experience. Thus, by age, shall we say 40, they have throughout their identical work careers, both earned exactly the same amount of money. Will they have the same net worth? Of course not. Although the income side of their ledgers may be the same, the outgoing side will be different for each. One person will save and invest a significant proportion of her earnings, while the other will spend on things of greater importance to her than a savings account. Each of these choices might be wise or foolish, but they flow from the beliefs of the individuals as to what they value. There is no laboratory test that will predict the eventual financial statements of these two different people. That will be determined by spiritual factors.

We do many things against our own biological interests. For instance, humans participate in extreme sports like BASE jumping, where young people jump from a tall building, a bridge, or a high tower with only one parachute and no reserve. On average, about 10 enthusiasts have died every year since the early 1980s. It's about 50 times more dangerous than conventional parachuting from an airplane. For that matter, even mountain climbing, at which about 30 people a year die in North America, is extreme.

No other creatures on the planet engage in highly risky activities for no discernible biological benefit. Some animals will put their lives at risk to save their young or in order to procure food. When animals fight, sometimes to the death, it is usually over reproduction, territory, or food, all easily understandable biological imperatives. But humans climb mountains, enter boxing rings or mixed martial arts cages, dive off stomach-churningly high platforms with nothing but a fat rubber band attached to their ankles, or line up in amusement parks to be hurtled around at terrifying speeds by diabolical contraptions. One of the usual explanations is, "Oh, I love the adrenaline rush!" However, that only postpones the question of why? No animals share that apparently urgent love of adrenaline.

When we speak of Faith as one of the 5Fs, we include two categories. The first part we discussed earlier, relating to things that are not measurable in a laboratory. The second category is all things God-related.

Here we are getting into the intersection of a spiritual world, which, as we say, affects all humans whether or not they believe in God, and specifically faith in the God of Abraham, Isaac, and Jacob.

Once we understand the existence of a spiritual world, we can begin to recognize how our views of God and His Bible impact all the areas of our lives. This is easier to see in our days than it was even only a few decades ago.

Few of the Jews living comfortably in Warsaw, Poland, in say 1935, had the faintest idea that life as they knew it was about to end. In fewer than 5 years, normal life in luxurious mansions would be replaced by unspeakable horror in torture camps so terrible that death itself was a relief.

We do not suggest that we shall confront such severe shocks to our lives over the next few years. However, wise people recognize that nothing lasts forever. Smart observers recognize that the challenging changes that have swirled turbulently around the foundations of our world over the past 10 years have consequences that will impact the quality of our lives in increasingly dramatic fashion.

One can ignore the soft sound of approaching boots and blindly await the cataclysm, or one can make the effort to peer through a telescope and spot the threats. It is possible to analyze current events through the lens of ancient Jewish wisdom and emerge with, if not a prophetic sense of where things are headed, at least a good idea of what the short-term future holds.

Some people condemn themselves to stumble through the dark forest at night snagged by branches and tripped by roots. Others wear night-vision goggles and cover the ground easily and safely. It is our goal in this book, to offer you the idea that the F of Faith includes an awareness of the most influential book in the history of civilization. We hope to equip you with night-vision goggles in the form of five permanent principles of the Bible. These will make sense of the treacherous landscape and help you to avoid the roots and branches awaiting the unwary.

Whether we examine uniquely American troubles or some of the bizarre sociopolitical problems being experienced on other continents, the picture we obtain will be clearer with these tools.

Five Permanent Biblical Principles

Permanent Principle of the Bible #1

People are not merely smart animals. We are an entirely different species, touched by the finger of God and possessing souls. This means that few lessons we learn from animals are applicable to people. For instance, if any animal is restricted to an adequately large area and provided with food, water, and safety, it will never endeavor to go anywhere else. People, even if confined to a very large area in which they can obtain all their hearts desire, find that their souls chafe at the restrictions. We seek the infinite. While animals protect their territories, we humans feel the urge to seize the territories of others. In civilized circumstances, we try to increase our holdings by purchase and trade. In less civilized circumstances, we do so by war and plunder. Animals act on instinct and are incapable of evil but are also incapable of choosing good over evil. People are capable of making moral choices and, in many cases, will choose war and plunder. We do not need to prepare ourselves to cope with evil animals; a mere fence will keep the wolves from our sheep. But we very much need to prepare to deal with evil people, or we shall not survive.

Those nations with a strong sense of their Biblical roots tend to build up their societies and allow their people to prosper in an environment of safety and security. Occasionally, straying from those roots, as Germany did when it temporarily turned to Hitler and his Nazi thugs, even Western nations will pursue predatory policies, but they seldom work for very long. The thousand-year Reich failed to make it past the 12-year mark.

By contrast, nations based on organizational principles other than Judeo-Christian deny their people prosperity and security and tend to prey on their neighbors. Shaka, the late eighteenth century Zulu chief, thought nothing of marching his warriors off a cliff to prove their loyalty and the 8-year Iran-Iraq war in which both sides needlessly sacrificed millions of their population was no less insane by Judeo-Christian standards.

Communism, the mirror image of Judeo-Christian faith, similarly denies its citizens the opportunity of improving their abilities to make a living while needlessly slaughtering them by the million, as did Stalin in the Soviet Union, Mao Zedong in China, and Pol Pot in Cambodia.

In general, those people who reject the Judeo-Christian model of human organization usually end up embracing its opposite, which is a materialistic vision of reality. In this vision, people are not united by the content of their characters and the devotion of their souls because people are merely smart animals. Just as animals are divided by shape and skin color, so are people, claims this mistaken model. In this age-old false vision of humanity, there must be strife between men and women, between black and white, and between rich and poor.

Permanent Principle of the Bible #2

The Judeo-Christian Biblical blueprint teaches life success. All individuals face two basic obstacles to physical survival: (1) Extracting a living from an often reluctant earth using as little of our time and effort as possible. (2) Preventing other stronger individuals or groups from attacking us and seizing our property and possibly also taking our lives.

The Judeo-Christian Biblical blueprint confers success upon its followers by solving these two problems. Firstly, it affirms the worthiness of work and the idea that we were placed into this Garden of Eden precisely in order to work it and become God's partners in creation by transforming jungle into cities and fetid swamps into fertile fields.

It then implants in us the idea that God does not allow individuals to take the property or lives of others and how borrowing from future generations is a bad idea. It inculcates in men respect for women and the goodness of protecting and cherishing women. Finally, it teaches the importance of specialization to produce God's desire of interdependence upon one another. Not surprisingly, those cultures that founded themselves on these precepts prospered in peace and tranquility.

Permanent Principle of the Bible #3

In isolation, individuals live short and painful lives. Only by organizing ourselves into families, communities, societies, and yes, nations, do we stand a chance of solving the two basic problems of survival.

Just imagine if you were the last person alive on the planet after some catastrophe wiped out everyone else. Your first sensation might be relief at being able to retain the remote control for the TV and being able to find a parking place downtown, but you'd soon be brought up short. No electricity (nobody to operate the power plants), no television or radio programing, no restaurants, and eventually no more food in the now empty markets. Pretty soon, for transport to help you in your search for food, you'd be reduced to riding whatever horse or donkey you could find, and like a subsistence peasant in the most primitive third-world neighborhood, you will have to plant something and hope it will grow to harvest before you starve to death. Our wealth *is* other people, provided they also subscribe to a common system of values that allows us all to communicate, cooperate, and above all, trust one another. Without trust there is no credit and no transaction, and without transactions, we are each on our own.

Human organization can follow one of four basic patterns: (1) leave each individual to live alone and cope with chaos and civic anarchy; (2) centralized planning by a tyrannical regime; (3) tribal; or (4) Judeo-Christian system of ancient Israel that created Western civilization in general and the United States in particular.

The first is unendurable, and the plight of those trapped in this environment is tragic. As for centralized planning, one would think that the twentieth century destroyed faith in this hopeless model, but it lingers with almost religious fervor among America's elite university faculties and Europe's secular fundamentalists. The tribal model has demonstrated an inability to build even bicycles let alone computer chips and seems incapable of even seeing the benefit of water-borne sewage systems. The fourth system, God's plan for human interaction, speaks for itself. With all the imperfections inevitable when mere humans try to implement a perfect system, it still remains the deep desire of most human beings. We see this as people vote with their feet.

Permanent Principle of the Bible #4

God created separate nations in the world instead of making all humans part of one big group. Several chapters of Genesis are devoted to showing how God's plan was for each nation to experiment with its own ideas of how human cooperation should be structured. Israel alone was presented with God's Biblical blueprint and, with it, the mission to share it with the world.

However, unlike some other faiths that also believe they possess the truth, Israel was never to use the sword to force others to accept its divine blueprint for human cooperation. The sword was unnecessary because it would quickly become obvious to all observers that God's Biblical model produced a wealthier, more tranquil, and freer society than all the other experiments out there. In their own interests, God hoped, everyone would adopt it willingly and peacefully.

By way of example, when the Soviet Union collapsed in 1991, the cars they had been making, the GAZ Pobedas, the Volgas, and the ZIL limousines were roundly rejected by Western car buyers. Those mediocre mechanical monstrosities were used in the Soviet Union because that is all there was. If you bought a car then, you bought a Soviet product at the point of a sword, as it were. You had no choice. Western cars were far superior because makers enjoyed competition. Nobody was forced to buy a government-made product. People picked the very best cars they could afford, and today, miraculously, most people in the West can afford a vehicle that will carry four passengers for 50,000 miles without any major mechanical work. Lexus, BMW, Mercedes, and even Cadillac do not have to force people at the point of a gun to purchase their vehicles. In their own self-interest, those who can, willingly and eagerly acquire those products, ignoring the poor experiments in car design that governments sometimes try to foist upon a docile public.

Similarly, God set up a system wherein different people in their own groups could experiment all they wished. Meanwhile, Israel and those who adopted the Biblical blueprint would build such vastly superior societies that others would flock to adopt the same system of organizing principles. Let competition of ideologies flourish and let people choose the right way. This was God's design.

For reasons that lie outside the scope of this discussion, what we think of as Western civilization grew from those societies that adopted Christianity, which, in itself, was an adoption of Judaism, the faith of Israel. Not surprisingly, more than 90% of the scientific discoveries and medical advances of the past 1,100 years came out of Christendom, an old word for Western civilization that we like. Not surprisingly, no capital market has ever emerged indigenously from a non-Christian country.

Sure enough, God's prediction that others would spot the success of societies following the Biblical blueprint and emulate them has been partially fulfilled.

Many societies have adopted the outward trappings of the West. Today, both banks and bathrooms in Beijing, Bombay, and Bangkok resemble those in Boston, Birmingham, and Berlin. However, in most cases, they have neglected to adopt the Biblical underpinnings of morality and law that ultimately make possible those outward trappings. This throws their durability into doubt and suggests the imprudence of the West trying to salve its conscience by throwing large sums of foreign aid to so-called developing countries. The idea that raising taxes on Americans and sending loads of foreign-aid money to badly governed regions of the world will convert those far-off populations into exotic versions of Highland Park, New Jersey, or Encino, California, is laughable.

Imagine a remote island whose primitive population spends most of its time robbing and raping, mugging and murdering. What do you think will bring about more change, parachuting in bags of cash along with officials of the World Bank or sending in 100 Christian missionaries?

Yes, the Biblical model is verified by the immigration patterns of the last 60 years. The greatest and most rapid human migration in history has been from non-Christian-founded countries to Christendom, or the West. To put it perhaps a little too bluntly, neither Saudi Arabia nor Somalia has an illegal immigration problem. People vote with their feet for what works, and what works in terms of allowing people to make a living and stay reasonably safe and secure is the Judeo-Christian-based West.

The disturbing deceit inherent in the idea of multiculturalism and its close cousins the communist dream of internationalism along with the left's childlike faith in the impotent United Nations are all futile manifestations of the attempt to overturn this fourth Permanent Principle of the Bible.

Permanent Principle of the Bible #5

Few more powerful motivators exist for human beings than a deep conviction in what their god wants from them. Part of America's inability to deal effectively with Islamic terror stems from this fatal failing: prior to 9-11, almost nobody working in the US State Department had ever met a human being willing not only to die for his faith but also quite willing to kill for it.

Islam may not have a god that did much to help its devotees build attractive and successful societies, but those devotees certainly are totally committed. Total commitment, even to something wrong, often trumps lukewarm commitment to truth.

Alcoholics Anonymous works so well for so many people precisely because its founder, Bill Wilson recognized the need to include a Higher Power when attempting major transformation. Not surprisingly, government anti-drug programs accomplish very little because they so meticulously banish God from the program.

Biblical Principles Applied

Using these five Permanent Principles of the Bible, we can gain better insight into what is happening as countries around the world struggle economically and militarily. These insights that have sustained Jewish culture for millennia even help us understand how China is so successfully maneuvering itself into twenty-first century global dominance.

Essentially, world cultures have enviously witnessed the wealth of the West since before the start of the twentieth century. They have lusted for the materialistic results of the Judeo-Christian system, but they have rejected the spiritual underpinnings that made it all possible. They mistakenly believe that all that stands between them and the affluence they see on American television are either their corrupt governments or alternatively that other countries bear the responsibility for their failures. However, without American global leadership that values our Judeo-Christian heritage and understands how its spiritual nourishment sustains our success, everyone faces increasing travail.

If the Judeo-Christian vision fuels your life, then your politics must conform. Winning is not everything; God is. For secular fundamentalists on the left their political creed *is* their religion. Thus politics for them is a form of religious war—a crusade if you will. For this reason, winning is everything. That is their religious doctrine—they have no other.

The left has succeeded in dividing America into many separate groups or gangs. By annihilating commonality and eroding love of a patriotic providential mission, it has set all against one another. Those who do not want to throw more money at a failed educational system are child-haters. Those who want relief for American families groaning beneath the burden of higher-than-ever rates of taxation hate the poor. Those who want a spiritual cure for multigenerational family dysfunctionality are bigots.

Today, secularized American culture is cut by a canyon. It doesn't separate whites from blacks; it doesn't separate rich from poor; it doesn't separate men from women. It divides those who regard Judeo-Christian values as vital for our nation's survival from those who consider the Biblical blueprint to be nothing more than a primitive obstruction to progress. And blacks and whites, rich and poor, those born in America and those who immigrated to America, and men and women are found on both sides.

Biblical Values as Obstruction to Progress

Atheism is as much a faith as Catholicism, Protestantism, Judaism, and Islam are. It is the belief in an unprovable fact, in the atheist's case, that God doesn't exist. Ancient Jewish wisdom expresses no surprise that as belief in traditional faith is pummeled and recedes, there is an increase in beliefs in other faiths. As the great writer, journalist, and thinker G.K. Chesterton said,

---

"The first effect of not believing in God is to believe in anything."

Writing about England in November 2022, our friend Melanie Phillips, an English political observer and author, noted that as, for the first time, fewer than half the country identified as Christian, there was a corresponding rise in those who identified as Moslem, as well as those who marked themselves as followers of paganism, shamanism, and witchcraft. When faith in God is absent, humans will develop faith in other systems and phenomena.

Will Durant was one of the most prolific writers and widely admired historians and philosophers in the second half of the twentieth century. Along with his wife, Ariel, he wrote a 12-volume series, *The Story of Civilization*, that popularized the study of history, and many of whose volumes were best-sellers. Durant abandoned the Catholic Church into which he was born. Yet he always retained a tenderness for the Church, and this led him into further introspection. Although he remained an atheist until the time of his death, he had the honesty to recognize the dangers and flaws in a society that abandoned God.

Ariel Durant says that her husband was tremendously concerned about where society was going, recognizing that much of it was in response to ideas in which he believed and which he helped spread. In *Will and Ariel Durant: A Dual Autobiography,* published in 1977 a few years before the authors died within weeks of each other, she wrote the following words paraphrasing her husband's thoughts:

Had not the apparent victory of the scientists, the historians, and the philosophers deposed the God who had been the very staff of life to the poor, and a pillar of support to the moral code that had helped tame the savage hunter into law and order, morality and civilization? Would philosophy or education or statemanship [sic] ever succeed in establishing an effective moral code without the aid of religious sanctions and beliefs? And if they failed, and religion continued to fade, would Western civilization lapse into a chaos of sexual laxity, political corruption, mutual violence, and a common, consuming despair? Could it be that all that enthusiastic slaughter of irrational creeds had undermined the secret foundations of civilization itself? Will repeatedly broached these problems to me....

The past few years have seen a number of notable atheists such as Ayan Ali Hirsi question whether the skepticism and rationalism that they championed, which is replacing the belief in religion, is actually leading to the same types of problems as did those religious systems they first criticized.

Faith Propels Us into the Future

Faith demands an ability to see what is not yet real and to commit to the future. Everyone is familiar with the word "amen." Its definition is trickier because like so many words taken from Biblical Hebrew, it represents a concept rather than simply being a word.

In Hebrew, the root letters of 'AMeN' have a number of meanings. We are familiar with the word as an affirmation given in response to a blessing or declaration. But we may not know the full meaning of this root, which leads us to use it in this way.

In classical Hebrew, this root appears commonly in the word EMuNaH, which is frequently translated as faith or faithfulness. Yet the English translation of Esther 2:7 tells us that Mordechai *brought up or fostered* (in Hebrew—OMeiN) his niece, Esther. The Hebrew word for the action he did uses the root letter E/A/O-M-N, exactly the same as the root of AMeN.

This same root appears in the final phrase in Song of Songs 7:2 translated as, "the works of the hands of a master."

Without knowing Hebrew, you would not know that the word for a master craftsman, or in modern parlance, a business professional, is also A–M–N.

What do a business professional, someone who rears a child, and faith and faithfulness have to do with each other?

In addition to the idea we mentioned in Chapter 1 that faith allows us to take actions without knowing the outcome, another part of craftsmanship (which shares the A–M–N Hebrew root) is the expertise that comes from repeated practice. A craftsman is someone who has done his craft over and over again until he becomes a true professional. He is faithful to his craft. He doesn't give it up just because his first attempts might have failed. In this way, faith, or an ongoing commitment to something despite not knowing how it will turn out, is required to be a true craftsman.

At the same time, however, faith *itself* is a craft. We need to practice the art of faith again and again to get good at it. Without the religious-born faith in training our "faith muscles," it is easier to succumb to fear and anxiety. Could it be that one of the reasons that so many youth today are expressing growing amounts of these emotions, as well as having increased thoughts of suicide, is because fewer and fewer of them are being provided with a belief in a loving God? Pediatrician and author Dr. Leonard Sax, who has studied teenagers intensively, makes this very case.

Fundamental to faith is the idea of, well, faith. In other words, there can never be incontrovertible proof of God because that would quickly eliminate faith. We know that objects in the vicinity of the planet are attracted toward the center of the earth by the force of gravitation. Incontrovertible evidence exists which makes that a matter of knowledge, not of faith.

However, even after watching the 10 plagues strike Egypt and experiencing the crossing of the Red Sea, the Israelites had crises of faith. Once the emotional impact passes, doubts filter in. "Perhaps it was just a fortuitous wind that blew the sea," "Maybe that *was* God's intervention, but now He is not going to act further." Those doubts are necessary! If something is a fact, the choice of faith is eliminated. And belief in God must always be a choice.

Many decisions in our lives that require faith to move forward are being chosen less in our days. For instance, fewer individuals today are marrying and even those who marry often hesitate or delay having children. Most Western countries are suffering a population crisis, experiencing fertility rates well below the minimum 2.1 children per woman needed for maintenance of a steady population. In almost every country, those with more than two children are disproportionately religious. This is partially because marrying and having children are both assisted by deploying faith. There is no guarantee that this person is the absolute best match for you. There is no contract stipulating that your children will bring you joy or that you will have the resources to care for that child.

Almost anyone who regularly reviews current business plans submitted by entrepreneurs will have noted the emphasis on quick "exits." Of course most venture capital investors do wish to see their money plus a generous multiple back to them as soon as possible. However, few of the entrepreneurs themselves seem interested in building a business with which they will remain involved over the long term. Fewer still think of building businesses for their children to carry on. When was the last time you heard of a new business called "Jones and Son" or "Jones and Daughter"? These days it is hard to find many original founders of a tech enterprise remaining with the company after its initial public offering. Cash out and on to the next thing.

Committing to a future, either by having children or by establishing an enterprise that one pictures lasting into the future, demands the type of faith that is encouraged by traditional religion.

Though taking leaps of faith is not completely reserved for the God-fearing among us, believing in God is extremely helpful in giving us the courage to face the unknown.

For one, the religious person takes for granted that God and His works are good, although we often struggle to understand how this can be. Therefore, the religious person more easily accepts that the future holds something positive. And he can more easily embrace it. In this way, faith is the opposite of hopelessness. When one cannot see beyond today's misery toward a better day, it is hard to get up in the morning.

Belief in a loving God, a central idea of both Judaism and Christianity, also usually brings with it the belief that God stands by to help us. In other words, as we leap into the unknown future, we are relying on more than our own talents or genius to support us. An invisible force leaps with us and will help us fight our way to the surface even if, at points, it seems like we're going under.

A person who has stretched and exercised his faith muscle has practiced the skill of seeing what his eyes cannot behold and his hands cannot grasp. That puts him at a huge advantage. Believing that a loving God cares about us allows us to have optimism for the future. Even when difficulties befall us, we trust that the sun will shine again. All the different meanings of the word E/A/O-M-N show us how intertwined these areas of life are.

Physical/Spiritual—Prescriptive/Descriptive

An important benefit of believing in the Creator is recognizing that the world is not random. Instead, a loving God deliberately fashioned human beings. Physiological particulars are not evolutionary coincidences. Rather, ancient Jewish wisdom sees spiritual parallels to the physical realities of our bodies.

Here is an example.

Images actually are cast on our retinas upside down. Incredibly, our brains interpret those images and turn them right-side up. It is hard to imagine any natural selection advantage for creatures in having a simple lens with its need for many lines of neural "code" to restore the optical image to an upright reality. Instead of seeing this as a blip, the oral transmission views this as a moral message reflecting the danger described in Numbers 15:39: "…and you shall not stray after your hearts and your eyes towards which you lustfully pull."

We understand that our hearts often tug us in the wrong direction. But why eyes rather than ears or nose? After all, there is an attraction in a sultry voice or a seductive perfume. Yet, our eyes are a stronger magnet leading us astray. Advertisers in the last century quickly learned that a tempting picture encouraged more sales than a wordy description. With the advent of TV, shocking pictures rapidly moved more voters' decisions than thoughtful debate. Sadly, pornography's popularity reflects the ease with which pictures can seduce men no matter how many statistics they may read showing its devastating impact.

We will come across more examples of how our bodies provide clues to spiritual realities later in this book. For now, let us suffice with one more. As experienced ocean sailors, we have had intimate acquaintance with seasickness. Here is how NOAA (National Oceanic and Atmospheric Administration) describes the cause of seasickness.

Seasickness is a result of a conflict in the inner ear, where the human balance mechanism resides, and is caused by a vessel's erratic motion on the water.

Considering that for millennia boat travel was a feature of trade and thriving societies, wouldn't it have made more sense for man to have evolved so that the balance mechanism would be found in the hips or shoulder blades? Those parts of the body are much more stable than our heads, which constantly move and turn around. Situating the balance mechanism between our ears confers no natural selection advantage; quite the contrary.

Once again, ancient Jewish wisdom sees a moral message being beamed to us by our Creator. In fact, the Hebrew word for ear, O-Z-N, is the root of the word for a balancing mechanism, a scale, mOZ-Nayim, found in Leviticus 19:36 when the Bible discusses having honest weights and measures. We find it interesting that ancient Jewish wisdom discusses an anatomical fact that scientists only understood in the late 1800s. Of course, to those who believe that the God who created us also dictated the Five Books of Moses, the fact that the language reflects a biological truth makes perfect sense. However, what is the moral message?

In Hebrew, hearing refers to all absorption of meaning. In other words, reading is about understanding meaning and thus is a form of hearing. The lines and dots on a page have no intrinsic meaning. A non-literate child can recognize a picture of a flower, but the written word conveys nothing. Only once writing goes through our brains and gets interpreted does it make sense. What then does the association between balance and our ears teach us? That hearing something gives us more time and opportunity to reflect, absorb, and think about information and to arrive at balanced conclusions, compared with an image that flashes before our eyes.

In our day and age, sound-bites are a distortion of hearing, whose goal is to sway us without our thinking. Compare a debate show such as PBS's William F. Buckley's TV show, *The Firing Line*, in the 1960s with today's sound-bite panels on morning talk shows, and you will see that fewer words leads to less intelligent reactions.

In order to understand how fundamental Biblical principles can improve one's life, it helps to recognize that they are descriptive rather than prescriptive. What does that mean?

Many of society's laws are prescriptive. In 1861, the United Kingdom introduced the idea of the speed limit, legislating a 10-mile-per-hour maximum. Travel around the world today, and you will find speed limits of all numbers on similar types of roads. Even within countries, maximum highway speeds vary. No great data analysis proves that a 55 mph speed limit works better than a 57 mph one, or a 60 or 70 mph one. Bureaucrats and legislators decree a number that becomes law. That law can change at any time.

Contrast this with another law—the law of gravity. This law says that anyone who steps out of a window on the 20th floor of a building will plummet downward to a sudden and fatal stop on the sidewalk below. There is no bureaucratic committee that can modify that law to apply only on Mondays or only in countries whose names end in "a." This law does not *prescribe*. Instead it *describes* how the world really works. This law was not created at the whim of Isaac Newton; he simply shared an understanding of the rules of gravity. People did not float like helium balloons around the countryside before Isaac Newton's time. The law was and will always be in effect in all times and places.

Many people tend to think of Scriptural laws as prescriptive: Do this. Don't do that. Keep the Sabbath. Do not steal. Yet many of the truths that God reveals to us through the Bible are descriptive. They describe how individuals and societies best function. One modern fallacy, a part of enlightenment thinking for a number of centuries, is that we are totally free to make any and all choices in our lives, relatively immune from unpleasant consequences. However, we do not thrive living alone. We all need to participate in the society around us in myriad ways as commonplace as using electricity or driving on paved roads. We depend on our neighbor not breaking in and stealing our possessions. If enough people in society do things to harm that society, the foundations of civilization collapse.

While the focus of this chapter is on Faith and Spirituality, the salient point is that this one of the 5Fs is completely integrated over every single part of our lives and every decision we make. We start our lives as newborns who are intensely physical. As we grow and mature, the spiritual side of us moves on to the main stage. We make decisions instead of only responding to physical stimuli and, as we shall see in the next chapter, even the most physical aspects of our bodies connect to our spiritual nature.

Chapter 4

Fitness: Bodybuilding

We devoted so much space to explaining what we mean by the words spirituality and faith because many of us understand those words very differently. But do we really have to define fitness? Indeed, the word is far less confusing. We can all agree that fitness is a healthy state of the body and revolves around health, diet, and exercise.

However, though we may understand what fitness is, where we are prone to disagree is on the variables that influence fitness. We know that our body is a system comprising elements like our hearts, lungs, kidneys, and blood cells. Thus it follows logically that anything that clearly impacts any of these elements will affect our fitness. What most of us are far less conscious of is that our bodies also react to additional elements that have as much to do with our overall health as our hearts, lungs, and kidneys do. These additional elements are Family, Friends, Finance, and Faith.

People Need People

Let's start by looking at this on the most basic level. Every year, we hear a number of sad stories of bodies that are found when neighbors smell a stench from a nearby apartment. These numbers may increase after a heat wave or when a cold snap aligns with a blackout. While precautionary measures include, "Visit adults at risk at least twice a day," it is indisputable that those who do not live alone, or who have strong relationships with people who might invite them to their own homes in an emergency, will fare better than those who are isolated. In so many ways, our health and our fitness benefit by being connected to others. Another way of saying this is: trying to be physically fit as an isolated person without friends and family is an uphill battle. If we add in a lack of money, it is verging on the impossible. The F of Fitness needs the other four Fs to flourish.

We repeatedly encounter reports of how much healthier married people are than their single counterparts. We do not know the definitive reason, but it is clear to anyone with both single and married life experience that spouses encourage one another to be diligent about health, whether it is eating well or regular doctor visits. Having children adds another variable to the equation. A rather daredevil young man of our acquaintance gave up his motorcycle when his wife became pregnant. All of a sudden, the potential downside struck him in the face. My (RDL) own experience is not unusual. My father, a heavy smoker for decades, resisted all attempts by doctors and friends to get him to give it up. But when I, as a 7-year-old, tearfully begged him to stop smoking because the smoke caused me to have uncontrollable bouts of sneezing—he immediately did so.

In the same way that Family helps Fitness, the reverse is also true. Being fit helps one with family life. Obviously robust bodily health and physical vitality make a person seeking a mate more attractive. Subsequently, the long and exciting process of building a family is also augmented by bodily vigor.

The crosslinks of Fitness with Finance and Fitness with Friendship are equally evident and also circular. One leads to the other that then circles back to the first. People who exude health find it easier to build friendships and business relationships. Healthy finances allow people to afford the relative luxury of a gym membership or even a private trainer as well as access to more preventive medical care. Those with a few dollars are known to eat more healthily while many of the same traits that encourage making money, such as delayed gratification and mindfulness, also apply to choosing how to eat.

Most of us recognize that unhealthy stress negatively affects our bodies. Whether it is suppressing our T-cells, increasing inflammation, or increasing our risk of illness while decreasing our ability to fight infection, chronic stress wreaks havoc with our physical selves. There are certainly physical ways to cope with stress, including exercising and eating well. However, restricting ourselves to those methods is like utilizing only half of a toolbox.

For example, continually being short of cash is stressful. Each time a bill comes due, each time we need to decline an invitation because we can't afford to attend, and each time we worry about how we will deal with an unexpected (yet inevitable) crisis of one sort or another, it taxes our body. We can try to avoid workaholism by remembering that no one ever engraved on his tombstone, "He spent an extra day at the office," but the people spouting that advice have a roof over their heads and food on their tables. Only if you are secure financially do you have the luxury of fixing your roof before it caves in, taking time off to visit a friend who needs support, or considering attending your child's soccer game. Financial insecurity is stressful. Fixing your finances is one way to improve your fitness.

"A sorrow shared is a sorrow halved." Having family and friends who support you makes even the most stressful situation easier. Although COVID-19 put a dent in the business model, a growing professional opportunity before COVID-19 overturned our world was being a professional cuddler. The power of human touch is immense. So strong is it that as people stopped creating families and putting in the needed time and effort to make friends, entrepreneurs realized that customers would pay for someone to hug them. Nothing kinky, no overt sexual overtones—just one human embracing a lonely individual starved for touch.

In 2018, United Kingdom Prime Minister Theresa May appointed a minister of loneliness to deal with what the government saw as a growing problem. She said:

> *For far too many people, loneliness is the sad reality of modern life. I want to confront this challenge for our society and for all of us to take action to address the loneliness endured by the elderly, by carers, by those who have lost loved ones — people who have no one to talk to or share their thoughts and experiences with.*

A summary of a 2021 article about loneliness in Japan said:

> *Increasing social and economic isolation is causing Japan's suicide rate to climb, with working women and single mothers most at risk. The newly appointed "minister of loneliness" plans to alleviate this phenomenon.*

Real Relationships

How many young people today carefully guard what they eat and exercise religiously, yet they are not making time for friendship, not marrying and having children? How many articles assure us that marriage is obsolete and women (especially) should feel empowered to have children without a spouse? Or that the rational and emotionally healthy decision is not to have children at all? How many misguided Gen-Zs think that going for a drink after work with coworkers is the same as having friends? Should a 20-year-old woman follow the recommended advice that family and friends should come in second place to her career and be reassured by hearing that a government loneliness commission will be there for her down the road? Our suggestion would not be to diminish or disparage the need for money or fulfillment. It would be to integrate that need—the Finance of the 5Fs—with Family, Friends, and Faith. Doing so may be the best investment in health (Fitness) that a person could make.

Advancing technology has presented an additional complication in forming relationships. For many, technology replaces time that they would spend with people in person. And while we can fool ourselves into thinking that we have so many more friends through social media, our interactions through technology usually lack the quality and benefits that true friendship offers. There is a difference in how we feel after scrolling through our phones or tablets with how we feel after spending an evening with a close friend. Our devices lure us away from real relationships, the kind that bring us happiness and help us handle stressful parts of our lives.

In fact, technology has in some ways redefined the word *friend* to mean a loose association formed over the internet, which may or may not have any corresponding association in real life. It is worth noting that ancient Jewish wisdom has a very clear definition for the word friend: in Hebrew, CHaVeR. The root word of chaver, in fact, is CHoV, which means obligation. A true friend, therefore, is not a loose acquaintance, but someone we feel a sense of obligation to, and who, in turn, feels a sense of obligation to us. Friends are people we show up for, and who, in turn, show up for us. If you're a beginning artist and you're having your first art show, your friends are the people who make it a point to show up. If someone you know loses a loved one and needs support, you are a friend when you visit, call, or bring a meal.

In this sense, friends are tied to each other not only through mutual enjoyment of each other's company, but a deep sense of duty. Having a life that is full of acquaintances may alleviate loneliness moderately. But having a life that is full of true friends can give us a sense of firm belonging in the world. The catch? To have strong friendships, we need to first be a devoted friend (and also be willing to overlook our own friends' occasional lapses in fulfilling their duty).

Headlines promise us that sex dolls will alleviate the problem of the incel (involuntarily celibate) man. We don't think we are going out on a limb if we say that dolls won't solve the travails of these men, who share an online community that is full of anger and hostility toward both women (who have rejected them) and many other men (whom they perceive as more successful with women than they are). No matter how lifelike these dolls are, and a burgeoning AI technology will make them even more so, nothing replaces human interaction. Perhaps the mightiest obstacle facing the sex doll industry is that in the Divinely designed male-female relationship, both partners' pleasure is enhanced by knowing that one is bringing pleasure to the other. The fatal flaw of the sex doll is not that it cannot provide some pleasurable frictional stimulation; it probably can. What it cannot do however is receive pleasure. Without that, it will never be more. Trying to treat sex as if it was only a physical activity has many problems. We would lay odds that these men's physical fitness will not be helped by fake females. The physical outlet, divorced from Faith, Family, and Friends, is a big dud.

Healing the Soul to Heal the Body—Healing the Body to Heal the Soul

We live in a time of incredible medical advances. We also live in a time of frightening medical errors and malfeasance. One of the greatest mistakes in the medical world is the overuse of Western medicine to treat maladies that are more spiritual than physical in nature.

Even though Pepto-Bismol won't cure an emotional stomachache, many of us are popping pills instead of dealing with the spiritual sores that are causing our bodies distress. Like so much of life, society tends to veer to extremes. We were justifiably outraged when "women's complaints" used to be dismissed as female hysteria. Many serious physical problems were ignored. It is true that sometimes, people go from doctor to doctor over years, only to discover finally that a chemical imbalance or a growth was missed. The other end of that spectrum has doctors prescribing medication when what is needed is emotional and spiritual solace.

We have been quick to reclassify what we used to consider as personality shortcomings as stemming from physical causes. In today's medical world, alcoholism is a disease with no character implications. (Even though the big book of Alcoholics Anonymous considers alcoholism to be a "spiritual malady," which requires a spiritual cure rather than a physical one!) Likewise, depression is understood as a simple matter of chemical imbalances in the brain rather than a symptom of an unsettled soul. Deep psychological and spiritual confusion precipitates a prescription for psychotropic drugs, hormonal manipulation, or surgery, rather than a response to the cry of the soul.

Indeed, the line between physical and spiritual is not always easy to mark precisely. Do some people have more of a physical propensity for alcoholism? Undoubtedly. Might depression for some be primarily linked to physical causes that can be treated? Yes. In some cases, physical cures to apparently spiritual problems will help. And indeed, due to the interconnections of the 5Fs, this shouldn't surprise us. At some level, all physical things have a spiritual aspect and vice versa. Yet it would be a mistake to overlook the need for truly spiritual "cures"—inner work, growth, and emotional healing—in favor of only medical treatments.

My (RDL) late father and teacher, Rabbi A. H. Lapin, knew from his religious training that the body and the soul were intimately connected. As such, he was an early student of psychosomatic disorder. Not long after World War II, a congregant with a paralyzed right arm sought his guidance. This man had undergone the entire battery of medical examinations and tests. He had seen learned doctors in every specialty, but nobody could find an organic, neurological, or anatomical explanation for his paralysis. After several lengthy meetings that included delving into his history over the past few years, my father recognized the powerful impact of his congregant's army experiences and was drawn to the notion that something traumatic concerning his right arm must have happened during that period. It turned out that in 1941 the man had been stationed at the Libyan fortress of Tobruk, which was under siege by the German army under General Erwin Rommel.

The man's mind drew back to one specific day. While desperately defending his position, with the barrel of his overheating machine gun glowing red, this soldier suddenly realized that his buddy who sat right beside him guiding the ammunition belt into the gun's breech, had been hit by a German bullet. Groaning in pain, his comrade pleaded for the water canteen.

Weeping now, the soldier continued, "I could have just passed it to him and instead I continued firing. When I paused to get him the water, he was dead."

My father had the man recreate the scene using the pillows from our living room couch. Sure enough, it was his right arm that would have passed the water canteen to the other soldier. My father spent much time explaining the duties of soldiers under attack as well as a lengthy discussion on life, morality, and death. Over the next 2 months the paralysis gradually diminished until by the end of that time, the agonized man had regained full use of his arm.

We see this again and again. Not only does our body provide a home for our soul, but it is also impacted by the condition of our soul.

The distinguished Dr. Lewis Thomas in his book, *The Medusa and the Snail*, discusses warts:

> *In one of these [studies], fourteen patients with seemingly intractable general-*
> *ized warts on both sides of the body were hypnotized, and the suggestion*
> *was made that all the warts on one side of the body would begin to go away.*
> *Within several weeks the results were indisputably positive; in nine patients,*
> *all or nearly all of the warts on the suggested side had vanished, while the*
> *control side had just as many as ever. . . ..*

In these wart studies conducted at Massachusetts General Hospital, Dr. Thomas described one interesting anomaly. One of the patients had lost the warts on one side of his body, as had been suggested in the hypnosis treatment. However, he had been told to lose the warts on his right side, yet it was the warts on his left side that disappeared. Later investigation established that this particular patient had general trouble distinguishing between right and left.

We do not know whether all warts absolutely respond to hypnosis or not, but a wealth of credible clinical data show that significant wart regression follows hypnosis and placebo treatment. Does this work for everyone or even for most? We do not know the answer to that question. We do know that there is no clinical literature suggesting that warts respond to birthday cake or freshly mown grass, yet there is a great deal of serious research into the extent that warts respond to spiritual suggestion, that of the mind and soul.

Mind-boggling, isn't it? As anyone who has had a wart knows, they are extremely physical. However, after knowing about Dr. Thomas's studies, are we still so confident that physical is all they are? The same is true for psychosomatic illnesses. The stomach pain caused by grief over the passing of a loved one or a dermatological problem caused by losing a job are very real. Trying to alleviate them only with medication offers short-term comfort at best and is clearly futile in the long term.

Acceptance of the loss and adaptation to a change is the only true cure for this kind of spiritually rooted pain. Our bodies and souls are not two separate entities but function interdependently.

At the Olympic level of athletic achievement, it is said that all the top competitors share an almost equivalent level of physical attainment. The paramount factor distinguishing winners and losers is mental, or as we categorize it, spiritual. When going for the gold or playing a high school sport or trying to become a Special Forces soldier, it is the unmeasurable aspect of ourselves that provides a greater ability to overcome pain and a stronger determination to extract yet one more joule of energy from a tortured body already delivering its maximum. A budding athlete blessed with a super-high performance body but possessing a tendency to pessimism and self-indulgence is at a decided disadvantage when competing against another athlete with less genetically developed physical attributes but far superior qualities of self-discipline, both of mind and body.

Placebos are any treatments such as sugar-pills or similar relatively inert substances that have no active properties. In countless clinical trials participants in the control group have been given placebos and yet report an improvement in symptoms. It does appear to be true that for many patients, belief in the effectiveness of a treatment is enough to change the course of the underlying health problem. The converse is also true for many patients. Developing the conviction that treatment is useless and that all hope is gone often spells doom for that patient. Though increasingly difficult to experience in contemporary health systems and medical environments, having a profound faith in one's doctor and treatment is surely one more valuable arrow in the recovery quiver.

Fascinatingly, just as we see that healing the soul can heal the body, we see that the relationship works in the other direction as well. Our minds can affect our bodies, but our bodies can also affect our minds. Are you feeling down? Put a smile on your face. Making that physical change will affect your emotions. While I might understand that going for a run releases endorphins leading me to feel energized and happy, smiling doesn't activate my hormones or even many of my muscles. Yet, it can jump-start a change in my mood.

Smile, Smile, Smile

When we were first married, I (SL) discovered that the phone rings constantly in a rabbinic home. This was before the age of cell phones; the phone was actually connected to the wall! My activities were frequently interrupted by callers wanting to speak to my husband or to ask me a question. To be honest, my voice sometimes reflected my irritation at being stymied in my fifth attempt to put a cake in the oven or work on a class I was preparing. Obviously, caller number five had done nothing different from caller number one, but my response to him was not as gracious.

My husband, having grown up in a rabbinic home, gave me the solution. As I pick up the phone, plant a smile on my face. This piece of advice has served me well over the years.

Although it may sound counterintuitive to us, taking action with our bodies can change our thoughts. Yes, the physical can affect the spiritual. Even when we know that we are trying to manipulate ourselves it works! Are you going for a job interview, possibly for a job that you are not confident you deserve? Among the many valid pieces of advice you may receive is that you should stand tall rather than slouching. It is true that this will make you seem more confident and competent to the interviewer. But it will also "trick" you yourself into feeling more confident and competent. You certainly can and should review skills and prepare in other ways. Yet how you hold your body will change your spiritual side, your emotions, and your thoughts.

Let's take this opportunity to discuss ancient Jewish wisdom's emphasis on a golden mean when it comes to our characters and practices. The great transmitter of Torah thought, Moses Maimonides (1138–1204), discusses at great length how to achieve this "middle path" in his magnum opus, the Mishneh Torah. Extremism, he advises, is almost always a poor avenue to follow. He recommends visualizing two extremes and then plotting one's path between them, usually at the geometric midpoint.

For instance, neither extreme sternness nor excessive compassion are desirable as full-time guides to life. The excessively stern person could never raise a child without injuring him or her physically and emotionally, whereas the intensely compassionate person could never raise a child without indulging and thereby also injuring the child's physical and emotional development. Imagine one parent never bending the rule on bedtime and never giving a treat, while another parent has no rules to bend. He thinks that the healthiest children raise themselves! One parent exerts too much discipline, and the other exerts too little. The parent who guides himself down the middle path will be able to reach into himself for the reserves of both stern discipline as well as soft compassion as the situation demands.

In another valuable example, Maimonides warns against both extremes of the generosity spectrum. Giving away all you have to charity only ensures that you will, in time, become needy and perhaps dependent upon charity yourself. Giving away nothing at all damages both you and your community. The golden mean advises us to donate generously but appropriately.

Similarly, there are two extreme attitudes toward our bodies. On the one hand, we can over-focus on our bodies. The gym rat who never enjoys a meal out with friends because he can't help but sneer at their food choices or find something that he can eat is going to damage his friendships. A woman who can't tolerate the idea of gaining weight is not going to be able to have a healthy relationship with her own body, let alone pregnancy. A man who focuses solely on a woman's physical attractiveness is likely to make serious mistakes. Anyone who cannot handle the idea of aging has some rude shocks in store.

On the other hand, ignoring or disdaining the body leads to ill health. Our bodies are gifted to us by God, and according to ancient Jewish wisdom, we have a religious obligation to take care of them. To neglect the body certainly isn't showing gratitude for the great blessing God gave us. An unhealthy body also makes us less able to take care of our families, finances, and friends.

Attending to the body, incidentally, includes not only physical care, but also grooming. We have listened to complaints from more than one woman about a man arriving for a date looking as if he had never heard of a mirror. Being clean and attractive for one's spouse is a Biblical ideal and that courtesy should certainly extend to someone we are hoping to impress. One of the lesser-known requirements for a

Jewish community is that women must have access to cosmetics. This not only assists the health of a couple's marriage in obvious ways, but also gives women a psychological and emotional boost.

In reality, when we go out in public, our faces and bodies are exactly that—on public display. Whether we show a frowning or smiling face and whether we look neat or sloppy does influence those around us. Workplaces do have different dress expectations, but in general looking put-together suggests to a potential employer that we are competent and capable.

Furthermore, just as there is physical pollution, there is also spiritual pollution. Most of us harbor legitimate anathema toward people who physically pollute the public space by littering or by driving a vehicle that emits clouds of noxious smoke and ear-splitting noise. They are diminishing the quality of our lives as we navigate the public spaces of our environment. Here too there is a spiritual version of the physical reality. We don't have the moral right to go out into the public space exuding a dark cloud of infectious despondency any more than we have the moral right to inflict a foul-smelling miasma of body odor upon, say, our fellow train passengers. Being of good cheer to the world is a Biblical value, and as hard as it can sometimes be, it is a value to which we subscribe. The late great Esther Jungreiss told of how, as a young girl in Bergen Belsen concentration camp, she was directed by her father that her job was to smile. Her smile would bring a brief sliver of happiness to the doomed prisoners and that was her moral obligation.

In Chapter 3, we spoke about the Hebrew word for clothing, LeVuSH, and how it is spelled exactly the same as the word LeBoSH, for embarrassment. There is another Hebrew word that means a garment, BeGeD. That word, too, can be read in another way, as BoGeD. (Remember, vowels are secondary in Hebrew.) A BoGeD is a traitor.

What's the connection between clothing and betrayal? For one, clothing came about as a symptom of our first betrayal in Eden. Until then, our bodies were complete reflections of our souls and did not need to be covered.

Now that we must clothe ourselves, however, there is an opportunity for clothing to constitute another kind of betrayal. Clothing, after all, is not essential to us. It is a covering. And it may or may not reflect the thing that it covers. In other words, our clothes have the ability to betray us. How so? On one level, perhaps, clothing can be used as a concealment or disguise. Spies rely on changing their clothing and appearance to blend in better with a crowd. In this sense, their clothing betrays who they really are. It is a lie. On another level, the clothing we wear can betray our inner dignity and divine soul. We have seen people whom we knew to be sensitive and compassionate, wearing T-shirts that sport repugnant slogans suggesting that the wearers are callous and cruel.

Somewhere between disdaining our bodies and elevating them as idols lies the correct path. The body is the vessel for the soul. Just as the salesperson in the jewelry store displays an expensive bracelet on a velvet surface rather than casually dropping it onto the counter and just as we prefer coming home to a nicely furnished room rather than to a messy dump, our souls reside best in tidy and attractive bodies.

In this sense, Fitness means not taking our bodies for granted. It means being mindful about our relationships with our bodies and about our efforts at maintaining them. If we see our body as a home for our eternal soul, then caring for our body becomes a purposeful activity.

Food: Filling and Fulfilling

Until now, we've looked at the powerful ways that Fitness, or bodily health, interacts with the other pillars of our lives, including our relationships with others and our own mental and spiritual health.

One area that we have not yet explored within the crosslink of Fitness and Faith extends to the always-in-vogue question of weight control and our relationship with food. Who doesn't want to lose weight? You'll see more "get-thin-quick" schemes advertised than even "get-rich-quick" scams.

Why do we have such problems with maintaining a healthy weight in our culture?

Revisiting the Garden of Eden, when God famously commanded Adam to stay away from the tree of knowledge, we discover an interesting command preceding that prohibition:

And the Lord God commanded (the) Adam saying, 'Of every tree of the garden you must eat, you must eat.' (Genesis 2:16)

Many English translations mistranslate this phrase as, "…of every tree of the garden you shall *surely* eat."

However, the original Hebrew does not say "surely." Instead, it twice repeats the commandment to eat, using the Hebrew words ACHoL tOCHeiL. Ancient Jewish wisdom explains why God's first explicit directive seems to have this repetition. God wants us to perform two separate and distinct acts of eating with every mouthful. We are to eat for physical sustenance, and we are also to eat for spiritual sustenance.

In this way, the first step in benefiting from the Food–Faith crosslink is realizing that we eat not only to become physically filled but also to become spiritually fulfilled. If we fail to extract the spiritual nutrients from food, we sometimes continue eating in the hope that even more food will fill the void. Recognizing the spiritual side allows us to extract the full benefit from every morsel of food, leaving us satisfied. In turn, we eat less.

Food provides vitamins, minerals, proteins, carbohydrates, fats, and other materials essential for the human body to function, repair itself, and thrive; it fills us. But eating also provides something else. It offers nourishment for the human soul to function, repair itself, and thrive; it fulfills us. Needless to say, gaining the former physical benefit is far easier and more intuitive than obtaining the spiritual benefit.

It is too easy to remain oblivious to the spiritual dimension of food, yet this comes with a price. As is evidenced by so many Westerners being overweight, most of us eat more than our bodies actually require. We eat more than our bodies need (as well as different foods than they need) because although the body is trying to communicate, "Hi there! Enough already!" its voice gets drowned out by our souls shouting, "I'm still hungry, feed me!" We keep eating.

Sometimes, we are stuffed to capacity and cannot eat any more. That leaves us feeling frustrated and dissatisfied. We feel as if we have been denied something and sense that we have not gotten what we wanted from the food. As soon as we can, we resume eating.

Though deriving a spiritual benefit from our food may seem like a tall order, we are trained from infancy to do it when as babies we derive more than physical sustenance from our mothers' milk. A closeness and a bonding take place through early feeding, and we retain an emotional link to eating throughout our lives, using comfort food to alleviate stress or banishing gloom with a good meal. Wise mentors warn against propping up a bottle for a baby. Doing so misses out on the intimacy of baby and mother looking into each other's eyes, the warmth of skin touching skin, and the experience of soul touching soul. Too many mothers are convinced that breast milk is the most nutritious food for newborns and babies (as it is) while they ignore the spiritual side of nursing. They desperately pump breast milk as they drive to their offices and on their lunch break, while someone else is feeding their baby.

We might say that there is a hierarchy in the ideal way that a newborn/infant should be fed breast milk:

1. Nursed by his or her mother.
2. From a bottle while being held by his or her mother.
3. From a bottle while being held by someone else who loves the baby.
4. From a bottle while being held by someone who feels affection for the baby.
5. From a propped up bottle.

If parents opt for a propped up bottle filled with breast milk rather than a formula-filled bottle held by someone who lovingly gazes at the baby, we suggest that the parents are focused on providing the physical food implied by the first "you shall eat" in Genesis 2:16 while mistakenly ignoring the second "you shall eat."

Now, there are all sorts of reasons that the first choice might not happen. Mothers are sometimes ill, physically incapable of nursing, distracted by a crisis, and so on. Some women simply find nursing unappealing. Nonetheless, it is always important to be aware of the ideal even if many times we must, or choose to, fall short of it. The other option, to pretend that there isn't an ideal, is more popular today, but it starts a downward spiral.

A mother who, for whatever reason, cannot nurse her baby has no reason to feel shame, but it would be completely appropriate to feel some sadness. We know a woman who lay close to death for a number of months after delivering her son. Others lovingly took care of the newborn. Obviously, she did nothing wrong, and she has a warm and loving relationship with her now grown son. But is she sad that she missed out on those precious early months? Of course, though she chooses to focus more on being grateful for her recuperation.

By stating an ideal, we hope to give pause to women who would not dream of giving their babies formula, but who assume that returning to work after 6 weeks comes with no cost. Yes, some women cannot miss work. But there are also many women who are working not to put food on their family's table but instead because they followed the trope that a career is the chief source of fulfillment in their lives. Even more young women are at points in their lives where they can make decisions that will reverberate down the road. We hope to shatter the myth that the physical qualities of breast milk are all that matter.

Breaking Bread

Though breastfeeding may be the foundation for children learning that eating is both a physically and spiritually nourishing act, as children grow, we try to retain that connection in other ways.

It is in the context of food that we usually impart the first lessons of socialization. Wise parents start training their young children to say thank you after providing food, often by modeling those words way before a child is capable of speech. As time goes on, recognizing the opportunities that arise around food leads quite naturally to the importance of family meals during which, once again, spiritual input accompanies the act of eating.

In the early years after World War II, European countries started talking about building an organization of European unity. The impetus was mainly the hope of avoiding all future European wars. Discussions during the 1950s revolved chiefly around coal and steel. The idea was that since these two commodities are essential to making war, if Europe could bring all coal and steel production under some kind of congenial umbrella, surely that would end war. Regardless of the naiveté and motivations, the conversations led to conferences that led to negotiations. It was finally decided to acquire a building in Brussels to serve as the official seat of the deliberations that it was hoped would lead to European unification.

The person most identified as the visionary father of the European Union was a French renaissance man, Jean Monnet. He was an amateur historian, a financier, a civil servant, a diplomat, and a business entrepreneur. Monnet rejected several suggestions of grandiose office buildings submitted to him by his agents searching for a suitable Brussels location to house the nascent organization. In his mind, his baby would one day need the gargantuan headquarters it now occupies in Brussels and Strasbourg, but back then he instructed his agents to find a large home, perhaps even a mansion. He insisted upon only one nonnegotiable requirement. The house in which nations who only a few years earlier were locked in mortal combat would now sit down to discuss peaceful collaboration, and even perhaps union, needed a grand dining room. Jean Monnet believed with all his heart that only over meals would the former antagonists gain enough trust and amiability to move the dream to reality.

Prison psychiatrist Theodore Dalrymple is the author of *Life at the Bottom*, describing his experiences over many decades of work with London's underclass. He reports that the clientele he encountered were people who literally didn't understand the term "family meal." Most houses he visited in the course of his work did not even have a dining room table where such a meal might be enjoyed. We're not claiming that young people who do not experience family meals will automatically grow up to become part of the criminal underclass. But not understanding how important the spiritual aspect of eating is and not recognizing the value of dining together are both signs of an unhealthy culture.

Have you ever wondered why so many young people nowadays suffer from eating disorders that were virtually unknown three generations ago? They seem to be "contagious," especially among teenage girls. Surely the reasons cannot be entirely disconnected from the spiritual desert in which so many young people now live. Eating disorders are treated by mental health professionals with nutritionists as an adjunct because there is a powerful spiritual component to eating.

In increasingly isolated lives, many adults have no one with whom to share a meal. The advice we would give is: avoid eating alone. This may sound unrealistic. Yet, we can tell you from experience that neighbors, coworkers, and others who surround us are surprisingly open to an invitation. Maybe you won't click, but maybe you will find a new friend!

If asking someone into your house is too big a step, invite someone to join you at a park for a brown-bag experience. Instead of taking an empty table in an office cafeteria, ask if you can join an existing person or group.

This analysis also should involve table conversation. Consider how weird it is that we absorb nutrition through the same facial orifice from which our voices emerge. After all, we don't smell and hear through our ears. Dedicated functionality seems, for the most part, to be bodily design. But mouths are different. When we advise people not to eat alone, we are also advising them to use their mouths for speaking while also using them for eating. This seems, in fact, to be the Divine design.

Punctuating our meal with conversation allows more contemplation while encouraging us to eat more slowly than we do when alone. Think about the pauses you take between bites when you are eager to respond to what your table mate just said. Eating in the company of others also feels more natural. Many of us rightly feel awkward sitting alone in a restaurant and eating a meal. In cities around the world, some restaurants maintain a large table for single diners. Whenever a diner enters alone, the manager of the restaurant politely inquires whether the customer would like to eat alone or join the group table. Some have reported to us that about three out of four diners take advantage of the offer rather than sit and eat by themselves. Eating with others helps the process of ensuring that eating is not only a physical activity but also a spiritual one.

But here is a caveat. For our best lives, table discussion should be uplifting and meaningful. The worst thing we can do when we sit down with other people is to gossip. Sharing the latest titillating news about a coworker's divorce or speaking begrudgingly or complaining about something someone else did will yield no positive results. It would be better to talk about vacation spots or upcoming concerts. Even better is to talk about ideas. What are you reading? What pleasant surprise have you had lately? Talk about history, religion, or human weaknesses and strengths if you dare. When you are dining with family, friends, or those you know well, plan interesting topics in advance. This doesn't have to add another burden to your day. Simply be aware of compelling things you read or hear. Once you are in the habit of saying to yourself, "This would make for interesting discussion. I'd like to know what my friend thinks of this," you will find that it becomes second nature.

While eating, try to be mindful of our constant human fight to prevent the powerful physical forces from overwhelming the soft but vital whisper of spiritual reality. Animals eat, and people eat. If we want to be more than animals, then we chew slowly and thoughtfully rather than gobbling. Even if we are alone, we can set a table and sit rather than eating on the run. What's more, taking a few moments to reflect with gratitude on having food elevates the meal. Opening a meal with prayer is one way to do this. Observant Jews say a blessing after eating as well as before, a practice that George Washington also followed. After all, when I am hungry, it is easy to pray; expressing gratitude for the food when my belly is full and I want to rush to my next activity is on an even higher level.

We can't end this discussion of eating without mentioning the serpent at today's table: technology. One easy and quick way to destroy many of the benefits of mealtime is by having a TV on in the background or bringing a phone to the table. What you have done is to invite an intruder to your meal. Every time you pick up your phone, you are making a statement to those you are with that you find their company unsatisfying and need outside stimulation. Feeding a baby while looking at a phone diminishes that experience as well. Yes, I (SL) know how often a newborn eats and how much time that consumes. Looking at a screen while nursing is an entirely different experience than reading from a real book or chatting with a friend. Electronic devices are brilliantly designed to trap 100% of our attention. What a shame to lose out on bonding with your baby or with the other people at your table because of this.

The Other End of the Mouth—The Indignity of "Crap"

We have looked at one end of the gastrointestinal (GI) tract, the mouth and associated digestive system; it is time to look at the other end, the excretory system.

You'll pardon us, but we have heard the word "crap" used in public as a synonym for feces by the hosts of popular television shows, by officials of the Canadian Civil Liberties Association and other organizations, and by news anchors, to name just three. We are not going to squander your time bemoaning the coarsening of the culture; we all know it is happening.

And it is not only the word "crap." There is another four-letter synonym for excrement that is just as popular though the self-anointed cultural elites have decreed that "crap" can be used on America's airwaves but not the alternative word for the same human by-product. Nonetheless, we hear it all the time when out in public.

Why don't people say, "He needs the earwax beaten out of him"? Or how about, "The breaching whale scared the saliva out of the kayaker"? Or why not, "I've never heard anyone speaking such nasal mucus"? Drivers never say, "Oh urine! I took a wrong turn!" Of all human body waste, why does only excrement enjoy such common usage in ordinary conversation today?

Ancient Jewish wisdom offers a clue by informing us that the most compelling form of idolatry is the worship of Pe'or that is mentioned several times in the Torah. Furthermore, it shocks us with the information that the sacrament of Pe'or is excrement.

What is this worship of Pe'or, which resulted in the deaths of 24,000 Israelites that we read about in the Book of Numbers?

Israel became attached to Baal Pe'or, and the anger of the Lord flared against Israel. (Numbers 25:3)

Moses recounts the incident in his final days, adding a pointed message.

> Your eyes have seen what the Lord did at Baal Pe'or, for every man who went after Baal Pe'or, the Lord your God has exterminated from your midst. But you who cleave to the Lord your God are alive, all of you, this day. (Deuteronomy 4:3-4)

The idolatry of Pe'or is viewed as more grievous even than the betrayal of the Golden Calf, which resulted in the deaths of 3,000 Israelites (Exodus 32:28). Why?

The long tube that makes up our GI system starts with the mouth and terminates with the anus. For animals, defecation is merely ejecting waste from food; for humans, the act carries greater significance. We don't just use our mouths for eating; we also use them for speech. The latter is one of the chief ways in which God uniquely created us in His image. In fact, ancient Jewish wisdom tells us that the meaning of the words in Genesis 2:7, "and He breathed into his nostrils the breath of life," is the ability to speak.

Animals make noises and communicate; people formulate abstract ideas and express them. Animals are bound to the present moment—they may be able to sound an alarm to danger or signal one another during mating season, but they cannot tell each other about a past or future event. Speech, however, allows us to transcend the immediacy of a situation. With words we can relate to a past and a future and to people and places not immediately before us. This means that we can connect with concepts that are abstract—including an understanding of spirituality and God. It also means that we can give over our experiences to a future generation though they may never witness what we tell them. If connections in time are an important part of how we connect on earth, speech is unquestionably the tool that allows us to formulate these connections. In this way, speech is the tool that declares us to be more than just animals, but rather exalted human beings with both body and soul.

One might say that the GI tract, which starts with the mouth, the organ with which we speak and thereby distinguish ourselves from animals and through which we can preach rectitude, ends with the rectum. What emerges from that orifice, a lowly waste product, is the very opposite of the exalted ideas that should emerge from the mouth. When we speak, we can convert the biological processes of life into the Godly sound of speech and prayer.

Ancient Jewish wisdom highlights that Pe'or represented the opposite of Moses, whose distinguishing characteristic was as a speaker and a teacher. In fact, in Hebrew, he is usually referred to as "Moshe Rabeinu"—Moses our teacher. At the beginning of his life, Moses refers to himself as "heavy of speech and heavy of tongue," in explaining to God why he is not the best choice as spokesman for the nation (Exodus 4:10). By the end of his life, almost the entire book of Deuteronomy is one long speech. Moses conquered speech. And speech is as spiritual as we humans get. Speaking to ourselves, to one another, or speaking to our Creator, uses the capacity that God granted exclusively to humans.

The Bible emphasizes that Moses began his final teaching of the Torah citing Beit Pe'or (House of Pe'or) (Deuteronomy 3:29), and after he died, he was buried opposite Beit Pe'or. The contrast between Moses and Pe'or highlights the polarity between humanizing speech and, well, crap—between following the path of Moses or straying after the path of Pe'or.

> And He buried him in the valley, in the land of Moab, opposite Beit Pe'or. And no person knows the place of his burial, unto this day. (Deuteronomy 34:6)

Moses and Pe'or represent two opposing extremes. To this very day, we need to choose where on the spectrum we want to be—on the end closer to Moses or on the end closer to Baal Pe'or. When rioters and convicts throw feces at law enforcement or when an intruder defecates on the living room floor of the house he is robbing, they are eloquently expressing themselves and thereby choosing where they belong. Rather than utilizing the exalted power of speech, they are descending not only to an animalistic level of behavior, but beneath it. They are worshipping Pe'or.

Brandishing synonyms for excrement in regular conversation is a way of publicly disassociating ourselves from God and opposing His creation of the human being as a unique talking creature closer to the angels than to the apes. Perhaps there is some existential relief in rejecting the omnipresent Divine eye by repeatedly invoking excrement many times a day. Using "crap" and other similar words in conversation roundly rejects human uniqueness and boasts that we are no more than any other animal.

Though Western society correctly discourages public nose-picking, ear-probing, spitting, and urinating under the general heading of good manners, these are merely social gaffes, not the conspicuous opposite of anything. Only defecation, with its uniquely malodorous product, is something that people feel a need to distance themselves from. Boys on a camping trip will happily urinate behind a tree, but most people, knowingly or not, obey the Biblical verse:

> Among your equipment you shall have a spade, and when you have squatted you shall dig a hole with it and cover up your excrement. (Deuteronomy 23:13)

Other than the cat, mentioned in ancient Jewish wisdom for being particularly modest in this area, most animals defecate and move on. For we humans, doing the same is not an option.

Distancing ourselves from excrement either by burying it or through water-borne sanitation and also by the refinement of not talking of it constantly, moves us away from anal preoccupation and closer to the mouth and the human greatness of speech.

One way many of us attempt to diminish the awkwardness of the bowel movement, the daily ceremony that is the closest we come to excrement, is by using euphemisms for the bathroom. "Do you know where the 'men's room' is?" What is a men's room? A place with sports playing on a large screen television and craft beer on tap? "I am going to powder my nose." Really? Even the word "lavatory" means a place for washing oneself, from the Latin word *lavare*. Which brings us to the last we'll cite of the many euphemisms, all of which exist to avoid having to say, "Excuse me. I am going to evacuate my bowels, and I'll be back in a few minutes." Washroom, that's right. "I'm going to the washroom."

And when we do go to the washroom, what do we find? The most over-decorated room in the house. Careful color schemes, pretty tiles, and monogrammed towels. All of these are statements that we stand proudly as humans touched by the finger of God, not adherents of Pe'or.

The Spiritual Message of Sleep and Struggle

Let's glance at our strange habit of spending up to a third of our time asleep. The function of sleep itself is one of the 125 greatest mysteries of science, according to *Science* magazine. It would certainly appear that any creature that managed to do away with sleep would enjoy enormous evolutionary advantage. First of all, it would have no extended period of vulnerability to predators. Second, it would have significantly more time available for food gathering and reproduction. Yet we all need sleep.

Have you ever experienced intense frustration at trying to recall something? Perhaps it is the name of someone you intended to call. Sometimes it is a tune that is dancing around your mind just out of memory's reach. We wander the aisles of the grocery store hoping to see something that might jog our memory as to what we need.

You scrunch up your brow, you rub your temples with your fists, and you contort your face into a bizarre mask of concentration. None of this helps. Finally, a disconnected thought pops into your mind or you run into an acquaintance and you stop to chat. A few minutes later you remember whatever it was that was tormenting you.

Isn't it amazing? All that sweating and stressing to remember and— nothing! Then 3 minutes of doing something else, and bingo! There it is. It came back to you as clearly as could be. The answer often comes when you back off. And sleep is an extended period of backing off.

One useful and practical tip is to keep a pen and pad alongside your bed. Before going to sleep, review any problem you are working on. (Don't try this if you can't compartmentalize and let go of the problem. You'll stay awake all night.) You will be surprised how often in the early predawn hours you will awaken with a creative thought breakthrough answering whatever baffled you the night before.

This shouldn't astound us. After all, this is one of those timeless truths of ancient Jewish wisdom. Human creativity is nearly always a process of thrust, retreat, and then thrust again. All areas of being creative, even the most basic and most creative such as conceiving a baby, work this way. When tackling a challenge, work the problem, back off, and then return to the problem. This way it will yield to you more rapidly than it would in one long protracted push.

This is the principle of both sleep and the Sabbath. Withdrawing from creativity one day of the week, focusing on family, friends, and God, doesn't lead us to lose one-seventh of our potential for the week; it enhances our creativity during the other six days. On a daily basis, many find that giving time for prayer or meditation similarly makes them more productive for the rest of the day.

We mentioned previously that physical biological realities contain analogies to spiritual truths. When we note these analogies, we gain insights into ourselves. One of the ways that our bodies teach us crucial lessons about our souls is in the area of resistance. Almost everything worthwhile and positive that we wish to accomplish physically feels like trying to roll a boulder up a hill. By contrast, indulgence feels easy. It's easy to lounge around in our pajamas and watch television; it is hard to exercise vigorously on a regular schedule. It is easy to eat as one desires but hard to maintain a strict diet. It is easy to laze the day away but hard to labor at one's work. Physical labor, which used to be the primary mode of work, but which many of us do today as a form of self-care, gives us practice for all other parts of life where we will benefit from doing the right, rather than the easy, thing.

It pays to notice, however, that hard physical work is not necessarily unpleasant. Consider the pleasure that an athlete experiences as he exerts himself on the court. Or the endorphin high that runners experience during a marathon. The pleasures of physical activity remind us that pleasure is also to be found in other demanding areas of life, even if the road seems grueling. And even if the pleasure of the exertion is hard to find, there is usually a worthy reward.

There is a wonderful biological example of this idea. One of the most aptly named physiological experiences in the birthing process is called labor. It is, indeed, hard work. Not only do most mothers' bodies go through a strenuous, grueling (if completely worthwhile) experience, but the baby is pushed and squeezed. One might think that, looking at it only from the baby's perspective, a Caesarian birth would be healthier. In reality, babies born vaginally tend to have a higher Apgar score—the classification of health done immediately after birth that measures the baby's appearance, heart rate, reflexes, muscle tone, and respiration. The very action of struggling to be born strengthens the newborn.

I (RDL) learned this lesson early in life. At about the age of 10, I had visions of becoming a tycoon. For some inexplicable reason, my parents would not give me money for everything I wanted, so I embarked on an entrepreneurial path. We had mulberry trees in our backyard, and silkworms feed on mulberry trees. People will pay for fabric made of silk. Bingo!

I kept a whole bunch of silkworms in shoeboxes. They are quite amazing to watch as their lifecycle is fairly quick. Over the course of a day or two, they spin a silken fabric and when the spinning has reached a certain point, the silkworm starts spinning a cocoon around itself. This little caterpillar wraps itself completely in what turns out to be a fairly hard shell and "locks" itself inside. After a few weeks, the shell starts moving and a tiny hole appears. After that, a small, slender limb starts pushing out, pausing, pushing, and pausing. The process is similar to watching a little chick break out of its shell. Finally, out comes a moth. This process can take an excruciating two hours, and the poor little moth comes out bedraggled and exhausted.

When I saw the time and energy it took to do all this, I realized that I would make money more quickly if I could speed up the process. I took a pair of small nail scissors, and I cut away a hole so that the moth could just pop right out. Guess what? All of those that I'd graciously helped, died. I remember going to my mom and saying, "I don't get this. I was just trying to help."

She said, "You can't improve on God's system. God set it up so that in order for this incredible transformation to take place, there has to be struggle."

Amazingly, astronauts who spend prolonged time in space shrink physically. Without their bodies needing to fight gravity, something we automatically do on earth, their bodies somewhat atrophy. While most of us have days where simply lounging around sounds like an exquisite idea, giving in to that impulse on any regular basis harms rather than helps us.

To sum up a bit at this point, if we have done our job well, it should be clear that no element of our life is unaffected by spirituality, intangible elements that profoundly affect us. In addition, our physical beings both reflect and influence all parts of our lives.

Chapter 5

Money and Morality

Having, we hope, made the case that Faith is an essential part of Fitness, and that we need to understand the spiritual side of reality and its impact on everything we do, our next step is to lay out the spiritual nature of money. You will recall that spiritual does not mean good or virtuous. It means that which cannot be measured in a laboratory. Whether we discuss generosity or greed, industriousness or laziness, we are expressing spiritual concepts. But what about money itself? Is money spiritual or physical?

On the African savannah, leopards wedge the remains of their last hunting foray up in the limbs of a tree in order to provide another meal tomorrow. On game photography trips with my family, I (RDL) remember occasionally spotting a partial springbok carcass up in a tree. We'd usually park ourselves nearby in order to watch and wait. The magnificent spotted predator would surely return, providing us with a wonderful photographic opportunity. I recall wondering what would happen if the leopard returned only to discover that some other meat-eater had discovered his larder and emptied it.

We humans have a similar problem. We may keep our food in a refrigerator, but what do we do with the money that allows us to buy the food in the first place? Stashing the cash in our mattresses leaves us vulnerable to callous predators who could break in and make off with the wherewithal for tomorrow's lunch and rent. We came up with a better idea. Let's keep our money in a safe place called a bank. But whether in 1931 or in 2023, banks do occasionally experience panic-driven runs on their deposits, and they fail. Governments might guarantee your money up to a certain amount, or they might not. Surely there is somewhere safer to keep your money. What is that expression again? Oh yes, safe as houses. Buying a house! Yes, that is the safest place to keep your money.

Between 2000 and 2003 and again from 2006 to 2008, home values in 20 big American cities dropped dramatically. Although people have often wrongly assumed that real estate prices constantly increase, obviously that isn't always the case. More than once, when people realize that the value of their home has dropped, sometimes to less than they paid for the house in the first place, we get asked the question, "Where did the money go? Imagine that five years ago I bought a house for $100,000 with $20,000 down and a bank loan for the balance of $80,000. Two years later the value of the house has risen to $120,000. My equity in the house has roughly doubled from $20,000 to $40,000. Three more years pass and for various reasons, the value of the house has dropped to $80,000. My equity in the house is now about zero. Three years ago I had equity in the house of about $40,000 and now, I have nothing. Where did my $40,000 go?"

In the final analysis, the value of anything has little to do with what you paid for it. The value is whatever someone or the marketplace is willing to pay for it.

What Is Money?

The indefiniteness of money is due to its spiritual nature. Money is a representation of a spiritual commodity—value. The woman shopping for groceries who sees that the same money can buy only a fraction of what it bought a month ago will not feel better if government surveys or a comment from her 8-year-old child (which often sound surprisingly similar) tell her that she is shopping with exactly the same total amount of cash as she did a month ago, so she hasn't lost anything. She does have the same amount of money, but its value is not close to what it used to be.

It is true that dollar bills, Krugerrands, and euros are physical. We can touch, weigh, and see them. However, they represent something spiritual. I may place a gold coin in a safe, go away, and come back in 2 weeks. The gold coin will still be there, looking exactly like and weighing exactly what it did previously. But if I take it to the bank to exchange it for dollars, I might find out that this week I will receive $50 dollars less than I would have received had I done the exchange 2 weeks earlier. When I ask, "Where did the money go?" I am actually asking, "Where did my coin's value go?"

While opening the walls of a home, one might find ten $100 bills that Grandpa stashed away in 1970 and neglected to mention before he died. The money is still there, but the value of what he hid in the wall cavity has shrunk to about 10% of the value he originally hid. Value is entirely spiritual.

Money, or more accurately value, is a bit like love. When a marriage sadly ends, one might plaintively remember the outpourings of love and the declarations of eternal dedication at the wedding years earlier. One might ask, where did the love go? The answer is that both love and money are spiritual commodities; they are not tangible.

Love is something that exists because a human being in concert with another human being (or sometimes perhaps with a thing or a place) willed into existence. Value comes into existence when one human being provides something that another human being wants. It is true that sovereign states or governments can print money, but they cannot create value. Thus, when the same aggregate amount of value in the entire system is now represented by many more units of money or currency, of necessity, each one must be worth less. That is called inflation. Just as a red heart represents love but it is not really love, physical coins and bills represent the current value of money, but they have no inherent value.

Most times when we say *money*, what we really mean is the value represented by those coins or that Treasury bill. What we really care about is what we can obtain in exchange for that metallic disc or that piece of paper. This is exactly what lies behind the tendency today in many societies for people to carry very few pieces of paper or metallic discs. We might tap our credit card on a point of payment device.

We might wave our mobile phone or use it to effect a payment over a digital payment system like Zelle or PayPal. We understand that we are trading away value that we have accumulated, not bartering away pieces of metal or paper.

Few examples are better than cryptocurrency in showing how a large market of people agreeing can impart value to a symbol. Whether it is bitcoin or any of its variants, the symbol we call money does not even have to be tangible. It can be the arrangement of ones and zeros in a cryptocurrency wallet that some car dealer will exchange for a large, modern, high-value automobile.

How Is Money Created?

Let's look at how money is created (in simple terms). A housewife says to the farmer, "I'd like five pounds of those lovely red tomatoes and three gallons of that rich creamy milk your cows produce."

The farmer asks, "What will you give me in return?" The lady offers some newly baked cake or some eggs from her chickens, but it turns out that the farmer has no need for cake or eggs. Now what?

Well, of course she could ask him what he does need and perhaps he tells her that he is shopping around for a saddle for his horse. The lady has no saddles, so her next step is to locate someone who is willing to trade his saddle for her cake and eggs. If she is successful in her quest, she can then take the saddle to the original farmer and effect the exchange she wanted in the first place.

It goes without saying that this process would be cumbersome and in most cases unworkable. Money is the elegant answer. The woman can give a physical representation of value to the farmer, and he can then take it to anyone else who agrees that those coins or bills or iron oxide stripes on the back of a credit card represent value.

But this is the question we must explore: why should the farmer who worked so hard to produce those tomatoes and that milk accept a handful of metallic discs from a lady he just met, in return for which he surrenders his valuable produce?

In order to make sense of that question, let's try another thought experiment. I'm about to take my children skating when the phone rings. "Is that Lapin the roofer?" asks a guy whom I vaguely remember from my children's homeschool co-op. "We have an emergency. Rain is pouring down into our kitchen. Come now!"

I am just about to share my disappointment with the children, who will undoubtedly be even more disappointed that their skating trip will be postponed, when I quickly realize that this is not the correct way to handle it.

"Children, we were about to go and have fun, but an opportunity has cropped up for us to serve one of God's children," is what I say instead.

We load up the truck, and they accompany me to the house with the leaking roof. My children help me get the ladder set up and pass me tools and shingles. In an hour or two we've solved the problem.

"How much do I owe you?" asks the happy customer.

Within hearing of my children I rephrase the question and answer it. "You want to know how many certificates of performance I want in exchange for my services? One hundred please."

He peels 100 dollars off a roll he holds and hands them to me. I explain to my children that I call them certificates of performance because they prove that I served another child of God, making his life better.

That evening, my wife and I go out for dinner. We enter a restaurant we've never before visited and once we are seated, the proprietor inquires as to what we'd like to eat. I tell him that we'd each like a large, juicy, well-done steak on a bed of fries. He looks at me in astonishment. "Do you seriously expect me to stand over a hot stove preparing you a delicious meal?"

"What!? Isn't this a restaurant?" I ask.

"It is," responds the proprietor. "But only for members of the club of people who serve other people."

"Oh," I say with relief. "I am indeed a member of that club."

"Can you prove it?" asks the restaurateur.

"Sure I can," I say, brandishing the handful of certificates of performance I received that afternoon.

"Oh, why didn't you say so?" says our now genial host. "Relax and quicker than quick I will have a delicious meal on your table."

Following our meal he asks for and receives 60 certificates of performance from me, some of which he exchanges later that evening in order to fill up his car with gas. The cycle continues with worker after worker receiving and expending certificates of appreciation.

In my own heart, and with complete freedom, I decided that I was willing to abandon my afternoon skating with my children for $100. I don't think I'd have been willing to do it for $50, and I was pretty sure that if I asked for $200, my acquaintance with the leaky roof would find another roofer willing to charge less. I asked for $100, and he thought about it and decided that, given my reputation for doing good roof repairs, he was willing to make that exchange.

Sticking to the roofing thought experiment for just a bit longer, that day I made $100, spent $60 on dinner, and decided to put away $40 into my savings account. My thinking was that if I put away a bit of every amount I earn, when I am old and unable to climb up onto roofs, I will have money to live on. Of course my main problem is how can I make sure that $60 will still buy me an excellent dinner for two in 30 years? What if I indeed manage to put away a million dollars but by that time, that dinner costs me $180? This means that in terms of the buying power of my working years, I don't really have a million dollars to live on; I have only the equivalent value of about $350,000 in today's money Can money really lose its value so easily? Yes, like love, money can vanish. Anything spiritual, such as a reputation, can vanish in a moment.

What Causes Inflation?

Here is yet another thought experiment. Imagine waking up tomorrow morning and discovering a duffel bag outside your front door. Opening it, you find it packed with cash, what you estimate to be about about a million dollars. It is then that you notice a label on the bag that proclaims, "This is a gift to you from your loving friends in the federal government." Your mind spins with thoughts of how you will spend this astounding windfall. The very first thing is to indulge your 20-year love affair with Bavarian auto engineering and buy yourself a Series 5 BMW automobile.

Getting ready to race over to the BMW dealership, you first call your best friend to tell him of your good fortune. Before you can begin to talk, his words tumble over one another as he recounts having found a duffel bag outside his door containing a million dollars. Your heart sinks. Somehow, intuitively, you realize that everyone in America received such a duffel bag of cash. You now know that through the amazing spiritual nature of money, your gift is not quite as valuable as you had first thought. Somewhat sobered, you make your way to the car dealership into whose windows you had often peered lovingly.

To your astonishment, a long line of people stretches from the door all the way to the end of the block. A young lady with a clipboard is making her way down the line. Taking your place at the end, she eventually reaches you. By that time, another hundred people are behind you. "Which model?" she brusquely asks. You firmly inform her that your heart is set upon a Series 5 with the 4.4 liter eight-cylinder engine. She shocks you with her next words. "That will be $160,000 dollars." You try to inform her that there must be some mistake because you know the car of your dreams was priced at $75,000 only last week.

She gestures at the line and explains, "You see all these people? About 100 of them want the same car you do. We only have six in stock, and we don't know when BMW will send us more, so we are basically auctioning the six we have. We have discovered that plenty of people are willing to pay over $150,000 for that car. Yes, I know it cost half of that yesterday, but somehow, it seems that today everybody wants one and is willing to pay a lot for it."

Don't let anyone mislead you. Inflation is not caused by foreign wars, climate change, or a technical interest rate error. It is caused by an immoral government willing to erode the value of the currency over which it stands guard by printing too much of it or by injecting too much money into the economy by an adjustment known as quantitative easing. People in government do this because it is fun spending money that other people worked to create; that is all there is to it. Spending other people's money and being given credit for your generosity and being rewarded with another few years in office is just plain fun. So why limit yourself to spending money you had to extract from often less-than-enthusiastic taxpayers? Taxpayers who, at the next election, might remember your vote for higher taxes. Much safer just to print money. The problem is that for a stable economy, the amount of money printed should never exceed the aggregate value of all the economic transactions in the region where that currency is in circulation.

In practice, that isn't easy. How do you discover the overall value of all transactions in your country so that you can instruct your mint to print the exact correct amount of currency? With a computerized society and a digital economy, it can be done, but how were stable currencies maintained before the age of the transistor?

For nearly 100 years during the Victorian era, the British pound sterling maintained its value so that for most of the nineteenth century, the price of a bushel of wheat or of a ton of coal hardly varied. This helped provide a period of unparalleled economic growth and financial stability. How did they do it? The answer again is free exchange, which is to say that the value of the pound was attached to the price of an ounce of gold. What is more, anyone was free to walk into the Bank of England and exchange his paper pounds for gold or the other way around.

Because a free market of even millions of individuals communicates so very effectively, merchants in London could feel when pounds were losing their value. At that point, because there were too many pounds in circulation, people entered the bank to exchange their paper currency for the safer solid gold. As the Bank of England saw their gold reserves walking out of the door, they stopped the printing presses, and no more currency was printed. Since it is not that easy to spend gold or to break up a 10-ounce bullion bar, eventually, as economic activity around the British Empire continued, people felt the need for more currency. City merchants walked right back into the Bank of England and, putting their gold bars on the counter, requested their equivalent in currency. That signaled to the bank that it was time to start up the printing press again and supply the Royal Mint with more paper money. This regular stopping and restarting the printing upon the reliable signal of the market is what preserved the value of the pound sterling for so long.

"We have gold because we cannot trust governments," said President Herbert Hoover in 1933.

In the aftermath of World War II, countries agreed at the Bretton Woods conference in 1944 to make the US dollar the world reserve currency and to make the dollar redeemable by gold at the rate of $35 for an ounce. That helped the United States of the 1950s and 1960s build unparalleled prosperity. Not only did America rebuild itself, but it also rebuilt both the foes it had so recently vanquished, Japan and Germany. As a boy in London in 1957, I (RDL) remember playing in bombed-out city blocks that hadn't been rebuilt yet. At the same time in Munich, and even in Hiroshima, reconstruction was almost complete.

In 1971, partially in order to camouflage the always-seductive printing of money, President Richard Nixon eliminated the connection between gold and the value of the dollar, launching American currency onto the destructive path of inflation. By 2023, just a bit more than 50 years later, inflation has averaged more than 4% a year, making it necessary to spend about $800 to purchase what just $100 would have purchased in 1970. Since the dollar became the world reserve currency, America has benefited greatly. However, due to immoral management of the economy and eroding the value of the dollar for short-term political gain, it is quite likely, in our view, that the dollar will soon lose its special international status just as the pound sterling did in 1944. This helps convey the extent to which an economy and people's money is tied to morality.

As long as people can trust the guardians of their money, their government, not to adulterate their money and erode its value, they will constantly create wealth by serving one another and by being obsessively preoccupied with one another's needs and desires. Free exchange between people, in other words, an ethical free market, builds and is built by connections among people.

Not only do citizens of an economically productive region have to be able to trust the guardians of their currency not to harm its value, but they must also be able to trust one another. Only through trust will they engage in transactions and thereby create wealth. In 1960, both Ghana and South Korea had about the same annual economic output. In that year, both countries had a gross domestic product of about $1.5 billion. Forty years later, Ghana was up to about $15 billion while South Korea was up to about $600 billion. While certainly a number of different factors help account for the difference, one highly significant difference is the disparity in the two country's size of the average circle of trust. Societies in which people tend to trust only family members and local friends are economically handicapped when contrasted with societies in which people's trust extends far more widely. Trust facilitates connection, and connection makes transaction and wealth creation possible.

When we board an airplane, it is with the trust that the mechanic who checked out the engines did his job with integrity. If we suspect that he substituted titanium bolts with cheap steel and sold the originals on the black market, we might not purchase an air travel ticket. When the erosion of common spiritual values in a society reaches a tipping-point so that individuals increasingly act in their own short-term interests, trust evaporates, transactions wind down, and Finance quietly dies. Of course, trust in government inspectors and regulatory compliance suffers from precisely the same dynamic. Thus, we see that our Finance depends upon spiritual factors like widespread trust, in other words, Faith.

Let's Connect!

It is no accident that every new technological development that makes it easier for more people to connect with one another results in a meteoric rise in wealth creation and prosperity. As Russian economist Nikolai Kondratieff (1832–1938) noted, we see peaks of commercial creativity roughly every 50 years. The proliferation of steamships in about 1800 and the spread of telegraphic communication and the railroads in about 1850 produced peaks of productivity and prosperity. It was around 1900 that we saw the arrival of radio and the telephone, and about 1950 it was television, followed by the internet in 2000. Each of these communication breakthroughs stimulated an until-then unprecedented height of wealth creation. Anything that makes it easier for people to connect under the umbrella of ethical capitalism creates value.

A story our friend Meir told us comes to mind. His New Jersey–based business provides people with disposable tableware for parties and entertainment. Not surprisingly, most of his manufacturers and suppliers are overseas. When we asked him about his suppliers, he didn't just give us numbers and logistics. As he spoke, we could imagine his overseas associates as real flesh-and-blood people. We could picture Andrew in Hong Kong, Steve in Malaysia, and Helen in Singapore. Meir knew a bit about their families, and he knew their business hopes and dreams. Turns out, whenever he speaks with them, he expresses his genuine interest in them and in their lives before he ever gets down to business.

A little after our visit with Meir, COVID-19 shut down the economy, and the response of governments around the world to the epidemic initiated the supply chain disruptions of 2020 and 2021. When we saw Meir again in 2022, his business was thriving. In fact, he had just expanded his warehouse substantially. We asked how he was doing so well at a time when others were struggling to stay afloat. He laughed and told us about a conversation he had with one of his friendly competitors who was bemoaning being unable to secure any merchandise from Hong Kong, Malaysia, and Singapore. This competitor assumed that he and Meir were in the same boat. In fact, Meir told us he knew that this competitor had tried ordering from the very suppliers who were still sending container-loads of product to him.

Meir quite correctly observed, "There is a shortage of product, and they don't have their usual availability. But they are choosing to supply me rather than him." To Meir, the friendship he had always demonstrated to his overseas suppliers was genuine. He enjoys getting to know the people with whom he does business and hearing their stories. Meir's interest was not manipulative at all; expecting a payback wasn't why he showed interest in their lives. He was just being the nice guy that he always has been. His competitor operated his business transactions on the basis of "just the facts." Not surprisingly, however, when these suppliers could not fill all their orders due to the unexpected reaction to COVID-19, they chose to keep doing business with Meir with whom they felt a friendly connection.

Not only customers and business owners, but competitors also exhibit warmth to each other. This sounds pretty unlikely to people in academia with its notorious fellowships of envy specializing in faculty backbiting. It also sounds pretty unlikely to those of us who watch movies and read news stories suggesting that greedy business owners constantly seek to benefit by taking advantage of and destroying the lives of their competitors and customers. That business people do care, not only for their customers, and not only for their vendors, but also for their competitors does seem to suggest superhuman or even angel-like qualities. It is harder for those of us inexperienced in the life of commerce to believe, but many successful business people not only know their competitors but also are friendly with them.

We have a dear, long-time friend in California named Oscar who is in the chemical shipment business. He contracts with various companies to package and ship their products in the appropriate containers. Oscar's is somewhat of a specialty business, and California has only four similar companies.

Similar to us, Oscar is a Bible-believing Jew. One Friday night, his family's Sabbath meal was disturbed by the police knocking on his door. They shocked Oscar with the news that his plant was engulfed in flames, and while the fire department was getting it under control, it was such a large conflagration that they had been trying to call him. They came in person because their attempts to reach him by telephone had failed.

Forcing down the panic he felt, Oscar quietly explained to the law enforcement officers that it was his Sabbath and he didn't use the telephone on that special day. They kindly offered to drive him to the scene of the fire, but he explained that not only doesn't he use the phone on Sabbath, he also doesn't drive for those 25 hours. He added that as soon as the Sabbath ended on Saturday night he would race over to inspect the ruins of his plant. Meanwhile, Oscar and his family did the best they could do to continue observing the Sabbath as a day of harmony and tranquility.

At synagogue on Saturday morning, the news of Oscar's disastrous fire had spread. (It was front page news seen by those who got the Saturday paper delivered to their homes.) To the fellow worshippers who stopped by his seat to express sympathy, Oscar smiled and said, "I'm not letting it spoil my Sabbath—I get only one of those each week. Tonight will be enough time to deal with the problem."

That night, after he had chanted the havdalah ceremony concluding the Sabbath, Oscar jumped into his car and raced across town to his plant. The devastation was complete. He fought down feelings of fear and even nausea as he realized that truckloads of chemicals from all over the state were due to arrive at his gates on Monday morning for processing. He later explained to us that he realized that not only would he be unable to fulfill commitments he had made, but once customers had to seek an alternative processor, it was exceedingly unlikely that he would ever win back their business.

It was while he stood there among the ashes, silently contemplating financial failure, that he realized that amidst the throng of officials milling around the still smoking heap was someone he recognized. It was the owner of one of the three competing companies in Oscar's field of chemical shipment.

Now, here is where you can participate in a little test. Are you attuned to the wonderful world of the marketplace? Do you have an instinctive sense of how enterprises of financial freedom work? The question for you to consider is this: was Oscar's competitor there that night in order to gloat?

While Oscar stood disconsolately staring at the wreckage of the company that had been started a generation earlier by his father, this competitor walked over. Putting his arm around Oscar's shoulder, the man who stood to gain most from the collapse of Oscar's business began to talk softly but firmly.

"You're going to get over this, Oscar," said his competitor. "As you know we are only about 2 miles from here, and I have some extra production capacity. Tomorrow you are going to arrange for all the trucks arriving here Monday morning to drive another 2 miles to my facility. We will do your processing there for you under your label and under your supervision. We will do everything in our power to serve your customers as well as you would have, and they will barely know the difference. We'll work like this through the week, and then we'll discuss how to handle the following week."

A second competitor stepped in to handle the second week, and before long Oscar's plant was rebuilt and back to full operation. Oscar lost no customers, and his business continues to thrive to this day. His friendships with his business competitors continue as well. This is not an exceptional story. It is not unusual for business professionals to feel warmly toward their competitors. They are competitors in business but often become friends as well. Just in our own personal sphere of acquaintances, without effort, we can think of another few stories similar to this one. All of these fall under the intersection of Friendship and

Finance, ways that we should relate to those with whom we have economic interactions. It doesn't surprise us at all that those with attitudes like this tend to do better in the long run, both financially as well as with the rest of their 5Fs.

Different Attitudes, Different Results

Think of the difference between how you are sometimes treated in a government-owned location, such as a big city's post office, and how you are treated in the same neighborhood when you enter a well-run private business. At the first location, the employees know that, barring egregious misconduct, their jobs are completely secure. Their pay is disconnected from how pleased their customers are, hinging more on external factors such as length of employment. In a private business, even if not overtly stated, an employee must be an asset. Whether a salesperson in a for-profit company is working on commission or on a fixed-pay basis, he must earn his keep. Someone who connects with customers leading to greater sales, fewer complaints, and returning customers merits job security and advancement.

The two types of places have entirely different vibes. At many post offices, it's not unusual for the employees to saunter to the counter and barely acknowledge you as a customer. This attitude echoes the way clerks in the defunct Soviet Union used to treat citizens. (We do offer particular gratitude to the occasional government employees who have gone out of their way to help us. However, that reflects on their personal ethics and values, not on the ethos of where they are working.)

You have probably had a similar experience to mine (SL) in predicting, without the help of crystal balls or Ouija boards, when a store is on its last legs. When I was shopping for a craft item, I went into a branch of a national chain. After wandering around unnoticed for a few minutes, I approached one of the employees at an empty checkout lane. Busy conversing with her counterpart at the equally empty lane a few feet away, she ignored me. My "excuse me" received an irritated look, and my question as to where I could find what I was seeking led to a shoulder shrug. No, I was not shocked to hear that the store closed down a short while later. Government entities, you will notice, never go out of business.

When a customer, having made a purchase or not, departs a private store, alert salespeople will say, "Have a nice day." Cynics critique, "They don't really care. They are just trying to get you to come back and spend more money."

And it is true that this farewell statement is more polite than heartfelt. But it is still genuine because on some level, free and open transactions generate authentic warmth between the participants in a transaction. Each recognizes the service the other is providing or may provide in the future. More than that, approaching the interchange with a good attitude actually leads to caring. Just as putting a smile on our face when we answer the phone causes us to feel warmer toward the person on the other end, speaking caringly toward other people actually leads us to care. We can tell, and we are sure you can as well, when a disembodied customer-service voice on the phone is reading from a prepared script or actually listening to and responding to us. The stores we enjoy frequenting have not told their employees, "We will dock your pay if you don't tell each customer to have a nice day." They have built a culture where the employees want to make a connection with those who cross their paths.

Food and Finance

Do you recall our discussion of the post-World War II vision of Jean Monnet as he strove to form a European Union in the hope that future wars could be avoided? We mentioned there how, while looking for a location for this new organization, one of his requirements was a dining room where representatives of different countries could break bread together. Leaving aside international politics, the business lunch is a well-known concept. Surely, business associates could meet in the office? Why do meetings so often take place over food?

Perhaps we can understand more about this from a familiar sight. When a business lunch meeting concludes, an interesting pantomime plays out. We would advise a novice student of the 5Fs to watch and see who pays the bill for lunch. Sometimes one business professional prearranges the payment by giving his credit card to the restaurant's maître d' before the other guests arrive. Sometimes there is a polite but perfunctory little debate about who is paying the bill. This "debate" is usually settled fairly quickly, almost as if everyone already quietly knew who the bill-payer, and thereby the luncheon host, would be. The issue of who shall pay seems of far greater moment than merely the financial amount involved. As a matter of fact, the sum is usually trivial to the participants and surely doesn't warrant even any discussion let alone the formal little ceremony that nearly always occurs. What is going on?

Ancient Jewish wisdom provides two Biblical stories that shed light on this dining phenomenon. The first occurs when Abraham welcomes three visitors whom he assumed to be pagan travelers to his tent, the home for his ministry of monotheism. Rather than opening any discussion of philosophy, Genesis Chapter 18 describes how he fed them. Ancient Jewish wisdom pinpoints Abraham as the epitome of loving-kindness. As such, his measures of hospitality were legendary. But another subtle point is being made as well. By the ordinary conventions of hospitality and the subtle obligations of guest to host, guests are more open to the host's opinions, ideas, and views. One of the reasons that Abraham and Sarah were so effective in spreading monotheism was because they fed so many people. Thus, if a business meeting is turned into a business lunch, the person presumed to be the host enjoys a slight advantage in the ensuing negotiations.

Indicating that this is a pattern, not a coincidence, Genesis Chapter 24 describes a negotiation carried out by Eliezer, servant to Abraham. He arrives at the home of Rebecca, whom he wishes to bring back to Abraham's home as a wife for Abraham's heir, Isaac. Verse 33 describes how Rebecca's family properly puts food before the visitor. Immediately, Eliezer responds by telling the family that he won't eat until he has had his say. Naturally, he does not wish to feel obligated in any way to the family from whom he is about to be making an extraordinary request. Only once the request has been granted and Rebecca has been promised to Isaac in marriage (verse 51) does Abraham's emissary, Eliezer, enjoy a meal with his hosts (verse 54).

While most business meals take place at restaurants or public venues, inviting a business associate to your home for dinner creates a bond hard to achieve in any other way. When the invitation is a sincere expression of wanting to get to know someone better, rather than a manipulative action (something that is felt quite instinctively by the guest), a side benefit is that those eating a host's meal often leave skepticism and combativeness at the door.

Earning Money Versus Receiving Money

We imagine that, like us, you have heard the saying, "Money can't buy happiness." Like most slogans, it is, at best, only half true. Life is just too complicated to yield timeless truth in one-sentence aphorisms. People are fond of saying that, "The pen is mightier than the sword." If that was obvious and undebatable, the idiom would be unnecessary. We don't make expressions out of basic facts. We don't say, "Ferraris are faster than Fiats," or even, "The sword is mightier than the pen."

Most simple slogans are contradicted by opposing ones. "He who hesitates is lost" is refuted by, "Look before you leap." "Out of sight, out of mind" is the opposite of, "Absence makes the heart grow fonder." There are nuggets of truth in all these sayings, but running your life on one alone would be foolhardy.

There is certainly an element of truth in the idea that money can't buy happiness but, aside from the fact that people who say that usually are not going to bed hungry, it doesn't question how one received the money. There are many accounts about how winning money in a lottery often doesn't make the winners happier. Not only does winning money at the gambling table or in a lottery (a government-sanctioned gambling table) usually not make the winners happier, but many follow-up stories reveal only a temporary economic bump, often followed by family breakup and other misfortunes. Many such "lucky winners" end up less happy, and occasionally even poorer than they were previously. Getting money in the form of a handout usually also does not make the recipient happy. If getting a handout did produce lasting delight, the happiest people in the United Kingdom would be the million or so British living on the dole.

One expression in ancient Jewish wisdom for someone who is down and out is, "One who waits at his friend's table for the crumbs to drop." What a sad phrase. In friendships, sometimes one is the host, and sometimes one is the guest. We take turns. It is not comfortable for one's soul to always be on the receiving end. This spiritual truth explains one of the reasons why the idea of "universal basic income," where the government guarantees everyone a certain amount of money, reflects a lack of understanding of how we were built. Practically, it won't work because of inflation (see the previous duffle bag of money story). More importantly, it won't work because it corrodes the human soul.

No, winning money or receiving it as charity does not lead to happiness for most people. But earning or making a reasonable amount of money often can and does. That is due to the Faith or spiritual aspect of money. We humans have a need for dignity and self-respect, not for a specific amount of money being put into our bank accounts on a regular basis. While getting something for nothing offends our souls, deep within us is the awareness that *making* money is the happiness-inducing evidence that I have served another human being.

When a customer pays you for whatever it was you delivered to her, an object she desired or a service she needed you to perform for her, she doesn't feel that you extorted the money. She willingly hands the cash over to you. Most likely, she would wish to do more business with you in the future if she had the same need again. Insurance brokers, car dealers, tailors, and so many other businesses boast of having long-term customers whom they have served, sometimes for decades. A Chevrolet dealer in North Carolina with whom I (RDL) was dining, once pointed out an elderly woman at the next table, and leaning over to me as if to impart a confidence, he proudly told me that he had just sold a car to her grandson, making it three generations of that family that he had provided with cars. To my friend, his customers were not merely the means of putting food on his own table; they were much more. They were part of his network of relationships, situated on the sliding scale somewhere between the starting point of acquaintance and moving to the side of friendship.

When someone voluntarily gives us money, it is because we pleased them in some way. It might be a customer or a client. Perhaps we served an employer or maybe a relative wanted to express how glad they were that we are family. Since relationships with other people are so important to us, it is deeply satisfying to have proof that we gave value to another party and that we are valued by them. When young children prevaricate to avoid disappointing a parent, for instance, they are reacting to the innate desire to please those with whom they are connected. Earning money or making money brings happiness in a way that simply getting money doesn't because it affirms our relationship with other human beings.

No, money doesn't buy happiness. But earning money does signal to our soul that we have served another of God's children. We have delivered value. This of course rests upon the foundation of an ethically based capitalistic system. In that world, making money is worlds away from taking money.

Some wealthy parents and grandparents provide a disservice to their offspring by letting those children know that they will not ever have to worry about money. A trust fund awaits them. Helping future generations is a wonderful idea that encourages people to work hard so that their children will have better lives. For this reason, an inheritance tax that cuts off intergenerational connection is highly immoral, not to mention, also ineffective. It has been all but terminated in many European countries, most recently Sweden.

However, taking away the need to be productive and to contribute to society by assuring our children of enough income to live comfortably, let alone lavishly, is a huge mistake. Those misguided parents who are seeking to care for their children's bodies are neglecting to care for the needs of those same children's souls.

Obviously, one could write entire books dedicated only to earning money, business, and finance. In fact, we have two best-sellers specifically on those topics, *Thou Shall Prosper: Ten Commandments for Making Money* and *Business Secrets from the Bible: Spiritual Success Strategies for Financial Abundance*. Despite recognizing the importance of the financial side of our lives, what we hope we did in this chapter was to point out how our views and handling of money specifically intersect with our beliefs (Faith) and our Friendships. We still need to deal with the elephant in the room: How do we integrate the Finance part of our life with our Family?

Chapter 6

Sex: Pleasure and Pain

The premise of this book is that the 5Fs in our lives intersect, depend on, and affect each other. Having discussed Faith and Fitness and the spiritual overtones of Finance at some length, it would be neat and tidy if now we could focus a chapter on Family, perhaps with a sprinkling of Friendship and a deeper look at the intersection of Finance and Family. However, while the 5Fs all impact one another and can only be understood through the lens of Faith (Spirituality), and while they are all impacted by and themselves impact Fitness, the areas of Family, Finance, and Friendship tangle together like a knotty and snarled ball of yarn.

Friendship, Finance, and Family cover the basic ways in which we relate to other human beings. Healthy societies and healthy individuals need all three types of relationships to function well. These are the areas where we find our greatest potential for fulfillment as well as our greatest potential for sorrow and dismay. They are also the areas where we receive the most confusing messages today.

This confusion is abetted by subtle and not-so-subtle changes in language. Do you recall that we looked at how the language surrounding animals has changed over the years? Dogs went from being working animals to being man's best friend, and frequently, people now refer to them as "fur babies." To mention only a few more examples, over the past few decades a major financial focus has shifted from the obligation of citizens to contribute to their nation's well-being to what citizens are entitled to receive from their fellow citizens via the government. The word "friend" has gone from describing a meaningful relationship to meaning an electronic connection not needing any emotional contact. Language surrounding marriage has also changed.

Here is just one example of how a change in language has turned the concept of marriage on its head. The emphasis in the media on spousal abuse has helped to train girls to fear marriage instead of yearning for it. Today, the term *spousal abuse* is, by legal definition in many advanced countries, abuse that takes place not necessarily between spouses (as we would assume) but includes abuse in dating and cohabiting situations, possibly even in hooking up scenarios. This misleading language change suggests to a young woman that abuse is far more prevalent among married couples than it really is, and so therefore she is safer dating or even living with a man (or many men) than she is marrying one man. The truth is that the potential for danger from someone to whom one is not married is substantially higher. Nonetheless, the almost blanket refusal by the government, academia, or the media to break down the abuse statistics to differentiate between husbands and non-husbands, all while using the language of marriage, results in demonizing marriage in the eyes of young women.

The examples of language given in the previous paragraph, along with the disproportionate one-sidedness of academic thought and government interference, have led to shifts in thinking. Women have been given preferential treatment in admission to medical and law schools, and the government incentivizes women-owned businesses, all while masculinity is labeled toxic. In many ways, including the unprecedented influence of social media and the strong thumb of government, these have been imposed on people rather than deliberated and discussed. Both the worlds of finance and family have turned upside down. Are we happy yet?

Unintended Consequences

A worldwide survey taken in countries with advanced economies (including America) revealed that family was the factor mentioned most frequently as a source of meaning in people's lives. Friendships are also high on that list, as happiness and fulfillment for most people depend on their relationships with other people. Yet, in our modern world, fewer people are forming new families or making new friends. The utopian dreams of a less patriarchal society did not include loneliness as an anticipated benefit.

The law of unintended consequences ensures that things often don't turn out as predicted. One might have thought that after more than half a century of promoting gender egalitarianism, half of marriages would occur after a man dropped to his knee and presented a woman with a diamond ring while the other half of all marriages would occur after a woman dropped to her knee and presented her intended with a fine watch. In other words, half of engagements should come about because a man proposed to a woman and half after a woman proposed marriage to a man. Anecdotally, you and we probably know of some cases where a woman proposed marriage to a man, but the overwhelming majority of marriage proposals are still made by men. Regardless of all the cultural experimentation, there remains in men the desire to be the initiator of the engagement. Women still hint and suggest that they want to get married, but there remains in women the yearning to be desired enough to be asked.

What has actually happened is that fewer proposals and marriages are happening all around, not that those that happen have followed these new-world suggestions for greater equity. Correlation doesn't equal causation, but the trends do coincide.

Attempts to change other patterns have also failed. At various times, there has been a strong push for women to retain their maiden names rather than take that of their husbands. Overwhelmingly, that has not happened. Even many women who have established a professional reputation under their maiden names and use that name in their career, use their husband's surname in personal settings.

Writing in the *New York Times,* columnist Maureen Dowd reported:

A Harvard economics professor, Claudia Goldin, did a study last year that found that 44 percent of women in the Harvard class of 1980 who married within 10 years of graduation kept their birth names, while in the class of '90 it was down to 32 percent. In 1990, 23 percent of college-educated women kept their own names after marriage, while a decade later, the number had fallen to 17 percent. Time magazine reported that an informal poll in the spring of 2005 by the Knot, a wedding Web site, showed similar results: 81 percent of respondents took their spouse's last name, an increase from 71 percent in 2000. The number of women with hyphenated surnames fell from 21 percent to 8 percent. "It's a return to romance, a desire to make marriage work," Goldin told one interviewer.

Another instance of male-female preferences that has not changed is the preferences of both sexes when it comes to height. For example, given that median heights in the United States for men is 5'10" and women is 5'4", one would expect most couples comprise a man taller than his wife. This pattern repeats in England and in most other countries. What is interesting is that, even given the average disparity, a far higher proportion of couples sport a husband taller than random matching would have brought about. The inescapable conclusion is that (a) men actively seek out wives shorter than they are, (b) women actively seek out taller husbands, or (c) both (a) and (b). Statistics suggest the third choice. Men wish to be taller than their wives, and women wish to look up to their husbands. We do know a number of outlier couples. Anecdotally, we will say that the taller wives in the couples we know still look up to their husbands, even if it is metaphorically rather than physically, and the men exude an aura of confidence in being able to physically care for their wives and families.

The hypergamy phenomenon, the desire of women to marry a man of higher economic and social status than their own, is of course perfectly normal and perfectly natural. Some see this as mindless molecular meandering as a woman's genes impel her to seek out a man best equipped to help her reproduce successfully. We see it as part of a vast and integrated divine plan that encourages men to build and create and develop the world in order to attract a high-quality woman.

Do we chalk this up to cultural conditioning? Could 60 years be too short a time span for change? Perhaps. However, trends suggest that there soon may not be enough marriages taking place even to be worthy of study. Is South Korea a bellwether? Despite efforts by the government to incentivize marriage and having children, allocating more than $150 billion for that effort, the culture is increasingly becoming one of singles and the childless. That certainly isn't what second-wave feminism promised.

Women in the United States in the 1970s and 1980s were promised that they could "have it all." As the widely viewed commercials in 1982 for Enjoli perfume told them, they could "bring home the bacon, fry it up in the pan, and never, never let [their husbands] forget [they are] a man." The commercial sang about working until five and showed these beautiful, joyous women then reading stories to their children before settling in with their husbands for a romantic evening.

That's not quite how it played out.

Over the years, the idea that a woman, her man, her marriage, and her children would be happier if she had a flourishing career (somehow all women were going to be top executives; there was nary a cleaning lady or cashier in sight) morphed into the idea that she didn't need a husband to have a family. Movies about career women hit by "baby hunger," like 2008's *Baby Mama,* showed this shift. Starring Tina Fey and Amy Poehler, this movie featured a high-ranking single female executive craving a child. A husband was completely optional. (Why are we not shocked that Mr. Right did show up anyway by the end of the movie?) What do we see today? The phrase *child-free* has entered our vocabulary. Who needs children at all? It is almost impossible for a young woman today to comprehend how different the message she is receiving is from the one given only one generation ago, let alone two or three. Is this progress, or is it contributing to a sadder, lonelier present and future for both women and men?

Having It All

Let's look at one of the myths that has shaped today's thinking: men can have it all—and women should be able to as well.

In its most basic form, when some people talk about men "having it all," they mean that men can have a powerful, fulfilling career while also having a loving marriage and a growing family (two of our 5Fs). Why can't women?

For others, the idea of "having it all" suggests that it has traditionally been socially acceptable for men to "sow wild oats" before marriage and keep mistresses after marriage. Here, too, women should be able to do the same. Men can have sex without worrying about pregnancy and so should women. Men curse, and doggone it, women should as well. Before smoking became vilified, the Virginia Slims cigarette company ran an entire campaign starting in 1968 with the slogan, "You've come a long way, baby." It promoted the concept that women should have the right to smoke publicly and frequently just as men do. Oops—that one certainly didn't turn out as intended. It seems that having the right to lung cancer, wrinkles, and yellow teeth is of questionable benefit.

Perhaps that is the roadmap of how to look at the other "perks" of being male. Leaving aside for the moment the premise of being able to enjoy (carefree access to) both Finance and Family, let's take a deeper look at the other male "privileges." We need to do this, because understanding the relationship between Family and the other four Fs requires us to question much of today's accepted wisdom.

People are flawed. We have mentioned this before, but knowing this fact deep in our bones is essential. Otherwise, we keep chasing after utopian visions. But pursuing elusive future perfection often involves harming the less-than-perfect but adequate present. Anyone with a few years on the planet knows that this is true. Examples of disastrous misbehavior can be found from the very first pages of the Bible and throughout literature and history. Nothing we can do and nothing we can legislate will ensure that everyone behaves well or that everyone is happy.

One of the consolations of having a culturally shared lodestar of morality is that even when strayed from, there is a point to which we can return. Those who opt to live according to the idea that God created us and placed us on earth, accept the idea that perfection on earth is unreachable. Perfection belongs to God. Earthly heaven is a myth. This means that human beings are destined to make mistakes. The challenge is to live in a way and to enact laws and rules that benefit the most people in the most circumstances. A corollary to that is to be charitable and kind to those who are hurting, to those who perhaps even suffer from the expectations of the norm. History strongly suggests that aiming for idealistic perfection more often than not achieves hell on earth.

Beyond the fact that men's bad behaviors are nothing to envy, it pays to ask whether it generally was universally accepted that men could and should callously have many sexual encounters? If that was so, author Oscar Wilde's Dorian Gray would be an admired character rather than a tragic one. Women, who are possibly more enamored with Jane Austen's novels today than their mothers were, dream of *Pride and Prejudice*'s hero, Darcy, not of the wastrel George Wickham. Were there communities, such as Hollywood and Capitol Hill, that celebrated deflowering (there's an old-fashioned word for you) young, innocent girls? Certainly. But both entertainment and politics were morally suspect and condemned by traditionally minded people for a long time before they became so adulated. And for many decades, the most popular movies glamorized gallant, moral, upstanding men. The idea that everybody thought that men behaving badly was a wonderful idea, or one that needed to be accepted, is simply wrong.

Perhaps the characters that populate the still-worth-reading and surprisingly popular books and stories of Louisa May Alcott, L.L. Montgomery, Grace S. Richmond, and Charlotte Bronte actually remain role models today. The women are intelligent and feminine, strong and tender. The admired men are honest, hard-working, as well as chivalrous. All the heroes are givers more than they are takers. They put their own needs as secondary to the needs of others. Message boards even across the latest technology are filled with individuals wishing to find such "old-fashioned" matches.

There is no question that in many countries and times, women did not have the legal rights that men did. There is no question that women were at a disadvantage if they were married to tyrannical and evil men. Were there problematic issues that needed to be resolved such as women being paid less than men for exactly the same work? Yes. But the idea that all women were straining at the bit to change the system or that all women were uneducated and passive is not accurate. Real life is much messier than that. It is not at all a sure thing whether the road taken in the past 60 years, the one down which modern society is now barreling, has not caused more widespread sorrow.

It is an ironic tragedy of modern feminism that "having it all just as men do" has led to women adopting many of the worst male characteristics. The person in the line behind us spouting foul-mouthed profanities is increasingly just as likely to be a woman as a man. When we read of a gruesome violent attack of the type that used to be committed almost entirely by males, today the perpetrators are too frequently girls or women. The rate at which women commit adultery is heading up. College-aged women are able to jump from bed to bed and boast about it. Women in politics are revealing themselves to be just as power-hungry and corrupt as the worst Boss Tweed cronies of yesteryear. Is this really a cause for celebration?

Gabrielle Union is an actress whose marriage to NFL player Chris Howard ended in divorce. In an interview, she explained that they had an "open marriage," meaning that they both could and did sleep with other people. Not to dismiss how dysfunctional that sounds to anyone who accepts the values of traditional faith, her words explaining why she thought it was okay accentuate the point we are making.

"I just felt entitled to it as well. I was paying all the bills, I was working my ass off, and I felt like that's what comes, the spoils of riches," Union continued. "Like my dad, before me, whoever has the most gets to do whatever the hell they want is what I thought."

Union adopted a worldview in which license, or the ability to do whatever one feels like, is the mark of successful living. She essentially followed a role model who taught her that the height of human achievement is freedom to live with appetites unchained as well as complete disregard for others.

Not only did she not seek a man whose standards were higher than those of her father, Union herself chose to emulate her father's behavior. In all fairness, she may not have known there was another option.

That still leaves her making a tragic choice. Instead of calling out males who behave badly, too many women have declared, "Me too!"

Men, just like women, can never have it all. The boys whose lives were upended by the draft in various wars did not "have it all." The men who worked from morning to night to support their families did not "have it all." The men who shepherded women and children onto the *Titanic*'s lifeboats in 1912 did not "have it all." The unemployed and celibate boys who are sitting on their parents' couches immersed in video games, depressed and anxious, do not "have it all." A bit later in this book, we will suggest how both men and women can come *closer* to having it all—although they will never reach that unreachable goal.

Male and Female He Created Them

Rather than accepting popular culture's slant on the subject of male-female relationships, we prefer to take our cues from ancient Jewish wisdom. Many of these foundational principles are laid out in the beginning of Genesis. We spoke in an earlier chapter of the real-life ramifications of choosing to live as if we came to the earth because God's hand placed us here or whether we arrived by a process of unaided materialistic evolution. Both alternatives are choices of faith, and we live completely different lives depending on which faith we opt to follow.

Another huge issue, not unrelated, demands that we make a choice without much conclusive evidence. Whether we decide to believe that men and women are biologically somewhat different but otherwise the same or that "male and female He created them" speaks to unchanging biological, emotional, and spiritual differences.

Society has been steadily moving toward functioning according to the first option, albeit with inconsistent application. Men and women should be encouraged to take the same professional roles. Men are as suited for staying home with children as women are. Sex is irrelevant in most situations.

If these chances represent such advances in our society, we might be surprised by how much people seem to be hankering after "the bad old days." *The Donna Reed Show* and *Leave It to Beaver* are two of many highly popular shows from the late 1950s and 1960s that portrayed a wise mother and wise father. Both depicted families in which he brought in the income and she managed the home, providing their children with guidance, safety, and love. Both these shows are much maligned today, but they still draw large audiences via reruns.

Likewise, the plethora of recent books such as Louise Perry's *The Case Against the Sexual Revolution*, Christine Emba's *Rethinking Sex: A Provocation*, Richard Reeve's *Of Boys and Men: Why the Modern Male Is Struggling, Why It Matters, and What to Do about It*, and Mary Harrington's *Feminism Against Progress* suggests that the past 60 or so years have not resulted in happier individuals, let alone more lasting and fulfilling relationships. Rising rates of depression, anxiety, and suicide cannot be disconnected from the confusion and disappointment that surround male-female interactions. Maybe we need to return to first principles.

We would be remiss if we did not make an important disclaimer before we proceed with the coming Biblical teachings about men and women. This disclaimer is that each of us is unique. It is a valuable nugget that emerges from the Genesis narrative. Genesis tells us that God created (the) Adam "in His image" (Genesis 1:27). One aspect of this, according to ancient Jewish wisdom, is granting human beings the gift of individual distinctiveness. Just as God is unique, so each person is unique.

This means that at the same time that we share certain traits with others based on age, sex, and other criteria, we are also each quite different from anyone else. In other words, there are exceptions to the general rules. For instance, as a 22-year-old, I (RDL) motorcycled through much of Africa on my BSA Goldstar twin cylinder motorbike. I covered about 7,000 miles without ever wearing a helmet or protective clothing. (Yes, I was young, dumb, and lucky. Very lucky.) Do we draw from this the conclusion that protective gear is not necessary? Of course not. The fact that I got away with it is irrelevant to anyone contemplating riding a motorcycle. The same is true in all areas of life, as well as in the area of male-female roles.

However, we need to think hard and clearly before we assume if and where we fall into the distinct minority when it comes to male-female differences. Though we might quickly take a medicine that has horrible side effects on only 1% of users, we would deliberate very carefully before taking a medicine that has these side effects on 90% of its users. Likewise, it is worth exercising some thought and care before deciding that we are the exception rather than the rule when it comes to basic truths about men and women. If all our close friends as well as most of our extended social sphere are also exceptions, a review class in statistics might be in order.

With that caveat, let's return to some lessons from the earliest chapters of Genesis. Did you ever play the guessing game, Animal, Vegetable, Mineral? The beginning of Genesis fits that scenario well. First, we meet the nonliving world—the world of minerals. We are introduced to water and land, then to the sun, moon, and stars. Following that, we see plant life, including grass and trees. The fifth day of Creation brings us insects, reptiles, fish, and birds.

What happens next is quite incredible. If we were writing the Bible, we would have added animals to the fifth day and reserved day six for humans alone. Surely, human beings would want to point to themselves as the pinnacle of Creation. But Genesis does no such thing. Animals, male and female, are created on the sixth day, followed by humans in Genesis 1:27: "... male and female He created them."

The Bible is informing us that one of the most compelling polarities of the world in which we live is that of masculine and feminine. This physical truth relates to animals as well as to people. Without both male and female horses or whales or humans, none of these species can survive. In this sense, humans and animals are comparable. Chapter 1 of Genesis describes the creation of the animal kingdom during Day Six and, without taking a breath as it were, moves to the creation of human beings. Chapter 1 presents a mostly physical biological depiction of reality, one in which men and women are indeed about 98% similar to one another, and what is more, men and women are very similar to the animal kingdom.

However, this isn't the end of the story. There is an entire second version of Creation that starts with Genesis 2:4. In Chapter 1, man and woman seem to be simultaneously created as a dual creature. However, the second chapter presents a tale of Adam's creation followed by Eve being separated quite dramatically out of his body. Chapter 2 introduces a spectacular story about sexual connection where a man and a woman come together and become one flesh, not merely through mating, but through the act of marriage.

These two separate and seemingly contradictory accounts of Creation reveal an important dichotomy. Chapter 2 of Genesis essentially says to us, "Now that we have established the physical nature of life, let's go back and view it through the other lens, that of the spiritual." In the same way that early twentieth-century physics revealed reality to be an integrated and hard-to-understand mixture of space and time, so is reality revealed to be a complex alloy of physical and spiritual.

Viewing the spiritual side through the lens of Chapter 2, we see that whereas male and female animals are largely identical to one another, men and women could hardly be more different. Even their very creation differed dramatically in a way that was not apparent in Chapter 1. So by the time we have carefully studied the first 56 verses of the Torah with the aid of ancient Jewish wisdom, we have the clear outlines of a critically important understanding of male and female. Physically, biologically, and anatomically they are largely similar to each other in the same ways that male and female bears are similar. They have different reproductive organs, different sizes, and somewhat different biological instincts, but they are basically the same. However human men and women, as seen in the second version of Creation, are spiritually, psychologically, and emotionally quite different from each other.

What are the implications of Adam preceding Eve in the Garden of Eden in the second narrative of Creation? If the initial narrative, where "male and female He created them," establishes their equal value in God's eye as well as their equal status as human beings in one another's eyes, the second narrative reveals an important additional aspect.

If you are a sports fan, you are familiar with the idea of home-team advantage. In the animal kingdom, the male Siamese fighting fish, also known as the betta fish, will fight any other male betta in its vicinity. They tend to fight until one dies or retreats. In general, the heavier, larger fish will win. However, there is a blatant exception! This is if a smaller, lighter betta fish is introduced into the tank about two days earlier than the larger fish. Under those circumstances, the original fish will defeat the new arrival even if the latter is up to 40% larger. That is the home team advantage.

Adam has the home-team advantage. How he uses it is part of the free will choice that is inherent in being human. No betta fish says, "I could overpower this other fish, but instead I'll invite him to work with me on reinforcing the aquarium." No male betta fish asks a female betta fish out for dinner before fertilizing her eggs. Yet human males do have the choice of whether they use their typically larger size and strength to behave like thugs or whether they use it for protecting and taking care of women. Men in Biblically inspired cultures follow an ethos of "women and children first" when people must be saved from tragedy. They march off to war and risk their lives to defend their women. By doing so, they also allow women the needed safety, both physical and psychological, that allows them to enter a state of increased vulnerability by becoming pregnant (and with that action risking their own lives) to ensure a future.

Needing Each Other

Harking back to our discussion of science losing its meaning and credibility when politics take priority over facts, we know that it has become unacceptable to acknowledge that men have greater upper-body strength than women do or that this makes a difference in various occupations. We "enlightened" people are supposed to pretend that gender is irrelevant when hiring firefighters or even prison guards. We are supposed to ignore the many instances of petite female prison guards having been overpowered by very large convicts. A cursory search on the internet for "convict overpowers female correction officer" reveals dozens of such cases. We are supposed to look the other way when ignoring these fundamental differences between men and women ends up causing sometimes severe harm. In this book, we choose to acknowledge reality instead.

Only in a relatively tranquil society of peace and safety functioning under a system of law and order can women live with the fantasy that they can entirely protect and take care of themselves. It is not coincidental that as laws lose their meaning and law enforcement weakens, female gun-ownership increases. Women know that guns offer them a fighting chance; in hand-to-hand combat, women are almost always going to lose.

While women can and do serve honorably in the military, ask yourself if it was incidental that the passengers who physically attacked the hijackers of Flight 93 on September 11, 2001, were all male. Flight attendant Sandy Bradshaw certainly acted heroically. On a call to her husband she spoke of throwing boiling water on the hijackers. She deserves full credit for doing what she did, but her contribution is of a different nature than that of the three men who initiated and responded to the cry, "Are you guys ready? Let's roll."

Even when it comes to building a developed society, men's physical strength is necessary. Professor Camille Paglia, a noted feminist and also a wonderfully honest observer of reality, stated, "If civilization had been left in female hands, we would still be living in grass huts." Drive around and look at construction sites. Only someone with an advanced PhD can think that the preponderance of men on the site doing body-breaking, dangerous labor is a result of social conditioning. Incidentally, we haven't noticed any calls to make the NFL co-ed either.

So, Adam is created first, and he, so to speak, welcomes Eve into his home, the Garden of Eden. This is replicated in American and in many other Western cultures that were built on Biblical principles when the bride reaches the altar (or in Jewish ceremonies, the chuppah) and finds her groom already there waiting for her. This sheds light, too, on why men typically still propose to women rather than the reverse, and why both men and women care about the height and other physical aspects of those they marry. Yes, women need men.

And men need women. We see this in Genesis in a beautiful passage after Eve's creation. Adam recognizes that a part of him was missing until Eve's presence filled that need. Listen to his words in Genesis 2:23: "This time she shall be called woman because from a man she was taken." In the English translation it is easy to miss that not one, but two creatures are getting a new name—man and woman. Up until now the male is called "the Adam." Eve's presence changes him. He has become a Man, in Hebrew, an *Ish*, only *because* a Woman, his wife, an *Isha,* is in his life. He is completely different and more than he was prior to her coming on the scene. Now that he is needed, his life has enhanced meaning. It is his job to protect and support her as she builds a home that, in turn, protects and supports him.

The Hebrew words for man and woman are each composed of three letters. The two letters they have in common spell the Hebrew word for fire. Fire is a metaphor for something that is tremendously potent. Fire keeps us from freezing, cooks our food so that it is digestible and tasty, and provides numerous other benefits. Yet, the same fire is also a metaphor for something that can be terribly dangerous, causing untold damage. Its very potential makes it a dynamic force for both good and bad. The Hebrew words for man and woman also each have one additional letter. Taken together, those two letters spell one of the names of God.

Ancient Jewish wisdom draws a point from this spelling. If God is within the interactions between a husband and wife, just as we saw in the spelling of the words, then the attraction between them and their uniting is a powerful force for good. If God is removed from the equation, what remains is the formidable force of destructive fire. We are sure that you have seen this lesson play out among people you know, though you might replace the word God with concepts like honesty, virtue, and loyalty, all Biblically encouraged traits that sculpt civilization.

We do not see it as accidental or patriarchal that Adam was created before Eve in the second creation tale. We see it as a depiction of reality by a Creator who wanted men and women to seek each other, need each other, and complement each other. Their contrasting masculinity and femininity are precisely what make them such a powerful team. This resembles the difference in water levels on either side of a dam wall that spins the turbines and generates electricity. If, in the interests of egalitarianism, we ridiculously insisted on the water level being equal on both sides of the dam wall, the energy-giving turbines would slow down and stop spinning. The peaks and lows of a roller coaster ride are what make the experience invigorating. The polarity of male and female is an immutable imperative of life. Once again, our basic operating system for the 5Fs, while acknowledging that individuals will do what they want to do, firmly posits that preparing for and carefully entering marriage, followed by having children (preferably starting while young), is part of the equation that leads to the most fulfilling life.

Tragically, we know of too many cases where men misuse women, whether they be their neighbors, employees, or wives. Sadly, church, synagogue, political, or any other affiliation isn't a guarantee against bad behavior. Women wanted the vote, the right to own property, and to sign their own contracts largely not as an intellectual Constitutional exercise, but because too many men failed to behave in upright ways. Women and children were suffering.

Yet, the pendulum has now swung way over to the other end. It is hazardous to be a young man on some college campuses because his word has no value against that of a female classmate. Rape allegations based more on morning-after-regret than upon assault as well as false accusations of child abuse sometimes receive the same unfair bias that used to go in the other direction. Men are told not to bother applying for a position because the hiring officer is only going to consider a female. The fraudulent biotech start-up Theranos only succeeded for as long as it did rather than being revealed as a scam because of the desire to show young, beautiful, blonde Elizabeth Holmes as a scientific, entrepreneurial whiz. See, technology appeals as much to women as it does to men! Bullying, bias, or bigotry in the opposite direction is still bullying, bias, and bigotry.

Society is never going to reach a state of human perfection. Encouraging men to be more feminine and women to be more masculine (often in the worst sense of the word) helps nobody. Inciting dislike and distrust of each other does not lead to a better world. Instead, the goal should be for men and women to use their particular gifts and strengths together to unite and form a better world for all.

Sexual tension between men and women is real. It has been around since Creation, and you see it all around whether you look in the pages of the Bible, read the works of Homer or Shakespeare, or glance at today's headlines. This tension is incredibly powerful and that makes it potentially a tremendous force for either good or bad.

Consider the potential damage that certain sexual relationships can have on the family, friendships, and institutions around them. Even in the hit 1990s TV show *Friends*, friendships among protagonists of the same sex went out the window as soon as competition for the opposite sex entered the picture. Not only are friendships, marriages, and families destroyed by destructive couplings, but companies have also been pulled down. Society, too, has been rocked when politicians' peccadillos became public as well as when blackmail or pillow talk led to betrayal.

Sex, the mighty force of cohesion, with marriage and social restraint removed becomes a force of disruption, discord, and decay. Viewing the detritus might have us thinking: maybe we would be better off subliminating sexual desire?

So deleterious can sex be, at times, that ancient Jewish wisdom relates an anecdote where the Jewish leadership of the Second Temple period looked at the damage done due to the sexual urge—the broken marriages, the rivalries between men, children born outside of marriage, and prayed to God to remove the sexual drive. God agreed. The next morning they found a passive and diminished world. No hens laid any eggs; no people got up to go to work. The world was empty of all energy and ambition. They understood that the sexual drive was an integral part of the energy that fueled the world and quickly prayed for their wish to be undone.

This story affirms the importance of sexuality as a part of our world, reminding us that despite the destructive potential of sex, it is also a profound force for good. Actually, we need to phrase this more strongly. Sex is powerful. Anything powerful can be powerfully bad or powerfully good. You cannot remove one option without destroying the other. At the same time, this underscores the need for the sexual urge to be harnessed. Something that is so powerful can lead to devastating destruction, both for individuals and for society. Therefore, we need to manage sex to live a successful life.

How do we manage it? Largely, by containing it within a sacred institution that harnesses the explosive potential of this powerful biological force. We speak, of course, of marriage. This is the foundation of the Family pillar. It is no accident that the entire modernist project believes that society cannot reach perfection until marriage and family have been abolished. This book is based on the opposite belief.

Sensitive Does Not Mean Silenced

One of the dilemmas for society is how to deal with individuals and their specific circumstances, while at the same time maintaining public policies and social norms. We want to be sympathetic and helpful to all, yet in doing so, we run the risk of normalizing things that we don't want to encourage. In the pursuit of making an outlier feel supported, we end up encouraging views that lead to heartbreak for many people.

Take the example of teen pregnancy. I think we can all agree that in the Western world, 15-year-old girls are not ready for motherhood. Can we also agree that if a 15-year-old girl does get pregnant and opts to keep the baby, she, her baby, and society will be better off if she finishes high school? However, when the school sets up a nursery on-site and provides extra support for this mom, it sends a message to other girls that this is a viable option. If she gets singled out for a lot of attention and praise, it might even seem like a desirable scenario. There is a mismatch between caring for the individual versus protecting the larger entity. Having more pregnant 15-year-old high school girls is not a good idea.

In that vein, we are well aware that not everyone who wants to get married does get married, that being widowed is a real-life circumstance, and that sometimes divorce is the necessary option. Not every couple who desperately wants children is blessed with them. We recognize that our words may cause those in these categories pain. This saddens us but nonetheless, we opt to speak.

We can see an analogy for why we do so in how views of disabled people have changed. It is a good thing that our society is aware of and configures things so that individuals in wheelchairs can access buildings and blind people can enjoy literature. We do need to make clear that having dyslexia or missing a limb doesn't make one a less valuable part of society. Caring for and about others is good. But as a society, we have a tendency to go to extremes. Decades ago, a major newspaper in Los Angeles refused to run an ad for an apartment stating that it had a wonderful view, calling that ad discriminatory against the blind. That was an indicator of egregious extremes to come. Something is wrong when the majority of students in a class are on medication and have a diagnosis of a learning disability, partially because that comes with added government-mandated benefits. We should not change the norm in order to make someone who doesn't meet that norm feel better. In the long run, doing so makes life worse for everyone. In real life, we have to do our best with reality. It is not compassionate to distort basic truths.

We are going to state that it is better to have sight than to be blind, better to hear than to be deaf, and better to have all one's body parts in working order. These are not cruel statements; they are reality. Should one not have these things, there are ways to compensate, and indeed, other senses kick up a notch when one is deficient. We have agency as well as the responsibility to make the best of the hand we were dealt. We can say that from the get-go it is good for our eyes to work; if they don't, then we move on and create a wonderful life without sight.

While we never can see "the road not traveled," we can speculate that sometimes what seems second-best ends up being a great blessing. When he was 3 years old, an accident with one of his father's tools left Louis Braille blind in one eye. Over the next 2 years, an infection affected his other eye, leaving him completely blind. We can be quite sure that his parents were devastated. They provided him with the best education available for blind people in France in the first half of the nineteenth century. Before his death in 1852, Louis Braille had refined his eponymous system that has brought education and joy to so many who are unable to see. His achievements do not negate the fact that, given a choice, he and his parents most likely would have chosen for the initial accident to have never taken place.

It is controversial today to state that it is better for an adult to be married than single, better for married couples to have children than not to have, and better for a child to be raised by his or her mother and father. Reading these words may indeed cause pain, but that is different from saying that writing them is cruel to those who are divorced or widowed, unsuccessful in finding a mate, are orphaned, or who are childless. Saying these things sets a standard. Aiming for the ground gets us nowhere; aiming for the stars means that we might reach a mountaintop. It also helps people understand that lacking any of those things means that they must make an effort to compensate for that lack. The very source of pain can even be turned into a blessing.

Today's culture insists that we can define words and norms as we see fit. By contrast, our lens for viewing the world is one that dates back thousands of years, one that has been tested and proven. We write this book to support those who share our views and, most importantly, to inform those who have no idea that these ideas are still very much alive that they, indeed, are.

Biology Lessons for Spiritual Truths

Earlier in this book, we expressed the concept in ancient Jewish wisdom that physical realities mirror spiritual ones. We spoke of our eyes seeing things upside down and our balance system being centered rather inconveniently between our ears.

Our knowledge of many of these biological concepts is the result of relatively recent biological and anatomical advances. For instance, science did not begin to understand the connection between ears and balance until late in the medieval period. Meanwhile, ancient Jewish texts from a millennium earlier address the relationship between the human ear and our ability to maintain our balance. These were not written as the result of early biological experiments but as a consequence of oral transmission passed down through the generations. This information was hinted at whenever the Hebrew words for ear and balance were used, since they share a common root. The authors of these texts relayed their knowledge, strengthened by the conviction that Hebrew was indeed the Lord's language that in itself described reality.

Something similar can be seen in the context of the space-time continuum which only began to be understood with the work of Herman Minkowski in the late nineteenth century and that of Albert Einstein in the early twentieth century. The former announced to the world that from then onward, space and time would no longer be perceived as two separate things. Instead, each would be known only as a kind of amalgam of them both. Five hundred years earlier, a Hebrew text by Rabbi Loew of Prague explicitly describes how space and time were really one thing. "As is well known to the wise," he concluded. Rabbi Loew didn't arrive at this amazingly prescient truth by seeking the flaws in Newtonian physics. That would have been impossible since Newton was yet to be born let alone pose his theories. To Rabbi Loew, the fact that in Hebrew the word for infinite space is exactly the same word as that for infinite time was a constant reminder of the ancient Jewish wisdom that hinted at this principle. The rest followed logically.

What are we to make of all this? Could it be that God was playing a joke on history? Are these merely examples of what computer engineers call Easter eggs—some kind of message hidden within a program's code as a private joke, intended to be discovered later by people exploring the program? Are we saying that similarly, God enjoys a little private smile each time human development catches up with one of the little surprises He embedded in the world of natural science?

God has not appeared to us and shared His thoughts so we cannot say what was in God's mind when He built these "hidden" features into the world. We can say that ancient Jewish wisdom stresses God's purpose of unity in the universe. What this means is that there can be no conflict between a true scientific fact and the words of the Author of that fact. While those looking through the lens of unaided materialistic evolution can find explanations for various biological anomalies, we come from a different perspective. We view them instead as being part of the purposeful design of a loving Creator. This yields more information that is helpful to us in living the most fulfilling life possible.

What is more, for those interested in learning what the world looks like when viewed through the alternative lens of divine design, these discoveries provide a form of ongoing revelation. We see history as a pair of inverse processes occurring simultaneously. On the one hand, our understanding of physical reality gradually moves, perhaps asymptotically, toward a distant perfection, a gradual process of multiple little revelations of physical truth, each leading to another one still far away and out of sight beyond the horizon. While suffering from fits and starts along with occasional dead-end rabbit holes and sometimes even a periodic reverse when a society's mistaken beliefs distort pure science for a short time, by and large, our grandchildren will know more about nuclear physics than we do.

On the other hand, the world's understanding of spiritual reality, in essence a tributary of Faith, dims a bit in each generation, moving further away from the early revelation of Truth. This process also endures its fits and starts and occasionally experiences a periodic reversal, a mini-revelation if you like, when an incandescent beacon of spiritual truth unexpectedly lights the landscape.

The immensely strong engineering shape, the triangle, is used in bridges, roof trusses, and truck underbodies. Two triangles superimposed upon one another, with one rotated one hundred and eighty degrees, gives us the ancient Hebrew symbol, the Star of David. One reason for that image's centrality in Hebrew culture is that it imparts graphical clarity to this fundamental idea. Physical knowledge tends to grow, becoming broader and broader as time goes by. That is represented by one triangle. The other triangle represents how spiritual understanding shrinks, ever narrowing with the passage of time in any given epoch. Keeping this duality in mind is the highway to wisdom.

Generally speaking, our grandchildren should wisely turn to the past for a deeper understanding of spiritual reality just as we should turn to the present and future to gain a glimpse into the stress energy mistakes in Einstein's ideas of gravitation. Just as a loving great-grandparent might leave a letter behind for his or her descendants, to be read when the progeny turns 25 but not give them the letter when they are 6 years old, perhaps God planted these truths that would only be uncovered down the road when His children would need them. This is why the unearthing of each of these Easter eggs that bring together physical and spiritual truth can serve as another exciting little spark of the light of revelation.

The Physical Depicts Reality

Male and female human bodies have certain unique features that are slightly awkward from the perspective of natural selection. For those of us who see biological features as suggestive of spiritual messaging, they help to explain deeply embedded cultural norms. Perhaps we can learn more about the spiritual realities of males and females from our very bodies. Instead of seeing some cultural norms as the product of years of misogyny and misguided patriarchy, we can see that they might serve a purpose that is hinted at in the very way we were created.

Are there any physical features that shed light on differences between men and women that relate to sex? Are there biological truths that distinguish people from animals? There are actually a few interesting ones.

Wouldn't it be noteworthy if the human male has a physical appendage that animals do not possess? Actually, let's ask the reverse question. Is there a physical appendage that most male mammals possess that human men do not?

The little-known answer is yes, the baculum. This penile bone aids reproduction by guaranteeing penile stiffness for penetration during mating. Most male mammals, including primates like gorillas and chimpanzees, possess it. Being baculum-equipped clearly is of enormous advantage to those lucky primates. They are always in the no-fail zone. No little blue tablets for them. The question is not why so many male mammals possess a baculum. It makes enormous sense from a biological perspective. The question we need to ask is why human males do not possess one.

For those of us who prefer a God-centric view of reality, another way of phrasing this question is: why did the Creator choose to deprive His beloved humans of this invaluable appendage?

Although a baculum undoubtedly assists in reproduction, when it comes to humans, reproduction is not the sole purpose of sexual intercourse. Indeed, while being fruitful is important, equally so is the idea of a man cleaving to a woman as we see in Genesis 2:23–24. Depending on their species, animals will mate freely or, in a few instances, cling to one partner. However, we don't find each individual lion or dove making that choice. The response is built-in to each species as its instinct.

Humans are entirely different. Men can choose to mimic animals and carelessly spread their seed in pursuit of ceaseless pleasure and maximum reproductive and genetic success. Alternatively, men can follow God's plan and choose to enter a covenant with one woman, build a family, and establish a home together with her.

If a baculum was standard male equipment, a wife would have no indication that she is the object of adoration and desire. It would all be rather physical, as indeed it is for men who gather sexual partners just the way rabbits do. Marriage changes everything. Having emotionally and spiritually committed to his wife, the arrogant jutting of masculinity that is not forced by a baculum represents the fullness of a husband's passion for his wife. When a man is aroused by his wife after years of marriage, after being by her side through pregnancy-induced nausea and exhaustion, after quarrels and difficulties, this arousal is as much a spiritual as a physical arousal. It makes sense to us that God wants His Adams and Eves to become one in overwhelming moments of joy, infatuation, unity, and love. And the couple knows this. They are fully aware that there are times when a man's body simply does not respond. No, a baculum is not for humans at all.

Is there any feature in a woman's body that is not found in female mammals? Actually, there is.

The hymen is found almost uniquely in the human female. The African elephant has a somewhat similar tissue, but Mrs. Jumbo's hymen rips only upon giving birth to baby Dumbo, not during his conception. It is hard to see a biological purpose that is served by the human hymen that is needed, apparently, by so few other mammalian species. This thin piece of tissue located at the opening of the vagina was not imposed upon women by an authoritarian patriarchy. Yet it does traditionally serve the purpose of letting a man know that his wife is a virgin.

A number of statements that were commonly told by mothers to their daughters in the mid-twentieth century are now seen as archaic and Neanderthal. Among them are the adages, "Men won't buy the cow if they can get the milk for free," and "Men sleep with one type of girl but marry another." More than two decades into the twenty-first century, surely those statements have as much purchase as the silly old, "Step on a crack, break your mother's back"? Perhaps not. Is it possible that, as women joined the sexual revolution, the declining popularity of marriage is partially related to our ignoring these "outdated" ideas?

We would like to be clear that nothing in the Judeo-Christian tradition approves of men treating sex casually. One way of achieving more parity between men and women would be to encourage men to adopt a more sacred sexual moral code. That would be our choice, and indeed still today in many religious circles, a man is expected to be a virgin at marriage just as a woman is.

However, upgrading expectations for men is not what happened over the past 60 or so years. Instead, women were told that having many sexual partners (just like men) was cool, that sex belongs anywhere and anytime rather than being confined to marriage, and that sleeping with someone doesn't have to carry emotional implications. In other words, women were told to suppress every natural feminine instinct and emulate the worst facets of male behavior. The invention of hormonal birth control, the Pill, coincided with the launch of this movement theoretically (and mistakenly) seen as removing any concerns of unintended consequences.

Could the presence of the hymen in human females, although absent in other mammals, suggest that men are built to want to be their wives' first partner? Could it even suggest that women do best having only one lifetime sexual partner? And while there is no physical sign that we know of that highlights fidelity, could we extrapolate from the hymen that wanting exclusivity when it comes to their woman is an intrinsic part of being male?

As unpopular in today's culture as it is and with extensive unofficial censorship of the data, there is evidence that the happiest and most durable marriages are when virgins marry virgins. "Contrary to conventional wisdom, when it comes to sex, less experience is better, at least for the marriage," said W. Bradford Wilcox, a sociologist and senior fellow at the Institute for Family Studies and a regular contributor to *Atlantic* magazine.

One of the most reliable predictors of divorce is premarital sexual experience with someone other than the eventual spouse. Virtually all studies of the relationship between premarital cohabitation and divorce have found this positive link. Researchers expressed surprise at this result because people had assumed that multiple premarital relationships would provide experience that would allow couples to choose a mate wisely with whom they could form a successful marriage. This is very clearly not the case. Furthermore, this is not symmetrical. The marriage is in greater peril if the wife had many earlier partners than if the husband did. Obviously there are biological reasons for stressing female faithfulness, such as a man's reluctance to raise a child that is not his. However, even if paternity could be guaranteed or if offspring was out of the question, most men would still be intolerant of sharing their woman.

One reason that the so-called "hook-up" culture exists, such as it does, is because the man possibly even subconsciously avoids developing any emotional bond with his one-time partner. Were he to begin thinking of her as his girlfriend, his woman, the thought that two nights later she would be "hooking-up" with another guy would be intolerable. From the woman's perspective, she often finds that telling herself that she wants sex with no emotional attachment doesn't make that statement true. The profound damage that this behavior inflicts on both participants and upon society in general should not be ignored. Sometimes we encounter a piece of information that arouses such cognitive dissonance that we instantly reject the notion. As time goes by, the idea lingers and gnaws away at the skepticism, gradually entering the realm of the "maybe." Such an idea is the ancient Jewish wisdom principle that de facto, intercourse equals marriage. In other words, there is never such a thing as casual sex. Almost without exception, when a man and woman experience intercourse, whether or not they acknowledge it, a permanent psychic or spiritual bond has been established.

It is even possible that something beyond the spiritual occurs. Apparently, there is something of a physical effect too. A sexual encounter can indeed leave minute chemical traces of the man regardless of how ardently the woman hopes never to see him again. After all, the vaginal canal lining is highly permeable, which is to say that semen, comprised largely of water and its solutes, can easily pass into the woman's body through her bloodstream. Semen contains many hormones, which may have something to do with fascinating data that suggest that women who engage in sex without condoms experience fewer female depressive symptoms than their condom-using counterparts. Although not the only reason, this may be partially why Biblical custom discourages condoms as a birth control solution.

If, indeed, there is a small hint of permanence to every sexual encounter, then the pain felt by a woman when abandoned by her "one-night-stand" is perfectly understandable. It is akin to a woman whose husband walks out on her the morning after her wedding. The pain can understandably transform into seething white hot anger. About two generations of women have now lived with the baleful effects of the sexual revolution, 60 years of casual connections. What percentage of Western women are nurturing subconscious anger at themselves and at the men with whom they slept with no thought to marriage? Could some of the widespread cultural hostility to men and masculinity have at its roots vast numbers of women angry at the men with whom they were meaninglessly intimate?

Increasingly we hear that a lot of the much talked-about campus rape culture stems from consensual sex deeply regretted by a hurt woman a few days later. The old aphorism has it that men seek many women for what they mistakenly perceive as their one need while women seek one man for their many needs. Like most enduring aphorisms, it holds a nugget of truth. Women often do seek one man, and once they sleep with him, they are sure they've found him.

One of the most discussed topics on some social media platforms is whether or not a woman should disclose her body count to her new boyfriend. Body count, for those readers who have enjoyed an enviably sheltered life, is the contemporary term for the number of men with whom she has shared physical intimacy. These women seem to experience considerable discomfort when asked about their "body count." Magazines and websites offer advice to women about how best to parry the question from the new boyfriend and how to camouflage the truth when a number is insisted upon. This is, of course, challenging to the secular vision of sex as nothing more than a spinal column spasm. If that is all there is to it, then naming a number should be as simple as detailing how many restaurants one ate at during a recent vacation.

The focus on female exclusivity has a rationale that probably satisfies both the God-centric as well as the evolutionary biologist. Namely, it is vital that every child knows his or her father. While, in almost all cases, it is physically obvious who a child's biological mother is, there is no such parallel for biological fathers. Thus, only the wife's unwavering fidelity to her man, whether a thousand years ago or today, is the basis of attributing fatherhood to him. By the time that anyone is demanding a DNA test, the marriage is in severe difficulty.

The "Dear Deidre" column of the British newspaper *The Sun* depicts the tragic aftermath of the eradication of marriage and normal family life. That agony column is filled with letters from women asking Deirdre what to do about not knowing who the father of their baby is. Other correspondents feel tormented at "accidentally" conceiving babies with everyone from stepfathers to work associates. The newspaper provides a valuable service by recording how quickly a normal, functional society deteriorates into underclass chaos once standards of sexual conduct are abandoned.

Throughout history, it has been vital for the safety of women and children that a man takes responsibility for his offspring's well-being. While some of us may be reluctant to admit it, this is still true today. A disturbing study showed that, "Preschoolers living with one natural and one stepparent were 40 times more likely to become child abuse cases than were like-aged children living with two natural parents." Statistics about children who grow up without fathers suggest that, today too, fatherlessness has a tangible and devastating association with negative trends. Our prisons would be emptier, our mental health services less needed, and our economy healthier if marriage was a stronger institution.

Societies with fathers who play an active role in the lives of their children are societies with stability and endurance. In past times, European aristocracy often appended a "von" appellation to their last names. You might remember hearing about the great German fighter pilot of World War I, Baron Manfred von Richthofen, better known as the Red Baron. You may recognize the Belgian fashion designer's name, Diane von Furstenberg. The "von" is nothing more than the transliteration of the Hebrew BN, meaning son of. In Hebrew the second letter of the alphabet carries the sound of either a B or a V, hence BN is equivalent to VN. On all formal religious occasions, such as a wedding ceremony, Jews are addressed as [name] son/daughter of [father's name]. Other cultures also acknowledge the importance of the father-son relationship. For example, the Scandinavian name Neilsson actually indicates "Neil's son." The idea is that one mark of being a solid citizen is that you know and have a relationship with your father. Conversely, having no relationship with your father, and perhaps not even knowing his name, indicated a lesser standing.

Since there is no equivalent of a hymen in men, is it possible that seeking exclusivity is hardwired more for men than for women? There have been a number of fairly successful polygamous cultures, cultures in which men marry more than one wife. However, it is tough to find records of even one viable polyandrous culture in which a woman has more than one husband.

Before COVID-19, it wasn't uncommon on the Venice beach on which the synagogue we founded stands, to see a man strolling happily with his arms draped over the shoulders or around the waists of two comely lasses. We don't recall seeing a woman with her arms linked with two handsome lads. Perhaps it is a reality that men would ideally like to marry a woman that no other man has "known." Considering that in many circles this is an unlikely find in these concupiscent times, they settle for the next best thing: a woman only a few men have known.

In all our counseling experience, and this is admittedly anecdotal but it is confirmed for us by numerous conversations with colleagues and marriage counselors, in marriages in which the man has physically strayed, it is easier for the couple to move forward to rebuild trust than in marriages where the wife has been physically unfaithful. This is not to suggest that a man being unfaithful to his marriage vows is not wrong, destructive, and incredibly painful for his wife. It is just to say that while it is tough enough for a man to come to terms with his wife's experiences from before they were married, a wife's sexual betrayal while married is almost impossible to overcome.

It seems as if the more prominent a man, the more off-limits his wife is to others. This can continue even after his death. The cruel (and defunct) Hindu custom of "suttee" in which the widow is burned upon her late husband's funeral pyre carries more than a hint of the same idea. When beautiful Jacqueline Kennedy married the, well, less-than-beautiful Aristotle Onassis 5 years after she became a widow, many of the bluebloods of the Northeastern seaboard were indignant even though they weren't quite sure why. It seems as if this idea of men having exclusivity over their woman is somewhat baked into the world.

A number of years back, when I (RDL) was just beginning to deliver speeches to audiences other than my congregation, I was engaged to deliver a speech to a certain group on Christmas Eve. I assumed I was invited because it made sense that only a rabbi would be available on that special evening. When I arrived at the venue, I found my audience was composed almost entirely of sad-looking women with red eyes. It was evident that most everyone in the audience was intent on their own private pain rather than on the pearls of wisdom I tried to provide. Only afterward did I discover that this was a loosely structured organization of women who were mistresses or girlfriends of married men. Since every one of them had a man who was spending that special evening with his family, the evening was a painful reminder of what they did not have. We find it difficult to believe that there would be a gathering of similarly sad and weepy men on Christmas Eve consoling one another because their married girlfriends were spending the sacred evening with their husbands.

We have provided examples that suggest to us that men and women do indeed have enduring emotional and spiritual differences. While we look at differences that we can see when comparing people to animals, some biological realities are also true for all mammals but serve to accentuate the distinction between male and female. These include the facts that male reproductive organs are external while female reproductive organs are internal, that males produce seemingly infinite supplies of sperm throughout their lives while females cycle through a finite number of eggs all present from the time of the female's birth, and that male and female bodies are different in qualities ranging from muscle strength in different areas to brain makeup. Take some time to think about what spiritual messages these may reflect. We may not like reality, but if these matters are really unchangeable, and if they reflect spiritual truths, then the sooner we accept the futility of fighting against them, the better off we are.

Relationships between the sexes, whether in marriage, at the office, or in every other sphere of activity, dominate much of our time and energy. How men and women relate in sexual and nonsexual settings affects our finances, friendships, and, indeed, our health. If these interactions were less perplexing and affected us less severely, imagine how fewer books and articles, shows, and movies there would be! Understanding the spiritual realities that God built into our world as it relates to men and women is imperative for running our lives. From our perspective, these realities begin to be laid out in detail from the very opening of the Bible. While thematically, these relate to marriage, they also express concepts that we need to know in the office, classroom, and wherever we may be.

Our never-ending challenges when dealing with men and women arise because men and women seem almost identical while also being incomprehensibly different.

Chapter 7

Some Tough Decisions

G iven our emphasis on the importance of properly managing relationships between men and women, the question remains of how to do that in a world where there are myriad interactions between the two sexes.

Men and women meet at work and at school, in neighborhoods, and in civic associations. Friendships and finance are not immune to the dynamics between the sexes. Many complications of our business and financial lives as well as of our social lives result from male-female realities.

Platonic Friendships—Not

We would like to make a suggestion that is almost impossible for our twenty-first century Western ears to hear. That doesn't make it wrong, but we do recognize that there might be a strong urge to hurl this book against the wall rather than contemplate this concept. Here it is: there is almost no such thing as a platonic friendship between men and women.

We often hear young women say, "We're just friends," when we raise this idea. They roll their eyes and say, "Oh, come on, I've had plenty of male friends, guy friends, who are *just friends*. There's nothing sexual about it; there's nothing romantic about it. We're *just friends*."

The male friend's response is usually different. The men, particularly younger ones, look down at their shoes, and they shut up. They know that they have been in many so-called friendships where the girl in the friendship thinks it's platonic and the males know that at the slightest opportunity they would gladly move it into the sexual zone.

There's been considerable research on this, which shows that in many of these so-called male-female platonic friendships, if the guy was married, the woman was even more inclined not to see any romantic aspect to it. For the men, it made virtually no difference if the woman was married or in a relationship with someone else. Regardless of whether women were attached or not, many men *still* sometimes fantasized about a sexual relationship.

A number of years ago, the phrase, "friends with benefits," came into vogue. No longer was there a taboo in adding sex to a friendship just as one might add enjoying seeing a movie together. Are you surprised that down the road the women in these relationships tended to be unhappy and the men confused? Psychotherapist Rachel Morris, whose specialty is sex and relationships says: "Most of the women in these cases are seeking a proper relationship. . . . The emotional consequences are huge—and someone is going to get hurt."

While that someone can be the male, it is overwhelmingly the female. As one of the men in a "friends with benefits" relationship said, "We probably shouldn't have slept together, but we did. [multiple times over the course of years] I was worried it might affect our friendship, but [she] seemed fine with us just being friends and sleeping together occasionally." That is, many of the women seem fine until they become hurt and jealous at their "friend's" serious pursuit of another woman, this time with marriage in mind.

If men have trouble leaving sex out of supposedly platonic associations, women have trouble leaving emotions out of the picture in supposedly "benefits" relationships.

That is why the female equivalent of pornography is not looking at pictures of scantily clad male surfers. It is reading romance novels.

Look at the top 10 fiction books of a random week in 2022 on the *Goodreads* bookshelf. The majority have to do with romances burgeoning between men and women who dislike each other, have no interest in each other, or start out as friends, and by the end of the book are much more. We'll go out on a ledge here and posit that these books are being read almost overwhelmingly by women, not men. Just as men satisfy their most basic fantasies, which are primarily sexual, with their own "visual literature," women satisfy their fantasies, which are largely emotional, with this literature of their own.

We are not saying that men and women have never interacted and can never interact without a sexual overtone. What we are saying is that it is folly to assume that men and women can interact with no romantic overtones or to rely on sex not rearing its head.

Precluding problems is easier than solving them once they have hit. On that basis, we install fire alarms in our homes or wear seat belts. While we can go overboard in avoiding risk, in many cases taking reasonable precautions is the wisest course. If someone knows that they have a predilection to alcohol, setting parameters such as never drinking alone or limiting oneself to a certain number of drinks is better than dealing with alcoholism after the fact. Self-made major crises usually don't come apocalyptically. Step-by-step, we head down a path. Very few of us will blow our entire bank account at one time. But we will overspend by a few dollars each month until our debt snowballs into a difficult-to-manage situation.

How do we avoid taking any steps down the path to sexual impropriety? There is an ancient Jewish wisdom principle: "Do not ever be alone in a secluded environment with a person of the opposite sex who is not an immediate family member."

Countercultural advice, to say the least. Not only does that sound extreme, it is extreme. However, think how many moments that resulted in "he said, she said," conflicts would have been averted by this simple principle. Way back in 1991, the nomination hearings for Supreme Court Justice Clarence Thomas riveted America when it was almost derailed by accusations from fellow attorney Anita Hill of earlier sexual innuendos and harassment. Depending on your politics for the most part, you either believed the accuser Anita Hill or you didn't. While these types of accusations are common today in high-profile cases, back then, this was revolutionary. So was the idea that either party would tell a bald-faced lie in front of Congress. The bottom line is that much of the drama would not have happened had the two of them followed the advice of ancient Jewish wisdom. Several times, lawyers Thomas and Hill were the only ones left at the office late at night. That left open both the possibility of compromising situations and the possibility of false accusations of misbehavior.

How many "Me Too" situations and accusations would not have been possible if, as a society, we agreed that men and women (not closely related to each other) should not be behind closed doors together? At one point, one of our teenage daughters interviewed for a babysitting job. When it turned out that the father was home all day while his wife was out, she wisely rejected the job offer. That doesn't mean that she suspected nefarious doings on the part of the dad. Following thousands of years of wisdom, she wasn't going to put herself in a situation that could go bad.

More recently, a congressional candidate in the 2022 election refused to allow a female journalist to accompany him for a day as he drove around. He based it on this concept of not being alone with any female other than his mother, wife, sister, or daughter. He did behave foolishly, but deciding not to be isolated with this reporter wasn't the problem. To avoid political backlash as well as to recognize the downsides of his decision, which could harm the reporter's career, he could have brought along his wife or another man for the day. But the principle of avoiding being alone with a woman he was not married to was sound. As the traditional virtue of truthfulness becomes less revered, it also would have been a prudent precaution.

We are not saying that this congressman would have been overcome with passion and made a pass at the female reporter. We are also not saying that he would have said anything verging on inappropriate. Neither are we saying that she was trying to set him up and was going to launch an unfounded accusation. We are not even commenting on the current political situation. What we are saying is that he deserves to be respected for having drawn a line around his marriage, not only at the point of infidelity but much earlier. In other words, ancient Jewish wisdom teaches us not only to avoid wrongdoing, but to keep ourselves far, far away from it. This congressman rightly placed a fence around his marriage, though he did it in a clumsy fashion.

Good Fences Make Good Marriages

Such "fence-placing" should really be a blanket policy and not based on a specific situation. What if the reporter was in her 90s or the most unattractive woman ever born? What if the candidate was head over heels in love with his wife? You can see how awkward it would be to have to evaluate each situation on its own. Do the following conversations sound like a good idea to you?

A man says: "My new associate is quite ugly and completely not my type. I think I can be alone with her with no problems. On the other hand, the sales rep assigned to my team is rather attractive. I had better not leave the door to my office closed when I'm with her."

A woman says: "I think of my accountant as a grandfatherly type. I feel safe being alone with him. But the carpenter who is working in the house? Now, he is hot. He even reminds me of my first boyfriend. I'd better leave the house when he's working there."

Having to assess each situation every time it arises is not a great plan. Do we think it a good idea for a man or woman to need to say to their spouse, "Since we had that argument last week, I'm not feeling as close to you as I usually do; I'd better not travel on this Tuesday's business trip with my coworker"?

How much better to have a blanket policy to avoid physical or emotional seclusion with members of the opposite sex at all times. Such a policy would save us from many broken marriages and damaged relationships.

A caller to my (RDL) radio show once confessed to me (and, incidentally, also to several hundred thousand listeners) of an affair he regretted having had with a female coworker on a business trip.

"It was a huge mistake, Rabbi," he said.

"No," said I. "It was not a huge mistake." Pause. "It was 10 huge mistakes."

I then detailed the series of terrible blunders on just that trip. Traveling together with his female worker. Staying at the same hotel. Socializing together at dinner after work. Walking her up to her room after the meal. Entering her room. Closing the door. You can easily fill in the rest yourself. Yes, each step was a separate bad mistake. At any step, he theoretically could have stopped. In reality, however, once that train pulled out of the station, it was increasingly less likely that he would call halt. Not having got on in the first place would have been far wiser.

Here are two personal experiences of ours. At one point, while I (SL) was homeschooling a bunch of our children, my husband's assistant was also working out of our home. Charla is a serious Christian, and while she did not know that she was echoing a Jewish concept, one day she said to me, "I usually close my door while I work so the noise from the family doesn't distract me. Tomorrow, a computer technician is coming to work on my machine. When my husband and I got married, we agreed not to be behind a closed door alone with someone of the opposite sex. So, I'm going to leave the door open while he is here, and I'd appreciate it if you could do something quiet during that time."

What a wise young couple they were!

While our examples so far focus on physical seclusion, emotional intimacy also needs to be guarded against. Camaraderie, congenial joking, concern for a coworker who looks troubled, imperceptibly and easily can lead one to cross a line. A female is not just "one of the boys," and a male is not a girlfriend substitute. On a business consulting trip, I (RDL) needed to travel with one of the women on our team. While there would not necessarily be any time I would be secluded with her, the very act of going to the airport, flying together, taking a taxi to the business, and so on would provide an uncomfortable amount of socializing time. We were going somewhere rather remote, so traveling on two separate flights was not possible. The time together could easily trip into emotional intimacy. In fact, Susan and I often shared Shabbat meals with this woman and her husband, so there was an easy relationship between us. My solution was to bring along our 10-year-old daughter. Not only would this give our entrepreneurially minded young one a good experience, but she would serve to prevent any conversation that could swerve from professional and courteous to overly personal.

Was I overreacting? We had the enormous privilege of enjoying a close friendship with the legendary motivational teacher, Zig Ziglar, and his wife, Jean. When we knew them, they had been married for many years, a covenant that they entered when Jean was 18 and Zig was 20. This master of sales traveled frequently and made a point of never being alone with another woman. "I made it clear that I was not doing anything but honoring my wife," he said. Note that he did not say that he did not trust himself to behave honorably or that Jean jealously demanded that he make this policy. Acting as he did was a way of honoring his wife, his marriage vows, and his God.

Our last few visits with Zig and Jean took place after a fall that left his speech intact but unfiltered. He told us over and over how fortunate he was to be married to his wife. "You and I both married above ourselves," was how he put it to me (RDL). Isn't that the type of marriage you would like to have?

Putting guardrails in place doesn't guarantee the perfect marriage. But it is one of many ways that spouses invest in their marriage by honoring each other. And it serves to keep wrongdoing far away. Why even be tempted to betray your life's most enduring relationship?

Progressive extremists mocked former Vice President Pence in 2017 when an earlier interview that he had given in 2002 resurfaced. They howled in derision about his commitment to avoid all secluded meetings with women other than his wife. The *New York Times* even commissioned a poll intended to reveal how out of touch the vice president was with the country and its contemporary norms. To the astonishment of the "paper of record," the poll revealed that a majority of women, and nearly half of men, said it's unacceptable to have dinner or drinks alone with someone of the opposite sex (other than their spouse). So much for being out of touch. But give the *New York Times* some credit for publishing their polling results even though the results were neither what they expected nor what they wanted.

The point is that apparently about half of all Americans know that it is a lot easier to avoid situations that could go horribly wrong than it is to allow oneself entry into those potentially intimate situations and then hope that one's morals and self-discipline are up to the task.

To wait until hormones and feelings are flying and the temptation is overwhelming, and *then* have to say, "I am not interested in a physical relationship," or "but I don't want to betray my marriage," is sheer folly.

An Unexpected Aftermath of 9/11

Pulling together our understanding from Genesis that men have a need to be needed as we saw from Adam only receiving the name "man" when he was needed by his woman, along with our wariness about platonic relationships, leads us to one rather shocking aftermath of the 9/11 terror attacks. On that frightful day in New York City, September 11, 2001, some firemen returned home from work, while many, many other firemen tragically did not.

For those who survived, it had been the worst day of their lives! They lost friends, those they often considered closer than brothers. Shortly after that horrific day, the New York fire department assigned one surviving firefighter to attend to the widow and children of every murdered firefighter. It seemed a comforting and generous thing to do. The widows weren't left on their own. One can understand that the widow of a fireman would find it more comforting to lean on another fireman as opposed to a random member of the community.

What happened next was reported in the *New York Times Magazine* section in May 2004. It was entirely predictable; a high proportion of these firemen who had been assigned to take care of a 9/11 widow divorced their own wives and married the widow.

Had the NYFD consulted ancient Jewish wisdom, it would have saved the department a lot of trouble. They would have heard, "Your thinking is right, your tactics are not. You *should* assign somebody from the fire department to each family, but it should be a fireman and his wife or two firemen together. At no point should one man alone be sent to take care of the widow."

When a 45- or 50-year-old man divorces his, say, 45-year-old wife, and he marries a 25- or 30-year-old young woman, we may not admire him, but we somewhat understand his urge, damaging as it is. But how do we understand a man who divorces his wife and marries somebody exactly the same age as his wife, from the same demographic, probably with the same number of children? He switches a situation that he's invested so many years of his life in and leaves his own family in order to marry a woman just like his wife, with children just like his own—except they're not. How do we explain that?

For that, we must remember that one of the greatest, most potent aphrodisiacs for a male is to feel admired and needed by a woman. It's as simple as that. It is one of the greatest and most powerful compulsions. It is almost irresistibly arousing for a man when a woman admires and looks up to him, expressing a need for him in any way at all. This instinct is so powerful that even if the woman doesn't articulate her need for him, but the man senses how necessary he is to her, his response is automatic and compelling.

Now we can see just what happened with the 9/11 widows. These widows were suddenly thrown into close proximity with men who were their husbands' buddies, their husbands' brothers. To the firemen in the attending role, there is a big difference between these widows and their wives. Their wives are busy and competent; their wives have a routine and a sense of security; their wives do not overtly reveal any sense of needing them in any way at all. If a wife does express a need, her husband often sees it as nagging as she points to her "honey-do" list. But needing and appreciating him in a visceral, deep way? So easily in a seasoned marriage, after a while, a wife doesn't express, or perhaps even feel, any real need for her husband (and he, in his turn, forgets to express his appreciation of her and may not even feel it). We are not blaming the wives here—both spouses put their marriage on automatic, and it went along until it hit this trauma.

Meanwhile, this widow who is alone and confused, hurting, and suffering encounters the strong man who is empowered to make many of her problems vanish and who is grieving in a similar way to her. They can mourn together, and she needs those broad shoulders and those strong arms around her, and she falls for him. Meanwhile, he is astounded by the thrills that surge through him and by the feelings of potency and virility that suffuse his entire being. What's more, he's being encouraged to be with her; he's a *hero* for being with her. In taking care of her, all his feelings of masculine protectiveness are aroused. In what became an added tragedy of 9/11, many firemen divorced their wives, shattered their families, and married the widows.

The potential damage from seemingly platonic interactions is, obviously, not limited to married individuals. Wouldn't it be wise to implement a policy that when a student and a professor meet, the door should be left open? And for that meeting to take place only when there is passing traffic outside that door? Would the abuses by Olympic team Doctor Larry Nassar have been possible if a third party was present at all appointments? Wouldn't it be better if no young law intern or aspiring business woman was ever asked to meet a potential client or a higher-up in his hotel bedroom? In the "bad old days" we had male and female dorms on campus. Visitors of the opposite sex were not allowed above the lobby. That didn't mean that sex between students never took place. It did mean that there wasn't the expectation and pressure to sleep together that there is today. What if just "going out for drinks after work" was seen as problematic rather than harmless? The wrongheaded attempt to say that we must pretend that male-female tension is not a reality has led us down an obstacle-ridden path.

Accepting Reality

Another example of this attempt to insist that sexual tension is no big deal harks back to our conversation of how the Hebrew word for clothing, BeGeD, can also mean "treachery." Just as wearing tailored, power clothing can make us feel more put together, our clothes can also mislead others in regards to us. This is the case when women wear provocative clothing. It is absolutely true that no man should make obnoxious remarks about how a woman looks and certainly not presume that because she is dressed a certain way she wants advances made on her. Decent men know this. However, it is also true that a woman who declares that she will dress as she chooses and men had better learn to behave is making a foolish decision. Demanding that men respect her character and value her brain while dressing in a way that directs onlookers' eyes to her cleavage, for example, is counterproductive. Her clothing betrays her—betrays the more substantial parts of who she is by directing others to focus on her body. Nobody has the power to legislate or change what is an intrinsic masculine reaction.

A woman may not be aware of this, and she may wish her choices had no consequences. She may well declare that, "Men should control themselves!" (And we agree that they should.) And she may find herself asking, in frustration, why she doesn't receive adequate levels of respect. But as long as she wears a form of dress that betrays what she wants to reflect as her essential nature, she is asking the people around her to discount what they see, to overlook the disguise, as it were.

Men, especially, are created to respond to visual cues and will be affected by what they see. If you want someone, perhaps a team member or your boss, to pay attention to your ideas, then your clothing shouldn't betray you by distracting them. We can feel irritation that this is how the world really works, but it might be wiser to accept a reality that we have no hope of changing.

When I (RDL) was a teenager, my parents sent me to study Torah in Israel with my great-uncle, Rabbi Elya Lopian. Watching and listening to a man who was a giant of ancient Jewish wisdom opened my eyes to spiritual reality.

Large numbers of young men from around the world flocked to study with him at his yeshiva (religious seminary), Knesset Hezekiah. A student, on one occasion, sought permission from my great-uncle to absent himself from his studies for a week while he returned home for a family wedding in Chicago.

Rabbi Elya inquired whether there would be women dressed immodestly at the wedding. My friend responded honestly that there was every possibility of this. He had moved in a more religious direction than his family. However, he assured our teacher that his spiritual level was so high that he would be immune to whatever exposed feminine charms he might encounter. He informed the venerable sage that he barely noticed attractive women.

My uncle granted his student permission to attend the wedding on condition that before he left, he was to meet with a friend of Rabbi Elya's. When the young man came to bid farewell, my uncle asked him about his appointment.

The student answered, "Well, I did call the number you gave me, but it must have been a mistake since it was a doctor's office!"

Replied Rabbi Elya, "There was no mistake. I am nearly 80 years old and blind in one eye, yet I am powerfully affected by the sight of women who are scantily dressed. Since you are a healthy young man, and you assure me that you are not similarly affected, I knew you must be suffering from a medical condition. I wanted you to be examined by the doctor whose name I gave you."

(Incidentally, please note that my great-uncle did not tell the student not to attend the wedding. He was well aware that Faith is harmed by damaging Family. Being part of a family celebration was important, though recognizing any perils one might encounter is imperative.)

Against the Tide

Perhaps all this focus on guarding ourselves, keeping in mind the goals both of being worthy of marriage and then of fortifying our marriages might strike many as extreme. They might ask, "Do we really need marriage?"

Obviously, those of us who take the Bible seriously must take marriage seriously. But even for those who don't, society certainly does need men and women to marry. On only one very basic level, most violent crime is committed by single males. Almost anyone finding himself alone late at night on a dark urban street would be nervous. That anxiety would ramp up if it became apparent that two silhouetted figures were approaching. Imagine how our feelings would change if the figures turned out to be a husband and a wife out for a stroll. Relief would replace fear.

As we saw in the last chapter, the best chance of raising a meritorious next generation comes when mothers and fathers who are married to each other are in the picture. Married people are physically healthier than unmarried ones, not only improving their own lives but also lessening the strain on the medical services.

In Chapter 21 of *Anna Karenina*, Leo Tolstoy wrote:

"Here is my opinion. Women are the chief stumbling-blocks to a man's career. It is difficult to love a woman and do anything else. To achieve it and to love in comfort and unhampered, the only way is to marry! How am I to put to you what I think?" And Serpukhovskoy, who was fond of similes, went on: "Wait a bit! Wait a bit! . . . Yes, if you had to carry a load and use your hands at the same time, it would be possible only if the load were strapped on your back: and this is marriage. I found out that when I married, I suddenly had my hands free. But if you drag that load without marriage, your hands are so full that you can do nothing else. Look at Mazankov, at Krupov! They have ruined their careers because of women!"

Men do better economically when they are married. The Federal Reserve Bank of St. Louis has a research department in which Guillaume Vandenbroucke labored during 2018 to study how married men out earn their single brethren. His findings included the startling statistic that on average, the married 35-year-old man earns about double what his single counterpart makes. Yet, employers do not inquire as to job applicants' marital status and then pay married men a large premium. So what is happening?

There are many possible reasons. Perhaps, on average, married men are more focused and motivated. They are more likely to seek promotions and higher job prospects. Likewise, they are less likely to take time off for spontaneous parties and less likely to sustain leisure time injuries requiring time off for convalescence. Maybe, most importantly, they are working for the benefit of their loved ones rather than for themselves, and they have a support team in their corner cheering them on. Through a combination of variables, being married brings a measurable money benefit.

Their wives, in turn, can bear children without the onerous burden of responsibility for financially supporting those children and without the emotional burden of child-raising falling on their shoulders alone. They have someone to lean on and who pledges to stay committed to them even as their physical youthfulness fades. When marriage is in the picture, the society that women depend on to live safe lives has larger numbers of strong men rather than brutish or wimpy boys.

Yet, for many people traditional marriage has become, if not completely quaint and antiquated, certainly completely optional. There were periods, such as post–Civil War society in the United States or post–World War I society in England, where women's opportunities for marriage were limited. In both cases, this was due to a lack of males, a result of carnage and death on the battlefield. (Even though it is not the topic of this book, we can't help mentioning that in many places and times, data show that after a war more boys are born than would be expected. The normative sex ratio of births changes. There are many theories but no scientific agreement on why and how this happens.) Nonetheless, for millennia, boys and girls have grown up with the assumption that being married and having a family was a natural part of becoming an adult. That is no longer so. Of course, in "advanced" cultures there is a lot less growing up in general going on.

Even more troubling, in today's cynical and bruising world, thousands of young people are reaching marriageable age as products of unhappy or broken homes. More young adults than in any previous time never had a father in the picture at all. It is easy to believe various academics who proclaim that marriages were never meant to last for 50 years and that as our expected life-span increases, it is only normal for couples to divorce and pair up with new spouses. The claim is made that marriage is obsolete and meaningless or, at the very least, can be embarked upon with the mindset that it may only be a temporary commitment. Studies that pop up now and then suggest that there is an "adultery gene." Experts advance the argument that people are helpless beings who can only act as we are hardwired. All these ideas augment the anti-marriage theme. We are told both that marriage doesn't matter and, if we insist that it does, we should feel free to modernize and redefine it.

What a dismal message to send. And how different it is from the message that God gave to Adam and Eve in Eden (when life spans were apparently even longer than they are today). With all our modern sensibilities, it is worthwhile to see if we can approach marriage recognizing how much happier and more fulfilling our lives can be should we be fortunate enough to share a lifetime and build a family with another human being.

As this book shows, without the cornerstone of marriage, the entire 5F structure collapses. As friends and as a society, we can support a few lonely people who, for whatever reasons, do not have family. When as a society, we destroy the idea of family en masse, we are in trouble. It is true that an individual does not have the power to guarantee he or she will be in a wonderful marriage, to eliminate illness and death, or to ensure siblings and children. That is worlds apart from not working to form, and be part of, a healthy, functioning, and thriving family.

Tragically, based on what society is telling them as well as their personal experiences, too many people today do not know and do not believe that successful marriages are any more real than Cinderella's pumpkin turning into a coach. Each of us needs to share stories of such marriages for our own edification and for that of those we love. We also need to ask what we are actively doing in our own marriages, or setting up for the future marriages we hope to be in, that will give us a fighting chance. Here are two true accounts we would like to offer.

We had the privilege to attend and participate on stage (RDL) at an event hosted by then-Governor and Mrs. Mike Huckabee of Arkansas. The focus of the evening was on promoting commitment in marriage. The highlight of the evening (SL: aside from my husband's speech) was a moving video by Dr. Robert McQuilkin, announcing his resignation from the presidency of Columbia Bible College and Graduate School in order to stay at his wife's side while she suffered from the ravages of Alzheimer's disease. We and 6,000 other couples watched, our eyes brimming, as he explained his thinking:

> *The decision was made, in a way, 42 years ago when I promised to care for Muriel "in sickness and in health...till death do us part." So, as I told the students and faculty, as a man of my word, integrity has something to do with it. But so does fairness. She has cared for me fully and sacrificially all these years; if I cared for her for the next 40 years I would not be out of debt. Duty, however, can be grim and stoic. But there is more; I love Muriel. She is a delight to me—her childlike dependence and confidence in me, her warm love, occasional flashes of that wit I used to relish so, her happy spirit and tough resilience in the face of her continuing distressing frustration. I do not have to care for her, I get to! It is a high honor to care for so wonderful a person.*

If there was any woman in the crowd who didn't choke up, we didn't see her. Fewer men had tears rolling down their cheeks, but we saw quite a bit of nose blowing. We saw many of both sexes murmuring a silent prayer asking for a marriage as blessed as that one.

Story number 2:

Rabbi Aryeh Levin, (1885–1969) was known as "the tzadik (righteous one) of Jerusalem," for his tireless efforts to care for the poor, imprisoned and sick. Stories abound reflecting his caring, Godly nature. Yet, one of the most circulated stories of his life relates not to his public works, but instead, to his marriage. At a doctor's appointment for pains his elderly wife was suffering, he explained their being there with the words, "Doctor, our foot is hurting us."

Marriages such as those still exist. What's more, most people still crave such marriages. Who wouldn't want to know that after 50 or 60 years, someone who adores you will still be at your side? It isn't far-fetched to think that children born within marriages like these will not only have more secure and loving childhoods but will also want to care for their parents if needed. At the same time, today's cultural rules make these marriages less likely and harder to achieve. Furthermore, the one commodity we cannot reclaim is time. Decisions we make that seem eminently logical and wise at 20 aren't easily undone when we are 35. It is incredibly difficult to ask a young woman or man how they will feel when they are 40 and 60 and 80 years old. Yet, once they get closer to those older years, they can't reverse whatever decisions their younger selves made. In today's world we are called upon to make all sorts of life decisions that weren't debatable in preceding generations. Frustratingly, more choice doesn't necessarily lead to more happiness.

Are Children Optional?

While individual couples make private decisions, public approval for not having and raising children is a different matter. Indeed, a condition of childlessness in a marriage contract was once considered an invalidating clause on the basis of it being *contra bona mores,* the Latin legal term for "against the public interest." You would be forgiven for assuming that we are talking of medieval England. However, a court ruling in New York as recently as 1959 announced that childless conditions in marriage contracts were not enforceable because they "violated public policy." Today, the expectation of having and raising children is less intuitive and almost countercultural. Our 5Fs are based on the assumption that Family is a vital part of the system and that after one moves beyond childhood, Family in the 5F system implies marriage and children. Yet our society often paints having children in a negative light. Many today will say, "I am close with my nieces and nephews. I don't need children of my own." Or they will explain that children simply don't fit into their desired lifestyle. Unfortunately, many have bought the line that not having children is the moral thing to do considering what a terrible and doomed world we inhabit.

Children represent the promise of the future. Without that, the present quickly becomes a place of fear, anxiety, and sadness. All of us need hope and optimism. We are sympathetic to those who fear having children because they themselves are products of dysfunctional homes. Some people claim that they know themselves and they don't have the patience or temperament to raise children. That self-awareness is wonderful, but it is not a life sentence. "I have a temper" is a call to improve oneself, not an excuse for anger. Some of us are born with a pull to art, others to nature, and still others to numbers. That gives us a head start in those areas. But all of us need to get basic proficiency in a wide variety of life skills. Some of us are, perhaps from birth, born with more difficult temperaments. Many of us had no built-in upstanding role models, and in fact, the ones we had may have been harmful. Negative inborn tendencies or challenging life-circumstances don't let anyone off the hook for not being able to function, find mentors, and improve in whatever domains are important.

Children force parents to grow up, to give more than they ever thought they would, to expand their very beings. They are the anti-self-centeredness energizer bunnies. Sadly, in the real world today, maturity and growth don't always naturally follow having children. Tragically, fewer and fewer of us have an instinctive feel for how to parent well, and much of the "expert" opinion out there is less than ideal. That is why, early in our lives, just as we need to learn how to be a friend and how to develop the skills and the desire to earn money, we also need to put plans into effect that push and prod us and provide us with the tools we need to become a great parent.

The need we all have for a visible future cannot be ignored, even if not all of us feel it, particularly when we are young. It's a lot like a body's need for potassium. We are quite unaware of the need, but a potassium deficiency will eventually create a problem. Just as those who lose a limb learn how to compensate for that loss, those not blessed with children need to actively seek how to build their future. For some, this will mean finding a charitable mission; for others, it will be investing in other people's children. It can be building a business that will provide honorable employment and valuable commodities to the world for future generations. This is worlds apart from being the "fun aunt" or occasionally helping in a soup kitchen. It is worlds apart from focusing on building one's bank account in order to buy a lot of toys or shoes and have fantastic vacations. Here is the clue. Investment demands focus, long-term commitment, and sacrifice. It can't be done only when it is convenient or when it makes a person feel good.

Will we soon be living in a post-family world? Over the past few years we read about many adults in their 20s and 30s who moved back in with their parents as COVID-19 changed their lives. Where does that leave them in 30 or 40 years when those parents might need to depend on them rather than the other way around? Do people understand that (while everyone should live and be well) in the normal course of events, those parents won't always be there? If your family and friends are either peers or older than you, what does that say about your future?

I (SL) listened to a thoughtful and what I found to be a terribly sad podcast with Meghan Daum and Mary Warrington, two women who are both happily married and both sure that they have made the correct decision not to have children. They spoke honestly about that choice. I admit to being shocked when the podcast ended with their discussing the thought they give to suicide as they recognize that there will not be younger people in their lives to love and care for them as they grow older. Meanwhile, Dr. Ezekiel Emanuel, a former advisor to President Obama, is only one of many talking openly about whether it is best to die when we reach a certain age. This scary cultural shift is one more step down the road of secularism that can lead to both the elderly and sickly being told that the decent thing for them to do is die at their own hands.

An October 2022 Pew survey reported that 44% of American nonparents between the ages of 18 and 49 do not think they will ever have children. Leaving aside that some of these may be sperm donors or unknowing fathers of children already (those men are breeding rather than having children) and that some will change their minds, that is a huge number.

On a very practical level, when China instituted its one child policy, we knew that it would end up hurting, not helping, the country's citizens. This is not because we are foreign policy experts but because it directly contradicts one of the first communications from God to humanity, commonly (if not very well) translated as, "Be fruitful and multiply." If God's message to humanity is descriptive rather than prescriptive, then ignoring that message won't end well for most individuals or for societies.

When we casually look at Genesis, it seems that "Be fruitful and multiply" is a command that God gives to fish and birds and then to people—procreate! However, if we look closely at the respective Hebrew in Genesis 1 verses 22 and 28, we see two important differences. Firstly, when referring to the animals, it says that God spoke. When talking to people, we read that God spoke "to them." Humans are participants in this activity in a way that animals aren't. Animals breed because that is what animals do. Humans choose whether to and with whom to procreate or not.

What is the second difference? "Be fruitful and multiply" actually comprises two parts, not two synonyms for the same activity. The Hebrew word translated as multiply is "RVu," which is, indeed, related to the word for many or multiplying. But it has another meaning as well. We see that meaning in the well-known word "rabbi" based on the same R–V(B) root, which actually means "teacher." In ways that we don't understand, animals pass on vital information to the next generation. Incredibly, generations of monarch butterflies migrate to the same locations as generations before them did. Butterflies that arrive at their Mexican mountaintop have never been there before, yet they know exactly where to go. We do not hear about good butterfly moms transmitting information and bad butterfly moms not doing so. When it comes to the birds and fish, the verse that follows after "Be fruitful and multiply" signals the end of that day of Creation. They will procreate, and instinctively, the mothers (and in some species, such as penguins, fathers as well) will know how to care for their young, and their offspring will know or learn how to be good salmon or competent sparrows.

That is not the case with people. The second verb implies teaching, the passing on of a heritage, just as it does for the animals. However, humans do not automatically pass on values, ideas, and ethics. It takes time, effort, and wisdom. Another verse follows the command to humans to be fruitful and multiply and continues with further elucidation of the goal of that teaching. We have an obligation to see that the next generation adds to the world, not diminishes it. They must be people who feel responsibility for the world and for other creatures. To take a very simple analogy, if we take our children to a playground, do we leave behind us litter and junk? Is the playground less appealing for the next round of visitors? Or do we teach our children not only to clean up after themselves, but also to think of what they might do to leave the playground in better condition than that in which they found it? If we, as parents, do our job well then, while our children have their own free choice, more times than not they will be assets to the world. If that is so, there is no need to worry that bringing them into this world is immoral—the world is improved by their being here.

The Flawed Premise of Equality

If you are ready to contemplate that getting married and raising children (not just procreating, but putting in love, time, and effort) are noble endeavors, we still have a question of what steps we can take to be successful in these countercultural activities.

There is an additional language change to the ones we mentioned in previous chapters that make it harder for this to happen. That is the redefining of the word "equality." How in the world can anyone other than the most bigoted, meanest, Neanderthal person be against equality? Yet, equality, like so many other words in our Orwellian times, isn't what it used to be.

Used as it is today, equality might mean either "equality of opportunity" or it could perhaps mean "equality of outcome." We also must question whether the words *equal* and *same* are synonymous with each other and what the word *fair* means. Could it be that much of society's push for equality and fairness, seen as a noble quest, is actually a push for *sameness*—a drab and dispiriting (as well as impossible to reach) condition?

The brilliant economist, Thomas Sowell, wrote, "One of the most seductive visions of our time is the vision of 'fairness' in a sense that the word never had before. At one time we all understood what was meant by a 'fair fight.' It meant that both fighters fought by the same Marquis of Queensbury rules. It did not mean that both fighters had equal strength, skill, experience or other factors that would make them equally likely to win."

While one of Dr. Sowell's area of expertise is in cultural differences in races and nationalities around the world, his words ring true to us regarding men and women in the workplace and in the home.

Meanwhile, when it comes to men and women, elementary, high schools, and universities increasingly teach according to an accepted agenda on this topic. Movies and other forms of entertainment do the same. This is just as misguided as previous generations who taught that, by definition, women didn't have the brains, temperament, or stamina needed for medicine or law. Replacing one set of false beliefs with another set of false beliefs does not lead to more successful living.

An online CNN headline in September 2017 read: "How to teach children about gender equality." The closing sentence after a fairly well-sized article and accompanying video says,

---

When I asked them [5th and 6th grade students] if they would tell their sons and daughters that girls and boys are different, they unanimously said they would tell their kids that girls and boys are equal.

That statement might get applause, but different and equal are not antonyms.

Equal is actually a meaningless word if you don't define what you are comparing. Two dimes and one nickel are equal in monetary value to one quarter, but they are not equal in weight or number. A bunch of weeds picked and presented to a mother by her 3-year-old son may be physically identical and equal to another bunch of weeds picked and presented to her by her husband, but we guarantee that it will not have anywhere close to the same emotional impact. In other words, depending on what you are discussing, physical, spiritual, and psychological factors can make the same not equal and the equal not the same.

Having delved into the unhealthy aspects of women wanting to emulate men at their worst, we're sure you noticed that we didn't yet respond to the idea about men being able to "have it all" meaning that they can have both meaningful and lucrative careers along with a flourishing family. Let's do that now.

There is a glaring flaw with the idea that men can "have it all" in this regard. The only way they manage both career and family is by partnering with a woman—their wife and the mother of their children.

The resentment expressed when that concept is articulated is actually not about one person being fortunate enough to have both Finance and Family. That takes a superhuman effort on the part of one person who sometimes needs to do this all alone under tragic circumstances, but it is certainly not desirable. The resentment expressed is rather about women not being able to turn the tables and easily find men whose focus will be on Family rather than Finance.

In this section, we want to question whether, if we want both Family and Finance (as we should and must), what are the necessary trade-offs? We never see obese giraffes or fat llamas because most animals stop eating when they have absorbed sufficient caloric energy. Enough is enough for animals, but humans have infinite desires. Many of us eat a little more than we really need. Many of us acquire and then need to store more things than we really need—hence the mini-warehouse industry. We finish a phenomenal vacation, and we start dreaming about our next one. However, although we always want more, we only have limited energies and resources to exchange for the goods and services we desire. We therefore must accustom ourselves to deciding which things we really want and which we are prepared to forfeit. What we want can only be acquired in exchange for what we have to offer, which of course, is not infinite.

Money and Masculinity

To determine the necessary trade-off, we first need to ask another question. This additional question has the potential to arouse an explosive reaction from critics. Here it is: does making money mean the same thing to a woman as it does to a man? Some will respond, "If it doesn't, that is due only to centuries of sexist indoctrination and nefarious cultural attitudes toward women." It is their hope that society can and will legislate and change attitudes until we reach a point where making money means exactly the same thing to women as it does to men.

That hope is based on viewing men, women, and money through only a physical lens. If we only had the first chapter of Genesis, we might agree. However, we know the second account of Creation as well. Based on this, you won't be surprised that we want to view this issue through a combined spiritual and physical lens.

Let's clarify from the outset that we are not talking about the *ability* to earn a living, nor are we discussing the intelligence or skills needed in the job market. Neither are we talking about enjoying one's job or feeling a sense of accomplishment. Both men and women can provide financially for their families. A growing number of careers today depend on factors that have nothing to do with biological functions that are unique to one sex. We find crossover in just about every field that was once considered traditionally male or traditionally female.

Many women are quite capable of making captain on a commercial air carrier or running a giant multinational corporation. Some women can competently weld rebar on the skeletal top floor of a skyscraper under construction, though fewer women than men wish to do so. Those things are not in question. Conversely, there is little doubt that most men are able to nurture toddlers and care for little children. They can certainly cook and put supper on the table. Our proposition, however, is that being capable of doing a job is not the most important concern. There is also the question of deep inner fulfillment, a springboard to happiness. The question that each of us has to answer for how we direct our own lives is whether doing certain activities answers most men and women's deepest spiritual, psychological, and emotional needs in the same way or in different ways.

Focusing on the spiritual differences between men and women, we contend that financially supporting a family fills a spiritual need in a man that it doesn't for a woman. A woman can obviously do it, but it doesn't fire up her femininity in the same way that making money ignites a man's masculinity. Sometimes it is easier to see the truth of a converse. Failing to make money does not make a man valueless, but it can erode the essence of his masculinity.

A woman who is fired or can't find work may indeed be worried, demoralized, and upset, but she doesn't feel less of a woman because of it. Perhaps she feels less valued as a person—but not as a woman. Failing to make money would likely create financial awkwardness. It might make her less successful career-wise, and it could affect her social circle, but it doesn't erode her sense of femininity.

Many women with enviable career skills opt out of the work-force in order to raise their children or care for family members. They often come under fierce attack for "betraying the sisterhood" by doing so, as happened to Anne-Marie Slaughter when she wrote an article explaining why she was leaving her prestigious, well-paying job at the State Department in the American government because she felt that her teenage boys needed her more on hand. Nonetheless, women like Slaughter, despite having put in years and hard work to excel at high-achieving careers, discovered that being available to their children was the important and soul-enriching work they wanted to do. Other women choose to be available for volunteer and community work or to provide support for their husbands' work. In no way is their femininity compromised; many women will tell you that it is enhanced.

When a man loses a job or cannot obtain one, it reaches into the very core of his masculine identity. For this reason his body often reacts with sexual dysfunction. (Ah—once again, the 5Fs, in this case Fitness and Finance intersect with each other.) This problem can deepen, rather than lessen, if his wife capably and expansively supports the family.

Our own anecdotal data, supported by studies in the United States and Denmark, reveal that as soon as wives earn more than their husbands, men suffer increased erectile dysfunction and usage of the necessary drugs increases. Apparently, men out-earned by their wives are more likely to use erectile dysfunction medication than their male breadwinner counterparts, even when this inequality is small. For their part, breadwinner wives suffer increased insomnia and anxiety. This is obviously not true for every single such couple, but it does seem to be a truth that is very inconvenient for the current cultural trend of diminishing the traditional family structure.

At an event, I (SL) was once seated at a table with a young, engaged couple. Unfortunately, he had just been let go from his job. His future bride kept saying, "Don't worry. I can support us until you find something." Each time she said that or some variation of those words, I saw his ego shrivel a bit more. Eventually, I took the opportunity of meeting her in the ladies room to explain that she was making him feel worse, not better. He needed to feel that he was going to be taking care of her, not to feel taken care of by her. She would support him more by expressing her faith in his abilities to get another job and her belief that she could rely on him rather than by assuring him of her financial prowess.

Some women neglect their due diligence during dating, paying no attention to their beau's bank account for fear of someone judging their interest in money to be unseemly. Or even more frightening, the girl with open interest in a man's financial prospects might be tarred with the unspeakable pejorative, gold digger!

We can scream, "Old fashioned! That's the way things used to be! If a couple is fortunate enough to be able to manage on one paycheck, it is irrelevant whose paycheck that is. Even when there are children, men can stay home with them just as happily as women can. Men who can't handle being supported by a wife are weak losers."

Maybe. And maybe that is a myth of our time. You can find anecdotes supporting both sides of the debate. Being forewarned, however, means deciding on what blueprint to run our lives rather than looking for stories that uphold our previous beliefs. Our conviction, based on how the Creator made men and women, is that the greatest odds of a happy marriage lie with the husband shouldering the burden of economic support.

A Different View

The Jewish marriage ceremony that springs from the pages of the Bible includes the husband giving a contract to his wife before two witnesses. As part of that contract, he commits to accepting responsibility for her sustenance. She makes no such counter promise. If Biblical rules are descriptive, not prescriptive, as we said in Chapter 3, then this suggests that marriages work better when this is so.

Let us elaborate. There is a principle in ancient Jewish wisdom that says, "the person who is obligated and performs is greater than one who is not obligated and performs." What does this mean?

Imagine the following scenario: You are visiting a friend whose elderly father lives with her. Mr. Green wasn't the pleasantest of men when he was young. Now in his 90s, crotchety would be a generous way to describe him. Nonetheless, your friend opened her home to her father and does her best to make him comfortable.

While you are visiting, Mr. Green thinks that he hears mail being dropped through the slot in the door, mail he is sure will contain the magazine he's been expecting. Knowing that your friend has already gone to the door three times in the past hour when no mail has yet been delivered, this time you rise and go to the door.

Who did the greater action in going to the door, you or your friend? Our first instinct might be to say you, since you had no obligation to "honor your father." You are just being a nice person. Ancient Jewish wisdom says exactly the opposite. When we are commanded or obligated to do something, part of our natural human instinct is to push back against that responsibility. Volunteering is easier. Since we are choosing of our own free will to take some action, we are in control. We are acting because of our own desire, not because we are compelled by an outside force. We can also choose inaction whenever we wish without a consequence. For these reasons, fulfilling an obligation is seen as a greater accomplishment than voluntarily choosing to do something, no matter how positive the action is.

Since a Jewish marriage ceremony obligates a man to financially support his wife, when he goes to work, he is fulfilling an obligation. As such, in relation to marriage, supporting a spouse is a greater act when a man does it than when a woman does. After all, he is the one who was told, "By the sweat of your brow you shall eat bread."

Clinical psychologist and professor Sherry Pagato is only one of many people today arguing (and as a professor we can assume teaching) that before marrying, women should get a written commitment to equality from their potential spouse.

In October 2017, *Harvard Business Review* ran an article bemoaning the fact that

More than half the men expected their careers to take precedence over their wives' careers, while most women expected egalitarian marriages. (Almost no women expected their own careers to come first.) Millennial men are often portrayed as more enlightened, but data complicates this picture: Surveys have shown that younger men may be even less committed to equality than their elders.

The article goes on to claim that this fact leads to many late-life divorces and advises couples how to equally respect and support each other's careers. We haven't researched the statistics, but we did find two of the three suggestions given for making sure that both careers are valued to be almost meaningless. The suggestions were for making regular time for "active listening" and being sure that there is regular "feedback." In other words, it is the same communication advice given most frequently for all marriages, friendships, and work teams. The underlying assumption (actually, it is openly stated) is that women are better at both of these things than men are, so men had better get with the program. Follow-up articles openly tell women to stay single if potential husbands don't commit to equally valuing both spouses' professions.

In her best-selling book, *Lean In*, Sheryl Sandberg, former chief operating officer of Facebook, wrote that a better world, ". . .would be one where women ran half our countries and companies and men ran half our homes." Many women and men agree with her. We vehemently disagree. She is seeking equality of outcome, a goal that rarely, if ever, leads to happiness.

Based on what we wrote, one should not talk of "equally valuing both spouses' professions." When it comes to relocating because of one spouse's career, for example, taking the psychic difference between men and women into account is as important as evaluating all the other factors.

That doesn't mean that a man's salary should be higher for identical work. In fact, that was one of the egregious wrongs that led to the formation of the modern feminist movement. It does mean that while both husband and wife might get a paycheck and while both, one would hope, receive emotional fulfillment from their occupations, he receives more spiritual and psychic fulfillment in going to work. Incidentally, this principle suggests that an unmarried man and a married man also relate differently to earning money. Obviously, this reality has some very practical ramifications for lifelong bachelors. It doesn't shock us that as boys stopped preparing themselves for marriage, many of them have lost all ambition to work as well.

As we have noted, some people's uniqueness comes out in an extraordinary talent and passion. That is as true for women as it is for men. History tells of the warrior Joan of Arc and of Leonardo da Vinci, of the prophetess Deborah and of Napoleon. Ruth Bader Ginsberg had a fire in her for the law as did her friend, fellow Supreme Court Justice Antonin Scalia. Being married to someone with exceptional gifts and drive may well mean that the couple's efforts go toward supporting that gift, regardless if it is the husband or the wife's. These usually play out on more of a local than a national or international stage.

Dr. Selma Wehl qualified as a pediatrician in Germany in the 1920s. As a refugee in the United States, she overcame numerous hurdles to requalify. She and her husband both recognized that God had granted her a gift of healing. She often diagnosed cases when other doctors could not. They decided together that he would focus on raising their son and she would concentrate on her unique area of strength. Nights often found him helping her with blood counts and patient care.

One mother whose child was in the hospital was surprised to find Dr. Wehl in her child's room after midnight. She expressed concern that it wouldn't be safe for the then (very) elderly doctor to go home. Dr. Wehl reassured her, "I am not alone, my husband is sitting outside in the car waiting for me." Her husband was 92 years old at the time. Dr. Wehl would have gone out in the snow in the middle of the night even had she won the lottery and never needed to work for financial reasons ever again.

Yes, if one spouse has such an obvious calling and is so clearly blessed with skills that the world needs, different calculations need to be made. But if earning a living for the family in a decent, honorable, and ethical way is the goal, then prioritizing the husband's work is our advice.

What are the societal ramifications if men and women, in general, relate differently to both money and sex, as ancient Jewish wisdom suggests? If that is so, then trying to level the field is an exercise in futility. We can only achieve equity if we force people to behave as we think they should, rather than allowing individuals the freedom to make choices for themselves. Interestingly, Scandinavian countries have discovered that the more gender-equal their political and social policies, the more different the career choices men and women make. Given the freedom to do what they wish, the sexes in general have different priorities and choices.

On a Mission

If we are correct, then we cannot minimize the added psychic benefit a man gets from doing activities that make him feel needed as a man. Being needed conflates with feeling a mission: I am doing something important, something where my masculinity is an asset. This is one of the reasons that men in the military, firemen, and policemen feel such a strong camaraderie for those with whom they serve. Knowing they are doing vitally important work and that their teammates depend on them in a very real sense is part of the reason that they do what they do, sometimes for less pay and greater danger than in other professions. Interestingly, many women are attracted to men in uniforms. Ideally, wearing that uniform tells a woman that the man is respected by other men, is able to consistently shoulder a burden, and can successfully work as part of a group. These are clues that he is worthy of her respect.

While a man can certainly be attracted to an individual woman who is in the military or serves on a police force, men as a group are not turned on by a uniform in the same way that women as a group are. Try entering a Google search for, "Are women attracted to UPS (or FedEx) drivers?" When we typed that question, an expansive choice of applicable sites discussing the topic popped up. The question, "Are men attracted to UPS (or FedEx) drivers?" got no bites.

Are we saying that being needed isn't important for women? No, we're actually saying that women feel no doubt that they are needed. Returning to the spiritual messages of the physical world, the world's existence hinges on babies needing the warmth and safety of their mother's bodies in order to survive. That reflects a truism that women know. They are essential. In the short term, women without men do far better than men without women. Widows do better physically and socially than widowers. Women, on the whole, make friends more easily and support each other better than men do. However, our lives depend on more than the short term. For civilization to continue, we need both men and women to thrive. Right now, in many first-world countries, men as a group are not managing, let alone doing well. That is not a cause for celebration. It bodes ill for everyone. Many women who wish to be married and raising families today are facing the problem of a male population that is floundering. And children, of course, are the ones who suffer most of all when they have limited or no access to their fathers.

We have been suggesting that much of feminism's mantra became a case of saying, "Whatever men do is valuable and fulfilling, so women must do it too." That misogynistic viewpoint is too widely accepted. We have devalued women's special talents, intuitions, and abilities. One result of this push has led to a pernicious problem that those women who find building a home and raising a family to be satisfying and who choose to focus on that are depicted as stupid, untalented, and lacking in ambition. We constantly hear how businesses and governments must supply more parental leave and on-site day care and subsidies so that women can do the really important job of working out of the home. Each of these efforts, of course, as well as more government regulation and higher taxation, leads to higher prices for everything so even more women are forced to work for money whether they want to or not. Society, in the United States at least, is tilted against mothers not because there isn't enough support for working mothers but because we have pretended that the only thing that counts is working for a paycheck and professional prestige. That is where life fulfillment lies. Talk about elevating mammon into an idol!

Microsoft was recently renovating its campus in Redmond, Washington. When the 500 acre campus opened in 1986, it was seen as a progressive vision for the future. There were restaurants and gyms; employees could eat, get their laundry done, exercise, and take care of their every need without ever having to leave the workplace! Stop and think about that for a minute. Is that really an advantage to employees, or is it a gift to the corporation that employs them?

There was a period when executive women boasted of negotiating deals while in the midst of childbirth. In between contractions, they could continue to work. As marketers know, packaging matters. A woman in the middle of a strenuous, life-changing and holy labor continues to work for her paycheck or esteem instead of focusing on the momentous event in which she is a star player. When peasants or sharecroppers were barely able to pause to have a baby, we didn't paint that as a gift to women. Exactly what type of behavior are we in our "advanced" society elevating as admirable?

Freezing a woman's eggs to extend her years of fertility is touted as yet another advance. Pardon our skepticism, but it reminds us of a feature of the Israelites servitude in Egypt. Exodus 1:13–14 recounts that the Egyptians worked the Israelites *b'farech,* usually translated as hard labor. Ancient Jewish wisdom adds another dimension to this unusual word.

Many Biblical Hebrew words exist on one level as one word, but on a deeper level we can treat the word as a compound word. The "b" sound at the beginning of *b'farech* is a prefix meaning *with.* The rest of the word can be divided into two part *PeH RaCH.* (In Hebrew, one letter makes both the F and P sound.) A *PeH* is a mouth, and *RaCH* means gentle. So the word can also mean, *"with a gentle mouth."* That certainly doesn't sound like hard labor!

No, it doesn't, but it is how hard labor often begins. Most demagogues and tyrants do not arise and say, "Support me and propel me into power so that I can make your lives miserable." Instead, they make wonderful promises and speak as if they are one of the crowd. We are told that Pharaoh initially joined in the great and noble enterprise of building new cities. It was an inspiring project that would grant fulfillment and meaning to everyone's life. Only after the labor had started with voluntary enthusiasm, did the screws begin to turn. Pharaoh went back to his palace, conditions worsened, and gullible people were now slaves.

We believe that women were and are being sold a pack of promises that separated them from their body and souls. They were seduced into believing that working for a paycheck was glorious and that the tasks of a wife and mother were menial. When women balked, and some in their late 30s and early 40s rued not having married and having children, a new scam was offered. You can have the fulfilling and lucrative career of your dreams and also have the family you crave. We will generously and nobly help you freeze your eggs so that you, just like men, can have children into your 40s, 50s, and beyond. This is not a gift from a benevolent government or corporate master; it is a gambit to keep women at work.

In the Western world, women in particular do have a rather long life expectancy. Why are we talking of working and freezing eggs rather than having children, raising them, and then having time left for a career if desired? Women's bodies are built to have children in their 20s. Having to choose between learning something new with a 45-year-old brain or tricking our 45-year-old bodies into gestation and then handling the physically taxing care of young ones, how do we end up thinking the second choice is better? Why do we equate raising children with turning off our brains in the first place? That is only so if we choose it to be.

This entire facade depends on convincing young women in particular that creating a home and family is demeaning drudgery while work done outside the home for a paycheck is meaningful and fulfilling. Will women who have bought into this sad vision feel vindicated in their 50s?

Majestic Motherhood

As a society we used to appreciate women who kept neighborhoods alive during the day and who nurtured their communities. They were there to offer a helping hand to those in need or to run local organizations that cared for the poor. They sat with sick neighbors and supported local arts, providing for the general welfare of their communities. They wrote books and explored crafts and did dozens of other worthwhile and growth-oriented activities, although not necessarily for a boss. We knew that women had a variety of talents and that deploying those for the good of their immediate and extended family as well as for the greater community meant they were performing a needed and valued service. Sometimes those efforts did bring in money, but the money was not necessary to let everyone know that those efforts were essential.

And, yes, bringing the next generation into the world and working to see that those children will contribute to the world rather than detract from it is a lofty goal. Individual women will find different parts of mothering and homemaking more and less fulfilling. Some women cherish the infant months, others delight in the toddler years, while some relish the growing independence of their teens. Some women love cooking, while others can't stand being in the kitchen. Some revel in decorating, while others couldn't care less. There are a thousand and one ways to build a home as long as the core is based on warmth, loyalty, and security. Just as one lawyer might choose to specialize in labor law while another prefers contract negotiation, or one construction worker specializes as a mason while another is an electrical contractor, motherhood and homemaking have a huge variety of scope when seen as a profession. Through the gift a man gives his wife and children by taking responsibility for earning the family's living and thus allowing her to use her talents and gifts without needing to fixate on monetary gain, she can expand her world and that of those around her. How pathetic is a society that condescendingly depicts being a mother, being a homemaker, as a one-track course of grueling mind-numbing grind that is only satisfying to loser ladies.

Once again, we posit that life works better when we accept biological realities than when we deny them. A man's biological contribution to the creation of a child takes a few minutes of his active involvement. A woman's body then nurtures and protects the growing baby for 9 months. After birth, her body incredibly produces the exact nourishment that the newborn child needs, changing as the infant grows.

We are aware that while some women revel in their pregnancies, others suffer miserably through them. (One woman can also have different experiences with each pregnancy.) Pregnancy, at one and the same time, is a natural process and a potentially life-threatening one. Some women luxuriate in breast-feeding while others find it painful or impossible. The bottom line is that while individual circumstances matter greatly to each of us, taking a 30,000 foot view, pregnancy and nursing are two of the greatest specialties and unique gifts possessed by women. For most women, nothing can compare to motherhood as a source of fulfillment. For a culture to present these uniquely feminine accomplishments as nuisances and impediments to a life of achievement is nothing short of cruel.

At age 17, Californian Chloe Cole, became a public voice against transitioning children. As an unhappy 13-year-old, she was quickly "diagnosed" with gender dysphoria, leading to being prescribed hormone blockers and testosterone at 13 and to a double mastectomy at 15. By the time she was 16, she knew she had made a mistake. The horrors and abuses taking place in the dubious field of gender studies are not the subject of this book. What interests us are the false messages young girls are getting and how they are imperiling the Family pillar of the 5Fs. In an interview with Jordan Peterson, recorded when she was 18, Chloe explained that as a preteen she heard nothing positive about being a woman. Women were oppressed, being pregnant is scary, having children is a negative experience, and female biological realities such as menstruation or menopause are horrible. Boys have the life!

Meanwhile, boys, too, receive messages that interfere with their ability to grow into healthy men. They hear that masculinity is toxic, that they are inherently oppressors, and that their inborn, physical traits are bad. Alternatively, the opposing message they get in nonfunctioning parts of society is that they are foolish patsies and wimps if they don't recognize that females are to be treated badly and demeaned. There is barely a healthy choice to be seen in the public sphere.

What terrible messages our children are getting! Make no mistake, these messages have an effect even on those young people who do not buy into them wholeheartedly. We are all affected by what surrounds us.

No Pain, No Gain

Of course there are difficult, boring, and exhausting elements of prioritizing family. Do you know any worthwhile occupation for which that isn't true?

I (SL) got a lovely Mother's Day card from one of my daughters that brought tears of joy to my eyes, but it also highlighted one of the enemies of successful living.

Among other sweet words, she wrote, "I am only now starting to realize how much of your own life and time and personal pursuits you must have sacrificed to raise us...."

The gratitude is appreciated, and the sentiment is lovely. It is also completely and unutterably wrong. It is wrong, not only in terms of motherhood but also in terms of marriage, work, and life.

Teachers often want their students to remain silent when walking down the hall. I once watched two first-grade teachers prepare their students for a trip past several other classrooms on their way to the music room. Neither teacher wanted her group to be disruptive. One teacher spoke about how important it was not to interrupt the other classes and how proud she would be if her students walked in a quiet and orderly fashion, two by two.

The other teacher spun a story, leading her students to picture that they were explorers going through the woods to spy on an enemy camp. One sound and they might be captured!

Both groups were quiet. First graders want to please their teachers. But the second group's faces were filled with expectation and joy. They weren't behaving well; they were having an adventure.

Our attitude toward what we are doing makes all the difference. Despite what my daughter wrote, I did not sacrifice to raise my children. That was my chosen vocation, and the normal and inevitable consequence was that I had less time and energy for other activities. As a human being living in a world with 24 hours in a day, I can't do everything and be everywhere. Among my friends I number social workers, CEOs, accountants, teachers, doctors, and pilots. The same calculus applies to them.

When I got married, I could have chosen a professional business path. I could have had fewer children. I had the option of paying tuition at a private school or using the public schools rather than homeschooling as we did. I even could have walked out on my family, unshackling myself from my obligations and responsibilities. Would that have gotten me "all"?

Did I sacrifice by staying in my marriage and devoting myself to my family? Not at all. I made choices and reaped the benefits from those choices while paying the associated costs. That is called reality.

It's easy to imagine the life that we did not choose through rose-colored glasses. We picture that alternative version of us as an executive wearing expensive, tailored clothing and jetting off to exotic vacation locales. We see ourselves saving lives as a surgeon or being feted as teacher of the year. Yet, somehow, we never picture ourselves as a bored lower-level employee struggling to make ends meet or as an executive cowering in the ladies room steeling herself to fire an employee she likes. Nor do we picture ourselves as someone earning a great living and relishing the challenges and successes of her career who frequently has to force a smile while yearning to be home with her child or having more energy to devote to her marriage. Sometimes that husband and child only exist in her dreams.

Were there days while my children were young when I couldn't see how I could possibly cope for 5 more minutes? Yes. I distinctly remember hiding behind some dresses in my closet to steal just a few minutes of quiet. That is no different from the nurse we know with a prestigious and lucrative specialty who threw up every single day after work for her first few weeks on her new job. She still has days where she is completely wiped out. Anything worthwhile has its difficult moments.

There is no job, career, vocation, or life that has only sunshine. It is up to us to focus on the positives in the life we choose rather than focusing on those things that our choice excluded. Our attitude, not our reality, decides whether we are sacrificing ourselves or finding fulfillment.

We know many women are working because their salaries really are indispensable. Inflation is rampant, and being a one-earner family is more difficult than it used to be. Even if living on one income is possible, we are not saying that a man should devote 100% of his efforts to earning a living and a woman should devote 100% of her efforts to building a home. If that was so, there would be no Friendship, Faith, or Fitness in either life, and the husband and wife would be a socioeconomic partnership more than being husband, wife, and parents. It does mean that both Finance and Family work best, not when every job and chore is split 50/50, but when husband and wife each has a sphere of responsibility and priority where they are the "alpha" and their partner plays more of a complementary role. Sometimes, life demands this balance to be 90/10; other times, it might be 70/30.

If you were being wheeled into the operating room, would you prefer to know that your surgeon has done whatever procedure you are facing 500 times or 1,000 times? Assuming equivalent innate ability, do we expect a musician who dedicates 4 hours a day to her music to be as proficient as one who labors for 10 hours a day at her art? Does anyone say, "Well, I'll choose the less experienced doctor because what matters to me is that she has good work/life balance"? It is illegal in the United States to ask a female applicant for schooling or employment if she plans to have a family. That may be politically correct, and we can and do ignore statistics that show how many female military members are on leave because of pregnancy as well as how many female dentists and doctors choose to work part time rather than full time. We pretend that women and men work the same hours and number of years, but that doesn't mean that the results of these ignored realities go away. We talk of how both men and women should have everything they want as if there is a great genie in a bottle who can grant us wishes. It is perfectly appropriate for a 5-year-old to tell us that she will be an astronaut, prime minister, and a ballerina. Maybe it's time for the rest of us to stop sounding like we are 5 years old.

Knowing Why We Do What We Do Is Important

We attended the funeral of a wonderful woman who passed away at 93 years young. As he eulogized his mother, her son provided some context for those, like us, who knew his mother as a vital, active, loving senior but who hadn't known her in her younger years. He spoke of his mother going to work as a secretary so that his parents could afford a private religious education for him. When she was directed to post an ad for a regional sales manager, she told her boss that there was no need to look for someone; she could do the job. Although in those years a woman sales manager was highly unusual, he gave her the chance to prove herself, which she proceeded to do. Yet, as her son pointed out, while she certainly took satisfaction in her work, the goal of working was to build her family and its future. Family and Faith were always the priority.

Contrast that with a podcast aimed at young mothers that ran within a few days of the funeral. The hosts of the show were interviewing a successful female writer who has two children, an infant and a toddler. The guest made the point that it is vital to get as much help as one can during the fleeting years that one has small children, so that one can retain focus on one's career. After all, she said, (we are paraphrasing) your career is going to be the entire rest of your life.

Being able to choose to hire childcare so that one can focus on work is, of course, a privileged woman's option. Mothers who are working so that there will be food on the table and a roof over their family's head do not have that choice. But the bottom line is, while working for money and family may need to coexist for many mothers, there is a subtle and not-so-subtle difference in how one lives based on which is the priority. Do we take time off from work in order to have children, or do we take time away from our children in order to work?

Reading old corporate manuals from the middle of the twentieth century can be strangely discordant. For instance, it was fairly common for large big-name American companies to interview the wives of the men they were considering recruiting for senior executive positions. (They did not interview the husbands of women they were interviewing because this career path was, for the most part, being offered only to men.) The companies recognized that they were hiring a team, not an individual.

The reason for this was the realization that every job in America was, in reality, a two-person job: a man, capable of fully focusing on the hour-by-hour and day-by-day work, providing financial support for the family, and a woman focusing on building a home and family, providing a haven and path to a future. Between them they built a family and a home and between them they kept the wheels of commerce turning. She was also frequently a sounding board and advisor for his ideas. She often organized events that made his work more valuable. The money being brought home was not his money or his earnings. It was theirs. The children and home were not hers but theirs. They were partners in every sense of the word. Employers concerned for the stability of their enterprise and the stability of the employees upon whom it depended, naturally had to assure themselves that men being hired for important positions were in stable and happy marriages.

It is easy to dismiss all this as shameful and primitive sexism (whatever that means), but is it even remotely possible that it worked better for men, women, and society than the contemporary morass of misery with which we've replaced it? In our own lives, what if instead of seeing Finance and Family as competing goals, we go with the 5F path of seeing a husband and a wife as a team that together can be successful in both? Instead of thinking of "my money" or "my family," the couple thinks in terms of "our money" and "our family."

When both husband and wife's external for-paycheck work have nothing to do with each other, keeping a marriage going and raising a family is a Sisyphean task. Both are being pulled away from Family. Harking back to more agrarian times, we understood the partnership needed, not only of husband and wife but also of the children. Many immigrants moved from struggle to success following the same path: husband and wife working together with children expected to pitch in as well. Whether they ran farms, grocery stores, or laundries, family teamwork was the answer. While this teamwork is less natural in many modern occupations, it is possible more frequently than people think it is. However, it takes a shift in thinking that both men and women need to be courageous enough to make.

Most of us, men and women, can find meaning and satisfaction following a variety of paths. Perhaps, when plotting a career path we should ask how our not-yet-existent family will fit in. Will incurring great piles of student debt for a degree make sense? After all, our futures will be filled with value from all 5Fs, not just from money alone. Marriage can make a huge difference in the path we end up taking. We know an actress who stayed involved in the arts, but she also took university courses in physics so that she could edit her physicist husband's papers. They, not he alone, made his career a success. Without Clementine, wife of Sir Winston Churchill, world history might have followed a different path, and she is not an outlier as a wife playing a less prominent but essential role in a famous husband's career. You may know of *Cheaper by the Dozen* as a not very successful movie or as a very funny book. Take the time to read the real story of Lillian Gilbreth and discover how partnering with her husband (while raising a large family) led her to become one of America's best-known engineers, a path she never would have contemplated or imagined before her marriage. Thousands of women whose names we will never know play this type of supporting role every day, and in doing so, the couple has an income, a stronger marriage, and a family.

Sometimes prioritizing in our own minds why we do what we do is needed. We almost can't recognize how alien and selfish "I need to work for my self-fulfillment" is. Yet, every year, young people enter college or advanced training opportunities keeping only their own wants and desires in mind. Then we wonder why we have so much trouble when it is time to become a "we" or an "us." Western culture in general places too much emphasis on being the "star."

How we think about marriage, how we avoid marriage, how we set up our marriages—all these impact our Faith, Fitness, Friendships, and our Finances. We will relate differently in all of these areas if we believe that human nature is completely changeable or whether we believe that a Creator expects us to constantly work on improving ourselves in those areas that are changeable at the same time as accepting that He has hardwired us in certain ways.

Closing the Circle

The 5F system tells us that for successful living, all five areas of our lives need to be in a state of dynamic growth. What is more, they all are crosslinked to one another. Though it might seem that ignoring everything other than work is the surest way to maximize income, it turns out that for the overwhelming majority of us this is not true. We might think of ourselves as completely rational, basing all our decisions only on what we can see and touch, yet by ignoring the spiritual, we would be missing out on understanding vast areas of life. We might see our friendships as completely separate from our marriage and end up destroying both. What is absolutely true for all of us is that joy and fulfillment in life do not come from focusing only on some of the Fs, but from nurturing and balancing all five.

We all are somewhat susceptible to group-think. To a greater or lesser extent, we operate parts of our lives on autopilot influenced by the zeitgeist—the cultural message that penetrates our beings. We brush our teeth somewhat unthinkingly, just as we do dozens of other actions during our day. In the face of so many decisions we have to make, our minds seek to place many of them onto autopilot. We are all familiar with driving home and upon arriving there being unable to remember going through a specific intersection. With crowded days and nonstop stimuli coming at us, it is not surprising that we relegate many of our opinions about important parts of life to those that the surrounding culture beams into us. But at the end of the day, we each have the agency and the responsibility to choose a foundation on which to base our lives. "Misery loves company" is not a saying that we wish to fall back upon 10 years down the road. The unified spiritual/physical view of how the world really works that this book describes is utterly irreconcilable with today's more popular materialistic perspective. Now is a good time to start deciding, without a crystal ball into the future, which approach you believe to be a better blueprint and therefore a superior roadmap for administering your life. Our goal is to let you know that you have a very real choice.

Chapter 8

Putting the 5Fs to Work

I n this book, *The Holistic You*, we have tried to present you with a blueprint of your life with the options stripped away—the five essentials necessary for living a complete and successful life. But that is not all. We have tried to depict the five essential Fs as part of a complete and integrated system with each F interdependent on the other four, imparting energy to them and deriving energy from them.

If you are ready to commit to redesigning your life with purpose and intent, now is the time to start. But that means making a new beginning and all beginnings are tough. This is because new beginnings involve change, and change takes energy.

When I (RDL) first started learning to fly, I struggled with several aspects of piloting a small airplane. One of the skills I found difficult to master was turning. When air traffic control directed me to turn 90 degrees left onto a new heading, it was not enough to turn the wheel and touch the rudder pedal in order to bank the airplane into a gentle turn. One also had to remember to add more engine power. Yes, turning takes energy, and without adding engine power going into a turn causes one to lose altitude because some of the energy that had been keeping you aloft is now being redirected into making the airplane turn. It follows that embarking on a 5F life rejuvenation plan will take energy because you are going to be significantly changing direction. The effort required might make you apprehensive.

However, having told you that rejuvenating yourself on the 5F program will take energy, we can also give you some good news. Unlike, say, a plan to build a house, you can launch your 5F rejuvenation in any one of the most immediately appealing of five possible starting sites. If you wish to build a house, you have to start digging foundations. That's all there is to it. There is no alternative, and we wouldn't take you very seriously if you spent your first day of house building at the paint and wallpaper store. No, there's plenty of time for that as there is for selecting light fixtures, but today you must dig. In your 5F rejuvenation plan, you can start with Finance, Fitness, Faith, Friends, or Family, depending on which will most easily get you out of the quagmire of resistance that accompanies all life-improving beginnings.

If you believe that starting off today in a gym is something that will get you off the starting block, go for it. If you feel that sitting down with an accountant or financial advisor and starting to plan your revenue increasing program and your subsequent investment intentions is the step you are ready for—do it. Maybe listing the friends you are going to reconnect with this week is your easiest launch pad. Remember, starts are hard. Make it a bit easier on yourself by choosing the F that is easiest for you to embrace. Whichever you select, just do it. Today.

Once you have commenced your program of improvement on any one of your 5Fs, as soon as you have taken a positive step forward, select the second of your 5Fs and attack it with an eye to a positive step that will move that F forward. In this fashion, during the course of the first two weeks of your efforts, review, assess, and take one positive step on each of your 5Fs.

We have mentioned that we have received many questions over the years. Here are a few examples of challenges faced by others tackling their own 5F rejuvenations, along with our responses.

Ask the Rabbi and Susan #1

Doris describes how health challenges have complicated her holistic journey toward 5F completion. We often feel humbled by the courage with which so many of our readers confront the difficulties with which life has presented them.

Good morning Rabbi Lapin and Susan,

I had my thyroid removed 3 years ago because of an enlarged nodule and cancer within a lymph node. My prognosis, as far as cancer, looks good. If you have thyroid disease like hypothyroidism, or have had your thyroid removed, like me, it can pose a challenge to get things working properly. It can be trial and error to find the right dosage. The last 18 months have not been good, and I am left feeling frustrated and a bit depressed because I wonder if I will ever feel like myself again. Also, I am very aware of how this is affecting those around me because I have not been in a good place.

I think about the 5Fs, and because of your teaching, I know that my health is impacting the other four areas negatively. I will give you an example. My father passed away this past summer at the age of 92. My mother, who is also 92, is still alive and well. However, she does have some failing health and so in December we (my brother and I) moved her into assisted living. She was not eager to go, to say the least.

Unfortunately, though, between my father's passing, trying to get my mother situated and my health and not feeling well, I was not always very graceful or patient with my mom. I know I am supposed to be a Happy Warrior, but I am anything but that right now; my physical body does not seem to want to cooperate. So, my question is, what does ancient Jewish Wisdom say about our physical body and how to live with a disease, chronic illness, etc.? I am really interested in knowing. Would God say, "Just deal with it and be happy"?

By the way, we are looking for a new doctor and are praying and hoping that they can get me adjusted correctly. I hope this all makes sense and I look forward to your answer.

Sincerely,

Doris

———

Dear Doris,

Most importantly, we are delighted that cancer does not seem to be a concern anymore. We also join your prayers that God grants your doctors the wisdom to find a medication and treatment regimen that restores you and keeps you healthy and feeling well.

Have you ever seen someone messing up really badly but remaining completely oblivious to the fact that they are doing so? I (SL) once cringed at hearing a teacher leading a class trip to the local science center who was not only using terrible grammar but, even worse, speaking rudely to her students. Yet, while I was suffering listening to her, she was perfectly comfortable. For many striving people, this works in the reverse. We are harder on ourselves than we would be on others.

When we human beings aim to improve, very often the first thing that happens is that we are tempted to become depressed at noticing our many shortcomings. We seem worse off than we were when we weren't paying attention. We see this phenomenon when our house is a wreck as the first step of a redecorating project or when we are in pain after the dentist begins working on our teeth. Instead of improvement, we experience an illusion of going backward!

This sounds like it may be happening to you. Rather than excusing your short temper with the excuse, "Well, I'm not feeling well," you are holding yourself to a higher standard. Meanwhile, you have been facing not only ill health but also the emotional and physical stresses that accompany parents getting older and the loss of your father. You are dealing with a tremendous amount.

Rather than God saying, "Just deal with it and be happy," we would phrase it as, "My beloved daughter. You have many burdens right now. Don't let aiming for perfection become an excuse for sadness or giving up. Each time you hold back a sharp word or put a smile on your face, I rejoice in your heroism. Love yourself as I love you."

Blessings,

Rabbi Daniel and Susan Lapin

#Fitness, Faith, Family

From time to time, people whose letters we have answered in our Ask the Rabbi *column write back to us later to tell us how things are going. We were so happy to hear from Doris a few months after we wrote to her and to discover how well she was doing.*

Ask the Rabbi and Susan #2

It is painful for us when we have to tell someone that they are on the wrong track. We much prefer being able to tell those who write to us with a problem that they are on the right track and all will be well. This is not often the case. Usually, the principles of 5F rejuvenation call for a change which we try to present as gently and as sympathetically as we can. Holly's question was an example of this.

Dear Rabbi and Susan,

My husband and I are reading your book on business as a result of seeing you on the 700 Club. I have been in business for 25 years in the Imprinted Apparel business and recently my husband lost his job. It made sense for him to join the business as he is 10 years younger than me and I have to deal with a lot of boxes and deliveries when jobs are completed.

My business has supported me for 25 years, but it is a small business and now we need to generate enough income for 2. We start our day everyday reading scripture and praying and then get to work. So far so good as the last Summer Camp order was double the size of last year. It is still a step in faith as we attempt to grow our business and ask God to help us.

Is there any specific advice you would give us? Thank you and God bless you today.

Holly

___

Dear Holly,

If you have been in business for 25 years and it is growing, you must be doing many things right. You clearly invite God to bless and guide your business, which is always an important step.

We'd like to limit our comments to the effects of your husband joining your business. While a temporary measure may sometimes make sense, it does make us uncomfortable for you and your husband to see his contribution as restricted to brawn. If his only role is one that could be filled by a strapping 16-year-old, then we would worry about the effect on his self-identity and your respect for him.

Additionally, it is a bad business move to overpay someone beyond his fiscal contribution to the bottom line merely because he is the boss's husband. We may have misunderstood, and he may be making other important contributions. However, if not, we'd suggest that he seeks another position elsewhere.

Even if your husband does contribute greatly to the business, we urge you both to be acutely aware of the effects on your relationship. Being your husband's boss can lead to emotions and ramifications that do not stay confined to the workplace. (A man being his wife's boss also has difficulties but of another nature.)

While each situation is unique, we would encourage you and your husband to "put the marriage before the money."

Wishing you both success in marriage and in business,

Rabbi Daniel and Susan Lapin

#Family, Finance

Ask the Rabbi and Susan #3

Human relationships, whether in a society, community or family, are exquisitely delicate mechanisms. Misunderstandings and miscommunications can make the difference between warm feelings of bonhomie and seething resentment. We can each probably do more than we are doing to lubricate interactions.

Dear Rabbi and Susan,

As a person who abstains from drinking (for reasons of self-discipline), I am often expected (usually by assumption or without asking) to be the driver for most events and parties with my family and friends. Does my personal decision not to drink bring with it the responsibility of serving others around me in this manner? Logically, why should others not enjoy themselves at a party (remain sober to drive) if I have already decided not to drink? I sometimes feel "used," though, because of my personal decision.

Involuntary Designated Driver

_____

Dear Involuntary Designated Driver,

We love how the questions that come into our *Ask the Rabbi* mailbox make us think. Your question certainly did that.

We would like to expand your question. In many ways, it is the same one as the at-home mother whose work-in-an-office neighbor asks her to sign for her packages or let the plumber into her house. We could brainstorm and think of a dozen similar situations. Basically, people are assuming that they are asking another person for something that is no big deal.

That isn't true, of course. Driving people home means that you get home later, and it also puts extra wear and tear on your car. Committing to answering the doorbell for the delivery man means interrupting whatever you're doing at an unexpected time and not being able to spontaneously go for a walk. The person asking may say to himself, "He's driving anyway," or "She's at home anyway," but he is making a mistake. When asking a favor of someone we should never minimize what we are asking. At the very least, we should never assume that help is available, and we should show gratitude. If it is more than a one-time occurrence, we should take care to show our thanks with a card, gift, or other gesture of appreciation.

So important is gratitude that God made Aaron rather than Moses bring the curse of blood upon the River Nile because Moses had been a beneficiary of the river, as it were, when he floated upon it as an infant.

On the flip side, you (and our hypothetical neighbor) have an opportunity to show kindness to other people. It seems from what you wrote that the difficulty is in your attitude toward driving people home rather than the technical details. You feel taken for granted, which leaves a bad taste in your mouth. If you saw it differently, it wouldn't be as much of a problem.

Can you examine your own life to see if you are ever on the other side of the equation? Is there one coworker who frequently heads out for coffee and either offers to pick a cup up for you or you call out, "While you're there could you get me...?" Do you assume that your spouse will do certain things and neglect to thank her each and every time? Do you ever say to yourself, "It's no big deal," when you ask a friend for what seems to you a small favor?

Your question is an opportunity for all of us to remind ourselves that anything someone does for us is a big deal. We should be on the lookout for those "small" kindnesses that make our lives easier and happier. We should make a point of expressing (and feeling) grateful for things others do for us even—or perhaps especially—if they are done routinely. And above all we should never have an expectation that others will do us favors. A sense of entitlement is repugnant while gratitude is Godly.

In your case, because you feel people are taking your help for granted, we would suggest a two-fold track. First, do some honest introspection to see where you can improve yourself in this area. Look for occasions to express appreciation to family members and coworkers. You will be doing the right thing, and maybe your actions will even influence them to do the same.

Then, the next time there's an event where you assume you will be expected to drive, think carefully. If you truly can't do it without feeling resentful, then let it be known in advance that you have plans after the event (and subsequently do something, even if it is going out for a cup of coffee) and, unfortunately, won't be able to drive. Don't sound apologetic or feel the need to say what your plans are. Ultimately, you need to decide if this is too big a thing for you to do or just one of the ways you can help out.

Safe driving,

Rabbi Daniel and Susan Lapin

#Finance, Friendship, Faith

Ask the Rabbi and Susan #4

Variations of this question fill our mailbox. Over the past years in many countries, on average, single young women started out-earning single young men. While this isn't the case with Jeff, his concern is the trend line into the future. The topic is not only incendiary but also very sensitive.

Dear Rabbi and Susan,

I have listened to a few of your podcasts that talk about the perils of income disparity between spouses, where the wife earns more than the husband. I'm a guy, and frankly the topic terrifies me because I'd rather drive nails through my feet than face the prospect of divorce because of this kind of thing.

I'm dating someone who does not earn more than me, but she has high potential to do so later. Am I heading for disaster?

Jeff

———————

Dear Jeff,

I (RDL) often speak about the connection between money and marriage on my podcast, and I (SL) frequently cover variations on the same theme in my Susan's Musings column. In this forum you get the two of us together!

A few years ago, we did a multi-day conference in Dallas on this topic. So, you have touched a hot-button subject for us and one in which, not surprisingly, much of what we have to say contradicts popular culture.

One of the sentences in your letter concerns us. We hope we're wrong, but you sound passively resigned to being terrified. Why isn't that fear fueling your financial climb to a new level at which that fear would evaporate? Part of being a male is developing and exercising ambition.

Here is the bottom line: There is no question that both men and women can provide financially for their families. However, making money fills a spiritual need in a man that it doesn't for a woman. In addition, failing to provide financially erodes the essence of masculinity for most men, but it leaves the core of a woman's identity intact.

When a man loses his job or cannot obtain one, it strikes a blow at the heart of his masculinity. For this reason his body often reacts with sexual impotence. This problem, with its capacity to damage the marriage, can intensify rather than diminish if his wife capably and expansively assumes the burden of supporting the family.

Your question relates to this concept. We wouldn't phrase it as "heading for disaster," but we do think that you are wise to think about this now.

Here are some of the questions we feel you ought to both be examining now. Is your girlfriend's work a "calling," or a job? Is she doing something that she feels defines her identity, or is she simply good at what she does? Do you ever get the feeling that her job is the priority in her life? If one of you was offered a career opportunity that required moving, meaning the other spouse would need to leave his or her current position, would your decision be based solely on who earns more? Do either or both of you see a commuter marriage where you only live together a few days a month as a viable option? What would inform that decision? Do you both mean the same thing when you use the words "marriage" and "family"?

When you and your girlfriend talk about raising a family, who do you see having primary responsibility for caring for children? Do you both understand why 50/50 is an unrealistic answer?

Additionally, we think that there are some really important questions for you to ask yourself. Why are you, at what we presume is a relatively young age, deciding that your own earning potential is so limited? Are you willing to do whatever is necessary to carry the primary burden of providing for a wife and family or are you counting on your wife to share that burden equally? If you were married and your wife decided after the arrival of your first baby that she wanted to be a stay-at-home mother and wife, would that delight you or terrify you? Have you expressed your preference to her in this area?

If you have listened to our audio program, *Madam, I'm Adam*, you know that ancient Jewish wisdom places primary responsibility for marriage failure on the husband. Earning more than your wife doesn't guarantee a successful marriage even though the opposite scenario is likely to pose problems. We encourage you to seek role models of enduring good marriages and openly ask for guidance from the husbands. Awareness of divorce is necessary in the world today, but if fear of divorce plays an outsized part in your thinking, we suggest that perhaps you need to develop your thinking and feelings before making a commitment to marriage.

Humming, "Here Comes the Groom,"
Rabbi Daniel and Susan Lapin
#Family, Finance

Ask the Rabbi and Susan #5

This question highlights one of the many counterintuitive aspects of life. One might think that having many interests and being able to do many things competently would be advantageous in earning a living. And while being a competent person in general definitely has great value, when it comes to serving our fellow human beings, which is of course the essence of making money, specialization is key.

Dear Rabbi and Susan,

I just recently discovered your material and I quickly became addicted to it. I would like to ask you something—what are your views on destiny? And more in detail—are some people destined to be failures?

I am 36 years old, and I have always been a passionate learner. Throughout my life I have been involved in various different fields—I have a Jazz drums degree, been cooking in some of the most prestigious kitchen in the world, got a Sommelier certification, I have been trading stocks for 4 years while studying various types of technical analysis (TPO, Market Profile, Point and Figure, Fundamentals and more).

While I am very proud of all the things I have learnt, I have never been able to monetize as much as I wanted. Once I felt I started to master a certain profession—I quickly began to lose interest and my attention and focus went somewhere else.... But now I am struggling to provide money for my family, and this is very frustrating. It seems to me that for some folks success just comes easily, while all my efforts for some reason don't produce the wanted outcome.

I have a great wife and daughter—and I am very grateful for that—but now I am just wondering whether I should just accept that I am a great fast-learning person, but making money is not in my destiny.

Hope to hear from you, thanks for your time.

Faithfully,

Phil

Dear Phil,

We are so happy you wrote to us. Your letter spoke to our hearts, especially since your decisions greatly impact the lives of two other people—your wife and daughter. However, we did say to ourselves, "Surely we've discussed this before?"

Yours is one of the most popular questions we have been asked over the past 10 years or so. Many have written with similar questions. But here's our not-surprising conclusion: each individual faces his or her own background, challenges, rationalization of behavior, and life-path. As such, each time we answer a similar question, we hope that we can add something additional to whatever we said before.

Here is one paragraph we previously wrote that you will find that in general summarizes our responses:

Leaving aside luck, acts of God. and genetics, 90% of everything that happens in your life is the result of things you have done or not done. This is particularly true in our business and financial lives. Now is a really good time to stop doing the wrong things and start doing the right ones.

Here is the new information we would like to add for you.

There are many myths that abound in society. If you and your wife have been married for any length of time, you know that the words with which so many fairy-tales close, "and they lived happily ever after," are misleading. More accurate phrases would be, "and they worked on themselves and their marriage to live happily ever after," or "and they faced challenges but were committed to facing them together and overcoming them, leading to living happily ever after."

Now let's examine your situation as you've described it. (And we admire your self-awareness and honesty. It bodes well for the changes you must make.) Here are about 30 words from a book called *East of Eden* by John Steinbeck. Do they remind you of you?

Alf was a jack-of-all-trades, carpenter, tinsmith, blacksmith, electrician, plasterer, scissors grinder, and cobbler. Alf could do anything, and as a result he was a financial failure although he worked all the time.

You see, Phil, God built a world in which He wants His children to connect with one another and need one another. We can most help other people when we become supremely competent specialists in some chosen field rather than being a little good at a lot of things.

Phil, how would you answer someone who wrote to us saying, "Successful marriage seems to elude me. Each time I'm happy with someone, I begin to lose interest and focus and my attention moves on to someone else. Am I just destined to have bad marriages?" We are certain you get our point.

Financial prosperity operates under the same rules. One of the enduring economic myths is the idea of "striking it rich." That implies a rapid change in circumstance. The odds of that happening are incredibly low. In general, financial stability and wealth result from building a reputation and acquiring skills by accumulating experience and connections in the specific field in which you've chosen to labor. For this reason, any professional who works 5 to 6 long days a week for a number of years will usually earn considerably more per hour than another who dabbles at the same profession, choosing to work only 3 days a week.

You have yourself accurately identified the very probable cause of your lack of prosperity. You seem to be confusing your love of eclectic learning with the work you do to serve others. By all means, keep growing and learning. Develop and maintain hobbies and interests. But direct a large portion of your effort to one field so that you build a continuous trajectory of accomplishment and service. You must be able to complete this sentence: People phone Phil when they need … You will undoubtedly need to work through difficult times at work. Those challenges are no excuses to quit and start over at entry level doing something entirely different.

Do we think there is such a thing as being destined to be poor? God is in ultimate control of our lives, but He most often leads us on the path in which we set out. Your self-chosen path is a tragic path to poverty, and we want to see you dramatically changing your own direction. We feel sure you can.

We are happy to welcome you to our teachings, and we look forward to hearing from you again with happy accounts of great success and prosperity,

Rabbi Daniel and Susan Lapin
#Finance, Faith

Ask the Rabbi and Susan #6

Some appliances, like washers and dryers, some computers, and even some cars come with a set of a few easily accessible switches and controls for the most common functions. Then, often behind a closed panel, one finds an array of controls for more exotic and less commonly used features. Similarly, with marriage there are several major principles that govern a large part of married life. However, behind the panel, as it were, are a number of additional ideas that, when applied, can greatly enhance the relationship. This question highlights one of these seldom discussed but nonetheless important ideas namely, how aware should children be of the physical nature of their parents' marriage.

Dear Rabbi and Mrs. Lapin,

Our question is about the modesty of parents. How private should the affection be between parents? For instance, is it acceptable for a wife to greet her husband with a hug and a kiss on the cheek in front of their children when he returns home from work?

With warmth,

William and Sue

Dear William and Sue,

Our guess is that some readers are scratching their heads saying, "Why is this even a question?" We agree with you that the topic does deserve thought, but we'd like to start by explaining why we believe that to be so.

Through the lens of ancient Jewish wisdom, the Bible emphasizes the difference between humans and all other creatures on the planet. The first two chapters of Genesis help to make this distinction clear. One difference is that animals operate on instinct; let's call it their operating system. They are not making judgment calls with respect to the spiritual consequences of their action. For humans, even the fundamental act of eating carries with it moral consequences that resonate down through the ages.

We discover the Bible using modest and refined terms when it comes to all physical activities that we share with animals. Furthermore, it emphasizes how we distinguish ourselves from animals when we eat, excrete waste, and reproduce.

Above all, there is modesty involved. Even in today's diminished culture the concept still exists, though it is usually called manners. We are taught to chew with our mouths closed in order to lessen our resemblance to animals. We are taught to relieve ourselves in private, unlike animals. Likewise, we are taught to be reticent about acts of intimacy.

We are, of course, each born into a certain time and place. When Prince William married, his wife Kate was widely admired for dressing in a classy and conservative style. Move Kate's outfits to sixteenth century England, and she probably would have been arrested for indecent exposure. A woman's exposed ankles do not cause men to blush today, but there was a time they did.

Similarly, today we are surrounded by public displays of affection. So common is this that it has its own readily understood acronym: PDA. Couples, some of whom only met a few minutes earlier, embrace in public in a way that would have not been viewed as appropriate for women sending their husbands off to battle a century ago.

Your question is whether something that is extremely common in the twenty-first century, shows of physical affection between spouses in front of their children, is a trend that should be encouraged or not. What timeless Biblical wisdom sheds light on this matter?

God created physical contact between a man and a woman as a powerful force. There is nonsexual contact between close family members (mother and son or father and daughter, for example). However, there is also a strong sexual urge that powerfully strikes men and women in slightly different ways and at somewhat different ages. The unique relationship called marriage combines both nonsexual and sexual aspects. We should relate with physical desire to our spouse, and we must also relate with respect and affection that is not dependent on sexuality.

The sexual relationship between parents is an intimate one that belongs to them alone. Many parents wisely keep their bedroom off-limits to the children. A few years ago, we wrote about our discomfort when friends, eager to display their new home, proudly walked us through the entire house including the master bedroom. Barraged, as our children are, by unhealthy relationship messages and with premature exposure to sexuality—even if it is not in the house but on a billboard or in a store—we prefer to let them see the sweetness of innocent affection between their moms and dads. Whether it is a welcome home kiss, holding hands while walking, or a tender brush of the cheek, in our day we think that it is important to be an advertisement for marriage in a way that wasn't necessary a few decades ago. It's been quite a few years since the Beatles song, "I Want to Hold Your Hand," was flirtatious. While holding fast to ideas of privacy and modesty, we do have to live in the world in which we find ourselves. There are so many harmful messages out there that modeling loving and innocent touch to our children becomes necessary.

Wishing you a loving marriage and wonderful children,
Rabbi Daniel and Susan Lapin
#Faith, Family, Fitness

Ask the Rabbi and Susan #7

Many young couples assume that since neither one of them is religious, their different faiths don't matter. Frequently, as they get older and especially when there are children in the picture, they discover that it often matters a great deal. Julie and her husband are one such couple.

Dear Rabbi and Susan,

Thank you so much for your podcast and your books, your work is tremendously enlightening and has enriched my life immeasurably.

I grew up as an atheist and discovered God as an adult. I am struggling to find the right path for me to learn about God and follow his teachings.

My own family background is Jewish on my mother's side, but my husband comes from a Christian background (but secular). We have started attending church because he is now also yearning to follow God's word. I enjoy church and Bible study but feel somewhat uncomfortable there due to my Jewish background. However, I want to support my husband and show a united spiritual front to our children, and I want my children to grow up in a Bible-believing community, instead of around the toxic secular values that my husband and I grew up with in school and society.

What is the right path for me?
Sincerely,
Julie

———————

Dear Julie,

Thank you for your warm and encouraging words. We really appreciate hearing that we are adding value to your life. We think that you are a wise and courageous woman. We say this without knowing you because you understand the importance of presenting a united front with your husband and of giving your children a spiritual reality and a safe community.

Little did you or your husband think, when you married, that it would matter that two people, both of whom came from families with a secular mindset, had different religious backgrounds. Yet, like most couples who have blithely ventured down these perilous pathways only to discover eventually that it does matter, you too have seen the same. It sounds like you are both on a growth trajectory and that takes honesty, courage, and strength.

We encourage you to allow the process to play out. While there are huge theological differences between Torah observant Judaism and Christianity, which we would never try to blur, the truth is that when contrasted with an atheistic or secular worldview, they have much in common.

We discourage trying to raise your family as both Jewish and Christian. Sometimes house-bound people try to look at a passing parade outside from the windows in two separate rooms. Unfortunately they spend so much time darting from room to room that they actually spend very little time gazing at the flowers and floats. Far better to remain in one room and derive all the benefit possible through the windows right there in front of you.

Nonetheless, this might be an opportunity for you and your husband to become more familiar with both religions. We don't know where you live, the ages of your children, or what church you have found, but many churches we know appreciate the Jewish origins of their faith. You can supplement church and Bible study with some Jewish sources (perhaps online) and begin to get knowledgeable about Jewish holidays and practices. Maybe there is a local synagogue you and your husband could occasionally visit as well. As with churches, you need to be careful to choose your guidance carefully—there is a great deal of nonsense available out there, and there are both churches and synagogues that sadly have little to do with the Bible and God's dominion over the world.

The important thing is finding a faith family with which you can affiliate as a family and in which each of you finds individual fulfillment as well as that warm surge of deep inexpressible happiness when engaged in something meaningful together with your family.

Initially, simply accepting the idea that there is a Higher Authority and rules for living is a major step. Recognizing that those rules for how the world REALLY works are formulated in God's message to mankind which he presented to Moses on Mt. Sinai is next. You and your husband ought to engage in a weekly Bible study together and into which you can include children as they reach appropriate maturity. Way down the road, it is entirely possible that members of your family might choose different paths and you will need to figure out how to make that work, but right now you are at the very beginning of your explorations.

Meanwhile, we applaud the steps you are taking and your commitment to your family and its exciting spiritual odyssey all together down one spiritual path.

May you thrive in your journey,

Rabbi Daniel and Susan Lapin

#Family, Faith

Ask the Rabbi and Susan #8

There is no virtue in being reactionary and automatically opposing any new social norm. Yet, sometimes we can't see what unintended consequences might develop if we go along with the culture. Justin and his girlfriend are wisely making a thoughtful decision about how to organize their relationship.

Dear Rabbi Daniel and Susan Lapin,

I have a question about dating. I am an old-fashioned kind of guy in a modern world. I am a millennial, but I like the old-fashioned way of doing things. I am in conflict a lot in relationships because of this.

One of the more recent conflicts involves whether or not me and my girlfriend should be at each others' places, alone. We each live alone, and could visit each other whenever, but I wonder if that is a good idea, or if we should keep the dating in the public space, as that might be more appropriate for Christian dating. I need to know what is proper, and what might be overdoing it on my part and being too restrictive. I appreciate your help.

Justin

Dear Justin,

Thank you for being an old-fashioned guy; we don't see "old-fashioned" as pejorative. Au contraire it is a tribute, and our daughters along with countless Godly young women also see it this way. This country needs more old-fashioned gentlemen.

By proactively thinking about how you and your girlfriend should behave now, you are setting the foundation for a successful relationship in the future, or alternatively for ending a relationship without unnecessary hardship and regrets. Either of these is a satisfactory outcome.

Ancient Jewish wisdom includes a timeless truth known as *yichud*. That Hebrew word derives from the root of togetherness. *Yichud* stipulates that men and women who aren't immediate family members should not be secluded together. Imagine how many "Me Too" moments and how many tears would have been avoided if coworkers and fellow students practiced this principle.

Because today, society is so clueless when it comes to male/female relationships, we published Gila Manolson's book on the topic. She makes the point in *Hands Off: This May Be Love!* that there are many psychological and physiological benefits to understanding the power of touch and confining touch to marriage. One point she makes, convincingly in our opinion, is that training oneself to desexualize attraction has its own dangers. Yet, what else can a couple do if they commit to not sleeping together but put themselves in isolated circumstances where that would be a natural urge? You are training your beings not to react to one another—hardly a good idea. That is exactly what you and your girlfriend would be doing by visiting each other's apartments. You would lose if you betray your standards, but you also lose by living up to them. In other words, we think that your concern is extremely valid and believe that you are showing intuitive wisdom.

On behalf of all old-fashioned gentleman,

Rabbi Daniel and Susan Lapin

#Friendship, Faith

Ask the Rabbi and Susan #9

Family businesses are often huge blessings for the people involved. It usually takes more than one generation to build significant wealth and a business staffed by family members who share the same cultural outlook and the same work ethic is a perfect platform for this project. But it can create considerable conflict as well.

Dear Rabbi Daniel and Susan,

As the mother of a son and daughter, I greatly enjoyed one of your podcasts in which you discussed father–son businesses. My son is currently employed in my husband's law firm. My son's background has not been stellar. He flunked out of the first year of a 3rd tier law school and had to take the bar exam 4 times to pass both sections.

Consequently, he has been working at the family law firm for 2 years and only recently been able to do anything court related. Needless to say he spent much of his time surfing the internet because there wasn't any work my husband could give him to do besides administrative work which my son felt was beneath him.

I realize the problem is much larger than just having your son in your business, but was hoping there were some books you could recommend regarding sons working for their fathers. I am thoroughly enjoying listening to your podcast, and your description of British Columbia has made me want to visit there.

Madeleine

———

Dear Madeleine,

We aren't familiar with any books to recommend, but a computer search on family businesses should bring up a few names. At a minimum, there would probably be useful chapters in those books, but they are probably better read before there is a problem rather than after.

You hint at understanding that there are three separate areas of concern that all impact one another. Your marriage: disagreeing about what is best for a child can cause tremendous strain. The business: it certainly can't be good for morale or the bottom line to have an employee surfing the internet instead of working. Your son: Any young person who finds paid work in a field in which he hopes to make his living "beneath him" is not thinking correctly. Is law what he wants to do or is this your husband's dream?

Of course, each area affects each other area, making this a quagmire of potentially painful conflict. It sounds to us as if some outside counsel would be very helpful. If your husband is amenable to speaking to someone you both respect, preferably someone with experience in both the business and family arenas, our guess is that this might be more useful than reading books on the topic.

Your specific challenge is a great one. Recognizing that your husband is acting out of love for his son, you see that he may be harming rather than helping him. You need to respect his role as owner of the business at the same time as you may be worried that he is damaging your family's income. Our suggestion would be to focus on getting you and your husband on the same page as the first necessary step.

We would recommend that together you explore the possibility of your son no longer working in your husband's law firm. Even if your husband dreams of having his son in his business, it is always best in these situations for the son to come back to his father's business after he has first been successful as an employee at some other firm. Clearly your husband has been providing "welfare" for your son. Maybe this should stop.

Try as best as you can to isolate this problem and initiate interactions with both your husband and son that are opportunities for shared stress-free, positive time. We pray that you can keep this serious issue from overwhelming your whole life.

Hope you find a silver lining in the cloud,
Rabbi Daniel and Susan Lapin
#Family, Finance

Ask the Rabbi and Susan #10

As a homeschooling family ourselves, Christina's letter resonated with us. However, a similar situation could arise in almost any community group.

Dear Rabbi and Susan Lapin,

I am a homeschool mom who is connected to a homeschool community. We meet on a weekly basis. The children are tutored by the moms, who are paid. The moms also are encouraged to help out and use their talents with organizing field trips, taking photos to create a yearbook, etc.

We have a situation concerning one mom who was very involved. Due to some circumstances, after paying full tuition to our little organization, she decided to remove her children from our program and register them in a school. In the contract it states that parents after paying tuition will not get a refund. She is very disappointed because she is being treated the same as a parent who did not lift a finger. What is a biblical approach to this case?

Christina

———————

Dear Christina,

Financial interactions and human interactions are intertwined. While money allows us to work together peacefully, it can also be the source of ill feeling and friction.

It's always a good idea to step back from an issue, which is what we would recommend doing in this case. The reason businesses or organizations (like a homeschool co-op) have contracts and rules is so that everyone knows the bottom line and is assured of being treated equally.

Imagine if you did refund this woman's tuition despite regulations to the contrary. From then on, wouldn't you have to refund everyone's money or to delete that contract item? Otherwise, you are not playing by the rules which is a certain way to cause dissension. Since we assume the rule was put in for good reasons, you do need to follow it.

At the same time, this woman feels that she, unlike many other parents, devoted volunteer hours to the co-op. Being treated like everyone else is leaving her feeling unappreciated. We doubt if the tuition money is the issue as much as her emotions. Perhaps the co-op could give her a gift acknowledging her role along with a heartfelt letter expressing gratitude for all she has done? In this way, you would be acknowledging her efforts while not undermining your organization.

This episode might be an opportunity to review your co-op rules. Maybe every parent should be expected to put in a certain amount of volunteer time or maybe "more than usual" volunteer hours should be reimbursed with credit toward tuition. You might also consider adding (with permission, of course) a pastor or community leader's name on the contract as the person selected to settle any disputes. Especially in a small-knit group such as yours, this might make decisions less emotionally charged.

Wishing you a successful homeschool year,

Rabbi Daniel and Susan Lapin

#Friendship, Finance, Faith

Ask the Rabbi and Susan #11

Questions such as Lonnie's renew our faith in our fellow man. At the same time, it is a serious question from a thoughtful person worried about getting something without paying full price.

Dear Rabbi Lapin and Susan,

A small coffee shop recently opened in my town and I visit them every day for coffee and sometimes a pastry. Because I enjoy the food and I appreciate being able to have a friendly conversation with the owner, and occasionally get a free refill on coffee, I like to leave a tip in the jar. Sometimes I'm even given free pastries, which are wonderful fresh-baked creations by the owner's wife, typically sold for a few dollars. I've even been given whole loaves of bread for free.

Here is where my dilemma comes in. I don't like to go around looking for hand-outs or expecting gifts; I prefer to pay for whatever I receive. However, I understand and respect that people like to give gifts without expecting anything in return. I'm the same way.

I understand that the coffee shop owner and his wife are likely allowing me their extra goods because it creates customer loyalty and it is also a sign of their appreciation for my patronage. I tend to feel guilty for receiving as much as I do from them because I feel like I'm not doing anything to really deserve it. I'm not sure how to adequately express my genuine thanks in return.

I want to give them more tips, but is that not being respectful of their act of giving a gift? What might be the best way to show my thanks, in addition to continuing to purchase my usual coffee and treats?

Thank you very much for your time and consideration!
Lonnie

Dear Lonnie,

While you may very well live downtown in a major metropolis, in our minds we're conjuring up a rural small-town atmosphere. Either way, your dilemma is a wonderful one to have.

We want to be clear that had you told us that a friend of yours worked for a cafe and kept on giving you freebies, that would be a completely different question. However, in your case, the owners are the ones giving you gifts. We think you are right to recognize their appreciation of your patronage as well as their desire to foster customer loyalty.

As you note, while I'm sure any tips you leave are appreciated, attempting to "pay" for your gifts in that way would be ungracious. They are making their own business/personal decision and you can pleasantly accept what they give you without feeling that it calls for a response. Indeed, as their clientele grows they may cut back on the gifts and it would be just as misplaced for you to resent that as to feel that you presently owe something in return.

However, you do want to support them and let them know how much you appreciate their business. One of the ways you can do that is by letting people know about them. This can include word-of-mouth as well as using social media such as leaving a review on Yelp or similar websites. (We would encourage you to talk about the pleasant surroundings and delicious coffee and food while staying quiet about the generosity. No need to set people up for disappointment when they have to pay for their pastries.) Let the proprietors know of your promotional efforts, not in a bragging way but because it will strengthen them as they cope with the inevitable difficulties that running a business entails.

You could also offer gift certificates to your friendly coffee shop when you want a way to thank someone local, for example a neighbor who takes in your mail while you're away or as a "notice of appreciation" to your mailman.

Some of us have more trouble giving than receiving while others of us lean in the opposite direction. Cultivating the ability to both give and to receive is desirable.

Enjoy a coffee for us,
Rabbi Daniel and Susan Lapin
#Friendship, Finance

Ask the Rabbi and Susan #12

As you can imagine, the Family F is a frequent topic in the letters we receive and a frequent feeling that we both experience is, "Why, oh why, didn't they speak to us before they got married?" It is never satisfying to have to write, "You should have…" and it is probably even less satisfying to read those words. One of our goals with this book is to encourage readers to be deliberate as early in life as possible. As you will see in our response, we wished that Anita and her new husband had been helped to walk through some important premarital conversations.

Hello Rabbi Daniel and Susan,

I really could use your help on this problem. I got married last August, nearly a year ago. I had always told my husband that I want to be a young mom. I am 26 now and my husband is 31. I really don't want to wait till I'm 30. I feel I'm so ready and in such a good place to start trying to conceive. He says I'll still be young even when I'm 35 or so but that makes me so, so mad! He has a job and makes most of the money but I do about 98% of housework.

Both our families are encouraging us to have a baby but my husband says he wants to wait till the perfect time, when covid is over and the world somehow is in better shape. I don't think there is such a thing as the perfect time to have a child, the future is so uncertain and right now we both are young, healthy, and have the time and energy to raise a family. We own a beautiful house with a lovely big yard.

I really try to respect his opinion but it's getting so hard and it's even ruining our private life. He is so obsessed with using birth control and avoiding me during the time that I am "most fertile" that it is starting to turn me off. I know we're newlyweds, and should be just having fun and stuff but I kind of feel I don't want to do it unless we're trying to conceive or at least not avoiding it.

Plus he says things like "WE don't want a baby right now" when he knows very well that it's the only thing I really want in my life. He says I should focus on my career. I'm a designer and I don't have plans to leave that behind 100% but I would be more than happy to stop for a while if it means I'll be taking care of my baby. I don't have much ambition towards my career but don't see that as a bad thing. Our families really want us to have a baby but his friends (all over 32) say it's too early and we should travel the world and stuff. I have absolutely no interest in that, he doesn't either. He enjoys our lifestyle as much as I do, we don't party and like staying at home, reading, going on walks, harvesting (we live in the country). His friends don't really get it but my friends do even though they are younger than his.

I would really appreciate some guidance. I feel as if I'm going insane and I feel anxious everyday about me suffocating him by my pressuring. I know also it's not all on him but I'm so afraid to keep waiting (even though we're practically just married). Also I don't want this to ruin our relationship, he truly is who I always dreamed of marrying.

Anita

_____

Dear Anita,

You and your husband both sound like good people who care very much about your marriage. Sadly, a clear conversation that needed to take place before you were married, didn't. Now we have a problem.

Every guide to marriage will tell you that communication is key. Part of communication is knowing that words mean different things to different people. It is also knowing that people are not always in touch with themselves. This means that even when they are sure they are speaking truthfully, they can be mistaken.

When you told your future husband that you want to be a young mother, that word "young" needed a definition. You could both agree on the concept, but if one of you thinks that 26 is young while the other thinks that 32 is young, you need to talk more. (Including discussing biological realities about fertility.) Other words that need expanded explanation before marriage are "financially comfortable," "close to my family," and words like large, small, or shared in whatever connection they are used. We are sure that readers can identify dozens of more words and phrases that mean different things to different people.

As to our second point about not being in touch with oneself, we cannot tell you how many couples we know who married with the agreement that they didn't want any children or only wanted one or two. Sometimes it was a second marriage for a man, and he already had a family and didn't want to add to that family. Down the road the woman (98% of the time it is the woman) who much earlier had been so sure that she did not want to give birth, became desperate to have one or more children.

Here are a few more points that you touched upon in your letter that we will comment on.

You say, "Both our families are encouraging us to have a baby." You also mention friends more than once. We cannot stress this enough: leave your families and friends out of this. Not only are their opinions utterly irrelevant, but this is a private discussion between husband and wife. Of course, your decision has family and community repercussions, which is an idea that springs out of the pages of the Bible. However, you and your husband should not be talking to or quoting any family members or friends on this subject. It is disrespectful to your marriage.

You say, "He has a job and makes most of the money, but I do about 98% of housework." It is time for you to communicate, first with yourself and then with your husband. Are you saying that since you do most of the work, a baby will barely affect his life? Are you upset at how little he helps you and is that bleeding into this issue? What does this have to do with anything? We have no idea but we think you should figure this out. What we hope you mean is that you both realize the fullest implications of the marriage partnership. He understands that without your manning the home front he wouldn't be nearly as successful and you, in turn, love and appreciate him for making it possible for you to build a warm and welcoming home.

These words ring alarm bells for us: "He is so obsessed with using birth control and avoiding me during the time that I am 'most fertile' that it is starting to turn me off. I know we're newlyweds, and should be just having fun and stuff but I kind of feel I don't want to do it unless we're trying to conceive or at least not avoiding it."

Physical intimacy has two functions in marriage, and ignoring either one is tremendously damaging. It sounds to us like you and your husband are each focused on only one of these functions: (1) sexual pleasure that is unique to marriage and (2) having children. The problem is that you're each focused on a different one.

This is setting you on a dangerous collision course, and young marriages are extremely vulnerable. While it would have been helpful for you to discuss and settle these issues before getting married, both of you are going to have to put on your grown-up clothing and deal with the reality before you. Our guess is that you will need outside help to ensure an affectionate, respectful, and productive conversation. This outside individual must be chosen with great care so that he or she does not do more damage.

Had it been both you and your husband asking for help in resolving this problem, it would be a bit easier, but it is only you. So although we wish we could help him understand what his dear wife is going through, we can only help you understand what is going on in his male mind.

Mainly, he is thrilled to be living with his beguiling wife and is hoping to have much more time with you alone before he has to share you with someone else with an even more compelling call than his. However, your husband needs to learn that asking you to ignore the cry of your body and soul isn't going to work. He got married expecting one thing, and real life is proving different.

You need to learn that getting mad is not productive. Consider it practice for being a mother—we guarantee that you will not be able to control children and bully or guilt them into submission. You are going to have to master your emotions until this is resolved. Meanwhile, the best thing you can do for your future children is to build your marriage, physically, emotionally, and spiritually.

We hope that your experience can serve to help educate other Happy Warriors. Not only are men and women quite different, but life throws curve balls at us. Before getting married, learn to speak the same language when discussing major issues. Do not assume or hope for the best.

Anita, this can be a tremendous building block in your marriage or it can be dynamite. You will know that it is a positive experience when you and your husband come to an agreement that lets your marriage win, rather than one of you defeating the other.

Praying for your success,

Rabbi Daniel and Susan Lapin

#Family, Friendship, Faith

Ask the Rabbi and Susan #13

We are nearly always skeptical when someone uses words like "over-priced" or "underpaid" because value can never be set by a committee. The value of an item or a service is exactly what a specific buyer and a specific seller decide by themselves. And anyone who has agreed to work for a certain pay cannot claim to be being underpaid because if he really believed that, he'd quit. Still, circumstances, especially those involving family, can be complicated.

Dear Rabbi Daniel and Susan Lapin,

I work for a developer who sells overpriced property. He tells me to go and see the people in the home and get them to like me first, then sell the property. Whenever I say anything about it being over-priced (I have mentioned it many times), the answer I get back is that I don't believe in the product.

Three months later and with only 2 properties out of 34 in our inventory sold, I'm struggling to know what is right as far as behaving morally toward my fellow man and doing right to my boss who unfortunately is my older brother.

Your advice would be much appreciated.

Bobby,

Dear Bobby,

Your question reminded us of a story our good friend, Zig Ziglar, used to tell. He was overseeing a group of sales professionals who were selling a rather expensive set of kitchen cookware. Despite having been given an explanation as to why the pots were a worthwhile investment and merited the high price, the sales people were entirely unsuccessful.

One day, Zig asked them all which of them owned a set of the pots they were selling. When no one raised a hand, he told them that evidently they did not believe what they were telling their potential customers. If they thought that the pots were truly an important and justified purchase, they would have bought a set themselves.

Good and honest people cannot sell something in which they do not believe. Since you consider the property overpriced, you see yourself as having to trick people into buying it. As a decent person, you can't do that. Ethical capitalism is when both seller and buyer win by making a deal. In your mind, you are being asked to make deals where you are the winner and the customer is the loser.

Your boss/brother is correct that you do not believe in the product. Is it possible that you don't have a clear picture of business expenses and that the properties are fairly priced? Are any other people in the company selling more successfully than you? Do they strike you as generally immoral and deceitful?

We would be interested in knowing how you arrived at the conclusion that the properties being sold are "overpriced." Here is not the place to delve deeply into the concepts of value and price. However, and meaning you no disrespect, since time immemorial, unsuccessful sales professionals have complained that the products they are paid to sell are overpriced.

Can you acknowledge your brother's allegation and ask him to explain the pricing to you so that you will be comfortable—or perhaps you will find out that your discomfort is based in truth? Perhaps your brother is inexperienced and the lack of sales is giving him a more realistic view of what the properties are worth? Both of these explanations assume the best of your brother and allow you to work with a clear conscience as both you and your brother learn more about the business.

Of course, it is possible that greed is the operative word here. In that case, we don't see how you can continue in this position. You can't do a job in which you see yourself as stealing from innocent victims. Because of the family relationship, you will need to be tactful in removing yourself from the business, but as a good person, it is no surprise that you cannot and should not sell something in which you do not believe.

Wishing you future prosperity based on ethical capitalism,
Rabbi Daniel and Susan Lapin
#Finance, Family, Faith

Ask the Rabbi and Susan #14

Sometimes there is a direct conflict between Finance and Friendship. This is the case for our following correspondent. When you add Faith into the picture, it becomes clear that short-term gain isn't worth the price.

Dear Rabbi and Susan,

Greetings from Croatia! Recently, I have been planning certain business projects with some people. In one of the most recent discussions with them, a friend who has more capital than I have, proposed that I become a director of his firm which is supposed to employ delivery partners, that is couriers for major online delivery startups.

Without going into too much detail about how this can benefit my long-term career, there is one concern that brings me nightmares. One of my other friends, whom I am thankful for helping me find a job as a courier when I lost my previous job as a stockbroker in a bank due to COVID-19–influenced lockdowns, has started his own firm that employs couriers. This means if I accept an opportunity to become a director in this line of business, I would compete directly with him.

I have been thinking about it and I see two negative outcomes right now. One is that I will very likely lose one friend because I will have to compete against him in the same business, which does seem to me as a betrayal since it will force me to use all the information he has given me so far against him. The other one is much less obvious, but I might lose reputation in a Catholic business network, a very ambitious and useful group of people which I consider very important for my private and professional development, because my friend is also a part of this group and interacts with others just as I do.

Based on the wisdom and experience you have, I kindly ask you to give me advice. Are my concerns justified and how could I possibly resolve this issue?

Thanks for your help!

Bardier

Dear Bardier,

We are thrilled with the growing numbers of Happy Warriors in Croatia. We appreciate your proper concern that this career offer presents you with a serious moral dilemma and personal challenge.

Our quick reply is that you should (probably quite painfully) turn down this opportunity. Now, we would like to take the time to explain why this is so.

People frequently confuse cause and effect. We watch a new law being enacted and congratulate ourselves on living in an advanced culture triumphantly moving forward on a just path. Frequently, however, the new law instead reflects the downfall of culture; something that used to be commonly accepted now needs to be stated.

Here is an example. One of the great rabbis of the Middle Ages whose works are still studied today is Rabbeinu (our rabbi) Gershom, who lived in Germany c. 960–1040. Rabbeinu Gershom instituted a ruling prohibiting anyone from opening mail addressed to another person. What an advance! Not exactly. Valuing and protecting privacy and personal property is a core principle of ancient Jewish wisdom. The fact that this prohibition needed to be articulated as a ruling was proof that people were no longer observing that long-held cultural and religious understanding. The necessity for the law showed a failure, a regression, rather than progress.

Companies today often require those they hire to sign a non-compete agreement. The worker agrees that upon severing the relationship with the company, for a certain period of time, he will not engage in certain activities. These might include setting up a rival company, accepting a position with a rival company, or working in a similar business within a certain geographical area. The details vary based on the type of business and the worker's position. The fact that this needs to be spelled out reflects a lack of confidence that an individual's conscience and faith will lead him to act correctly without a contract.

Your friend shared his knowledge and experience with you. He did not make you sign a non-compete because his help was based on relationship, not law. We think that were you to accept the position you are being offered, you would feel yourself to be a smaller person, and indeed, be turning yourself into one. And yes, the Catholic business community of which you are part and which emanates an aura of respectability and trustworthiness will possibly see you as not worthy of being one of them.

Evil will never depart from the house of him who repays good with evil (Proverbs 17:13). While there are many circumstances in which you could morally compete with the company that educated you such as, for instance, where you paid for an apprenticeship and the company declined to hire you or where any first offer of refusal was not exercised, your case is perfectly described in Solomon's ringing denunciation. You must decline the offer but with the following steps.

You should sit down with both parties separately. Explain to your friend about your offer and why you are turning it down. Reassure him that you are telling him not to make him feel guilty in any way at all but to let him know how much you cherish his friendship and how much you appreciate what he did for you. Then meet with and explain to the person who made you the attractive offer your reason for turning it down. The man who wants to employ you should understand how much you value his offer. It is possible that one or perhaps both of these parties may respond with ideas that surprise you. Most importantly, you will smile at yourself in the mirror.

Much business used to be (and some still is) conducted with a handshake rather than with a legal tome. Contracts are wonderful, but the need for more specifics and more words reflects a failing of society, not a success. May God bless you with prosperity as becomes a man of integrity.

Please stay in touch,
Rabbi Daniel and Susan Lapin
#Friendship, Faith, Finance

Ask the Rabbi and Susan #15

Marriage is a training ground for character development. We often need to recalibrate our individual desires and our relationships with other people so that we and our spouse are both fulfilled and happy.

Dear Rabbi Daniel and Susan,

I live in the Bay area, which is a popular tourist destination. I would welcome having visitors as guests in our home but my wife absolutely rejects the idea. She gets all stressed about it.

Isn't it a good or Godly deed to host old friends or relatives? What are your thoughts on this?

Ted

Dear Ted,

Oh, we have so many thoughts on this. While we love hearing from you, we really think that you should be speaking to your wife and not to us.

You are certainly correct that God looks kindly on hospitality and kindness to others. There are also many other deeds that make Him smile. Just to give you a few ideas, do you regularly visit the sick and religiously give charity? Are you a Big Brother, and do you offer handyman help to any neighbors who might be widowed? The point we are making is that there are many ways in which to reach out to others, and we all tend toward ones that fit our time, talents, and personalities. You might enjoy having guests, but perhaps your wife would prefer cooking for new mothers or driving an elderly neighbor to a doctor's appointment as her "Godly deed" activity.

We personally love having guests. Even so, as Susan began devoting more hours to creating and editing our teaching resources, we have not extended ourselves in this area as much as we used to. None of us can do everything. You may be picturing sitting and chatting with relatives, and your wife may be picturing extra laundry, cooking, and clean-up. Or perhaps she relishes quiet time at home because her days are hectic. We don't know why she doesn't want guests, but we suggest you find out without being critical and implying a lack in her for not wanting them. If it is a matter as simple as doing laundry, you can assure her that you will take care of it. If it doesn't fit her personality or her current schedule, then the two of you might decide that she will welcome your childhood best friend and you won't even ask about having over that second cousin with whom you never speak.

This difference of opinion is an opportunity for the two of you to learn more about each other and to show how much you value each other's desires. The discussion can be glue that holds you together rather than a wedge that drives you apart. One thing you can know for sure. Striving for harmony in the home is a good and Godly deed.

Wishing you a peaceful home,

Rabbi Daniel and Susan Lapin

#Family, Friendship

Closing the Circle

In all our responses above we employed the 5F principles. We wanted you to see that most real-life puzzles can be resolved provided one has a value system such as the 5Fs that help keep one focused on the things that really matter. Vacations, pets, sports, hobbies, art, and culture all can enhance the joy of living, but it is helpful to see them as, if you will, optional. Whereas Finance, Friendship, Faith, Fitness, and Family are indispensable essentials.

Working 16 hours a day on a new business or even just going off each and every day to a job one may not love can be grim and grueling. Knowing that you're doing it all for a small group of special people, your spouse and children, who are pulling for you all the way, can change it all from drudgery to purposeful. Knowing that you are caring appropriately for your body gives you the drive to push the boundaries of your endurance. Having friends who inspire you with their commitment to the values that sustain your faith makes your walk more joyful. In this way we begin to sense the vast array of benefits that flow from the 5F crosslinks that you have studied these past chapters.

You are surely already discovering that you see yourself as more multidimensional than in the past. Those often awkward gatherings at which, going around the table, everyone describes themselves should hold less fear for you now. Whereas most people intuitively feel that they should describe the work they do, you have absorbed deep into your being that your work is important, but it is one-fifth of the important things that form the core of your consciousness. You could just as meaningfully speak of your Family, your Faith, your Friends, and your Fitness.

We are happy that you are on this journey, and we look forward with eager anticipation to meeting you at one of our appearances or hearing from you and being able to congratulate you in person for having made the change to the 5F path, mindfully and deliberately living your life.

Index

Gross domestic product (GDP), 46, 117
Group-think, 198
Guests, obligations of, 124

Hands Off (Manolson), 219
Happiness:
 balance for, 3
 connection for, 25–27
 and cultural views of men and
  women, 138
 from earning money, 125, 126
 equality of outcome and, 185
 giving others, 94
Happy Warriors, 203, 228, 231
Hard labor, 189
Harrington, Mary, 138
Harvard Business Review, 184
Harvard University, 132
Having it all, 133–137, 179, 193
Hawking, Stephen, 52
Health, *see* Fitness
Hearing, 80–81
Heart, being misled by, 79
Hebrew:
 amen in, 76–77
 clothing in, 64–65, 94, 168
 eating in, 96
 friend in, 87
 hearing in, 80, 148
 hidden messages in, 148–149
 man, woman, and *fire* in, 143
 numerical values of letters in, 5
 son of in, 156
 translations of, 7–8
 truth in, 61
Hebrew Bible, 10. *See also specific
  books and parts*
 on building connection, 33–35
 descriptive principles in, 81–82
 on differences between men and
  women, 137–141
 on marriage, 139–140, 183–186
 on private ownership, 48–49

 visualizing scenes from, 39–40
Heh, 5
Height, of husbands and wives, 132
Hierarchy of five needs, 7
Higher Power, 73
Hill, Anita, 161–162
Hinduism, 157
Hirsi Ali, Ayaan, 76
Holistic systems, 14–17
Holmes, Elizabeth, 144
Homemaking, 188, 190–191
Homeschooling, 193, 221
Home team advantage, 140
Hook-up culture, 153–154
Hoover, Herbert, 116
Hopelessness, 78
Hormonal birth control, 152–153
Horowitz, Yaakov, 47
Hospitality, 123–124, 234
Howard, Chris, 136
Huckabee, Janet, 173
Huckabee, Mike, 173
Humans and animals, differences
  between:
 blushing, 62–64
 in defecation habits, 63, 105
 in eating behavior, 63, 101, 180, 214
 modesty, 214
 Permanent Biblical Principle on,
  68–69
 in reproductive anatomy, 151–152
 speech, 103
Hymen, 152, 153
Hypergamy, 132–133
Hypnosis, 90

Identity, 181–183
Idolatry, 47–48, 102–103
Immigrants and immigration, 73,
  197
Income:
 of men vs. women with
  same job, 185

Well-being, 25
Western civilization, 14, 33,
    70, 72–73, 76
Western culture:
  anthropomorphizing of
    animals in, 63
  childlessness in, 78
  hook-up culture in, 154
  individualism in, 197
  male–female platonic friendship
    in, 159–160
  manners in, 105
  predatory policies of nations in, 69
  prolonging fertility in, 189–190
  teen pregnancy and, 146
  treating spiritual maladies in, 88
  wedding ceremonies in, 142
  weight control and, 96
Wholeness, 53
Widows, 146, 157, 166–167, 187
Wilcox, W. Bradford, 153
Wilde, Oscar, 135
Will and Ariel Durant (Durant and
    Durant), 75–76
William, Prince of Wales, 215
Wilson, Bill, 73
Winning money, 125
Wisdom, x–xi, 21, 152. *See also* Ancient
    Jewish wisdom
Witchcraft, 75
Women. *See also* Men and women,
    differences between; Mothers
  attitude of, about caring for family,
    192–195
  benefits of marriage for, 171
  biology of female animals vs., 152
  career for, 98, 180–182, 185–186,
    188–190, 195–196
  consequences of gender
    egalitarianism for, 131–133

  cultural messages about being a
    woman, 191–192
  having it all for, 133, 135–137
  on male–female platonic
    friendships, 160
  meaning of making money
    for, 180–181
  men's bad behavior against,
    143–144
  need for both men and, 141–145
  need to be needed for, 187–188
  preferential treatment for, 130, 144
  prioritizing career of, 185–186
  protection for, 141–142, 167
  provocative clothing of, 168–169
  respect for, 70
  who out-earn husbands, 136,
    182–183, 208–210
Work. *See also* Career
  balancing rest and, 106–108
  worthiness of, 69–70
Workaholism, 85
Working mothers, 98, 188–190,
    195–196
Work/life balance, 194–195
World Economic Forum, 50
World reserve currency, 116–117
World War I, 17, 26, 171
World War II, 17, 67, 69, 89–90,
    98–99, 116–117
Writings, of Hebrew Bible, 10

Yeats, William Butler, 30
Yehuda HaNasi, 28
Yichud, 219
YouGov, 32

Zeitgeist, 198
Ziglar, Jean, 164–165
Ziglar, Zig, 164–165, 229